BREAKSPEAR

BREAKSPEAR

THE ENGLISH POPE

R.A.J. WADDINGHAM

Adrian Waddingham

The
History
Press

To Angela

First published 2022

The History Press
97 St George's Place, Cheltenham,
Gloucestershire, GL50 3QB
www.thehistorypress.co.uk

© R.A.J. Waddingham, 2022
Maps © FourPoint Mapping

The right of R.A.J. Waddingham to be identified as the Author
of this work has been asserted in accordance with the
Copyright, Designs and Patents Act 1988.

British Library Cataloguing in Publication Data.
A catalogue record for this book is available from the British Library.

ISBN 978 0 7509 9954 0

Typesetting and origination by The History Press
Printed and bound in Great Britain by TJ Books Limited, Padstow, Cornwall.

MIX
Paper from
responsible sources
FSC® C013056

Trees for Life

CONTENTS

LIST OF ILLUSTRATIONS

MAPS

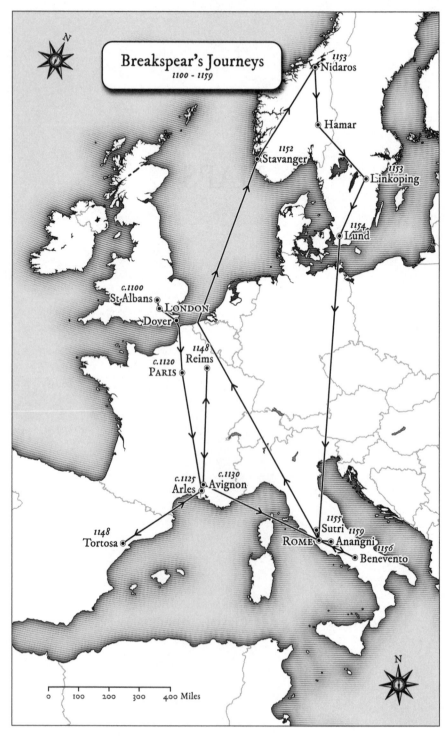

Breakspear's journeys 1100–59. *This map depicts modern borders.*

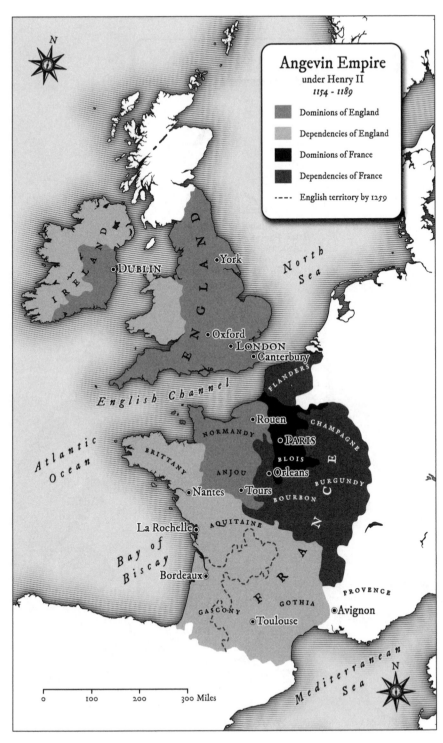

Twelfth-century England and France.

Twelfth-century Italy and the Mediterranean.

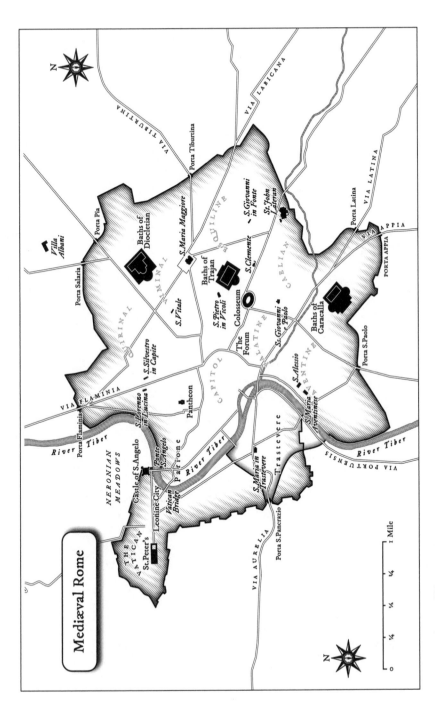

Rome in the twelfth century.

PREFACE

The English reader may consult the *Biographia Britannica* for Adrian IV but our own writers have added nothing to the fame or merits of their countryman.

Edward Gibbon[1]

Nicholas Breakspear was elected pope in 1154, choosing Adrian as his papal name. He is the first and so far only Englishman to sit on the Throne of St Peter. To be elected pope is an achievement at any time; to have been elected at a time when all of Europe, sovereigns included, were in thrall to the papacy is doubly so. That such an honour could fall to an Englishman of low birth is almost unbelievable. Nicholas Breakspear, born near Abbots Langley early in the twelfth century, perhaps around 1105 and probably illegitimate, was elected pope unanimously by the cardinals. Despite this great accolade, his fellow countrymen seem to have completely forgotten him: Gibbon wrote his complaint in 1789 and little has changed since. Apart from a seventy-eight-page cameo by Simon Webb in 2016 and a collection of most helpful academic essays edited by Brenda Bolton and Anne J. Duggan in 2003, there has been no biography of Breakspear published since that by Edith Almedingen in 1925.[2]

Most English people know about Thomas Becket, the murdered Archbishop of Canterbury, born in London to a minor Norman knight only a few years after Breakspear. Yet few in England today know anything about Nicholas Breakspear even though his story is the more remarkable. London abounds with monuments to England's famous sons, but the capital has neither plaque nor statue to commemorate Breakspear. His family's descendants are better known in England for brewing beer. The Brakspear Brewery was established by distant relations in Oxfordshire in 1711 and to this day its logo is a bee, copied from Pope Adrian's seal. They appreciate the greatness of their ancestor even if the rest of England has failed to acknowledge him.

Bishop Louis Casartelli, an Edwardian biographer of Breakspear, wrote in 1905:

> It is not easy to account for the comparative neglect into which the memory of this really great Englishman and great Pope has fallen among us.[3]

There are reasons. Becket achieved what he did within England, whereas Breakspear spent but few years in his home country and as an adult was out of England's sight. Becket's exciting story centred on his quarrel with the English King Henry II, and his dramatic murder when armed knights stormed into Canterbury Cathedral. This English political story stole the limelight while Breakspear was left unnoticed over in Italy, where he was apparently just doing mundane churchy things. His activities in another country could not compete with a gory murder on people's doorsteps.

British interest in happenings in wider Europe started only much later when adventurism began, and the seeds of empire were being sown. Even then, British universities, the source of most of our historical research, remained focused on events directly involving Britain. British giants on the world stage were kings, soldiers and, later, colonialists. Breakspear was none of these, so even in these later years, he continued to be overlooked. Nonetheless, the pope was supremely powerful in the twelfth century when Christianity was the beating pulse throughout the western world. There were heresies from time to time, but these concerned the interpretation of faith rather than challenging Christianity itself. The pope had temporal power too, although much less than Germany, France, England or Spain, whose kings nonetheless all recognised the spiritual leadership of the pope. In an age when the powers of Church and state were intertwined, the pope's support for a nation's political endeavours was crucial. William the Conqueror invaded England in 1066 with full papal support. Even the mighty Emperor Frederick Barbarossa of Germany, intent on re-establishing the lapsed authority of the Roman Empire within Italy, craved papal support. He was desperate to strengthen his position in Germany by being crowned by Pope Adrian in Rome. King William I of Sicily had defeated Pope Adrian's forces in battle but he still gave him generous terms in return for papal recognition of his kingship. Despite being greatly respected by his powerful peers abroad, English historians failed to recognise Pope Adrian's importance or seek to scrutinise his life.

That Pope Adrian had to stand up to the powerful Emperor Frederick Barbarossa, and that Adrian's reign lasted but five years whereas Frederick dominated Europe for thirty-five years, left Adrian vulnerable to after-the-event imperial propaganda. With no sympathetic historians to champion Adrian's cause or balance the story, German historians were free to belittle Adrian's achievements unchallenged and unfairly accuse him of deliberately sabotaging the close links between empire and papacy. Furthermore, the papal schism on Adrian's death in 1159 clouded judgements. The full story has not been fairly told.

Perhaps Pope Adrian received less attention because, by the time writers from the eighteenth century onwards began analysing history, Breakspear's memory was suppressed along with the Roman Church. Breakspear was a devout churchman but his legacy is not one of liturgy, or of the minutiae of canon law, and his exclusion is unwarranted. Adrian was one of the twelfth-century popes who exercised the most influence in the political affairs of Europe, leading armies into battle and making and un-making states and their rulers. Despite a schism, he handed the papacy on to his successor in better shape than he had found it. His political power tempered by strong integrity contrasts sharply with our age, when many politicians are seen to be unscrupulous. In 1896 the *Manchester Guardian* acknowledged Adrian's power:

> There is no more striking illustration of the openings which the mediaeval Church gave to humble worth and ability that the like of a poor Hertfordshire lad who, leaving England almost penniless, came to reorganise the Scandinavian Church, to beard the mightiest monarch of Western Europe since Charles the Great, and himself to dispose of kingdoms.[4]

My second Christian name is Adrian. I have always been aware of my papal namesake, and my interest was piqued on a bike ride through Morden Park in London. A notice at the ruined Merton Priory claims that both Thomas Becket and Nicholas Breakspear attended its school. I tried to discover if these two Englishmen really had schooled together but found that there is no evidence that Breakspear was at Merton. Nonetheless, I had stumbled upon a gap in the pantheon of English heroes. Having spent forty-seven years working with numbers as an actuary, I decided to turn to letters and right this omission.

Nicholas Breakspear was a mystery to me before embarking on this project. I have scoured as much as possible from the sources available in English covering twelfth-century events. The monk chroniclers of the twelfth and thirteenth centuries provided background even though most had too little detail to satisfy the curious twenty-first-century mind. Two noted English chroniclers, Roger of Wendover and William of Newburgh, were both laconic.

Contemporary writer John of Salisbury proved helpful and was refreshingly frank about his conversations with the pope. Notable by omission is the Laud Chronicle, the version of the Anglo-Saxon Chronicle that reaches 1154, which never deigns to mention Breakspear. It is odd that the election of an English pope seemed not to be newsworthy in 1154, although William of Newburgh, writing in the thirteenth century, was in no doubt about Breakspear's impressive achievement:

> He was raised as if from dust to sit in the midst of princes and to occupy the throne of glory.[5]

I might have expected more help from Matthew Paris, the chronicler monk of St Albans,[6] writing 100 years after Breakspear, but he gave us not a word about Breakspear's Scandinavian work, even though that had won for him the papacy. Fortunately two Scandinavian chroniclers, Saxo Grammaticus and Snorri Sturlason, offered some detail, not to say colour.

Adrian's confrontations with Frederick Barbarossa dominated this period in Otto of Freising's biography of Frederick, which was continued after 1157 by Rahewin. Both were partial to Frederick's point of view but tell us much about events that we would not otherwise know. I am also indebted to the nineteenth-century writers Horace Mann, Alfred Tarleton, Edith Almedingen, Richard Raby and Louis Casartelli,[7] whose hagiographies have taken me to places that I could not have reached on my own. John Freed recently wrote a weighty tome on Frederick which is well balanced on the all-important relationship between Adrian and the emperor.[8]

Breakspear: The English Pope is not a religious essay and there are as many cannons as canons in his story. My aim is to delight the reader with a human story of an astonishing rise from a low birth in England to what was then the highest elected office in the world, an exciting tale set in a turbulent twelfth-century Europe. From his cradle in Hertfordshire to his grave in Rome, Breakspear's life was a literal journey. There was effective free movement within twelfth-century Europe, especially for scholars, and people thought nothing of long travel even though it was so much harder than it is today. This account follows Breakspear's footsteps through Europe and for most readers this is a journey into the unknown. Let us begin.

MAIN CHARACTERS

Anacletus II,
Pope
When Pope Honorius died in 1130 two popes were elected: Innocent II and Anacletus, who was backed by the German Emperor Lothair III (1125–37). However, supported by Bernard of Clairvaux, Innocent won the recognition of most European countries. Anacletus died in 1138.

Anastasius IV,
Pope
The 80-year-old Anastasius was elected pope in 1153 after the death of Pope Eugenius III. He reigned for only seventeen months, succeeded in 1154 by Breakspear as Pope Adrian IV.

Arnold of Brescia
Born in Brescia around 1090, Arnold was a priest who studied under Peter Abelard. He became radicalised and campaigned for the Church to renounce wealth. He became the leader of the rebel Commune of Rome and was hanged in 1155.

Bernard of
Clairvaux, Abbot
Nobly born in Burgundy in 1090, Bernard founded Clairvaux Abbey in 1115. He defended the Church against heresy and was the driving force behind the Second Crusade. He died in 1153 and was canonised in 1174.

Boso,
Cardinal

Boso was an Italian prelate serving in the Curia, and Cardinal of SS Cosma e Damiano from 1156; he died in 1178. He was chamberlain to Pope Adrian and one of his closest advisers.

Conrad III,
King of Germany

Born around 1093, Conrad became King of Germany in 1138, using the title of Roman Emperor although he was never crowned as such. He died in 1152 and was succeeded by his nephew, Frederick Barbarossa. Together with Louis VII of France, he had led the disastrous Second Crusade.

Eskil of Lund,
Archbishop

Born to an aristocratic Danish family around 1100, Eskil entered Church service in 1131, succeeding his uncle as Archbishop of Lund in 1137. A close follower of St Bernard of Clairvaux, he resigned his archbishopric in 1177, retiring to the Abbey of Clairvaux, where he died in 1181.

Eugenius III,
Pope

Bernard of Pisa was born in 1080 and became a Cistercian monk at Clairvaux Abbey in 1138; he was pope from 1145 to 1153. He was a gentle man guided by his mentor, St Bernard of Clairvaux. Eugenius brought Breakspear into the Curia.

Frederick
Barbarossa,
Holy Roman
Emperor

Born in 1122, Frederick was King of Germany 1152–90 and Holy Roman Emperor 1155–90. His forays attempting to restore imperial control in Italy dominated Adrian's papacy.

Gregory VII,
Pope

An Italian, born of peasant stock in 1015, Hildebrand of Sovana became Archdeacon of Rome in 1049 and reigned as pope from 1073 to 1085. He was a champion of papal supremacy, insisting that only the pope could appoint bishops.

**Guido of
Biandrate**

An Italian count who controlled Novara, some
30 miles west of Milan, Guido was among the
defenders of Milan in 1158 when it surrendered
to Emperor Frederick. Nonetheless, he retained
Frederick's favour.

**Henry I,
King of England**

The fourth son of William the Conqueror, Henry
was born *c*. 1068 and reigned from 1100 to 1135.
He seized the throne when William Rufus died in
a hunting accident while his elder brother Robert
Curthose was away on the First Crusade.

**Henry II,
King of England**

Born in 1133, the son of Geoffrey of Anjou and
Empress Matilda, Henry was the first Plantagenet
King of England from 1154 until 1189, also ruling
much of north-west France. He married Eleanor
of Aquitaine after she had divorced King Louis VII
of France.

**Henry IV,
King of Germany**

Born in 1050, Henry was King of Germany 1054–
1105 and Holy Roman Emperor 1084–1105. He
sought to extend his control in Italy, pitting himself
against Pope Gregory VII. The struggle between
emperor and pope, centred on the power to appoint
bishops, was called the 'Investiture Controversy'.

Henry the Lion

Born *c*. 1129, Henry was Duke of Saxony from 1142
to 1180 and Duke of Bavaria from 1156 to 1180. A
cousin of Emperor Frederick Barbarossa and a noted
soldier, he married Matilda, the daughter of King
Henry II of England. He died in 1195.

**Inge,
King of Norway**

One of the three sons of King Harald of Norway,
(1130–36) he was born in 1135 and nicknamed
'Inge the Hunchback'. He ruled mostly alongside his
brothers Eystein and Sigurd but outlived them both.
He died in 1161 during a battle with his brother
Sigurd's son, who succeeded him as King Haakon.

Innocent II,
Pope

Innocent II was one of two popes elected in 1130, and, with the support of Bernard of Clairvaux, eventually prevailed over his rival Antipope Anacletus II. He reigned from 1130 to 1143, spending much of this time in exile in France.

John of Salisbury

John Little, born in Salisbury around 1110, moved to France in 1136 to study in Paris and Chartres. He was a noted writer and philosopher and became a close friend to Breakspear. After 1148 he became secretary to Archbishop Theobald of Canterbury, and later Thomas Becket. He became Bishop of Chartres in 1176 and died in 1180.

Jon Birgensson,
Archbishop

Jon was the Bishop of Stavanger when Breakspear arrived in Norway, and was chosen by the cardinal as the first Archbishop of Nidaros. He died in 1157.

Louis VII,
King of France

Born in 1120, Louis was King of France from 1137 to 1180. His first wife, Eleanor of Aquitaine, later married King Henry II of England. He was joint leader of the failed Second Crusade.

Manuel Comnenus,
Byzantine Emperor

Manuel was born in 1118 and ruled as Byzantine Emperor from 1143 to 1180. He was keen to restore the Byzantine Empire to its former glories and in particular to re-establish a hold on the Italian mainland and to oust the Normans from Sicily.

Matilda,
Empress

Born in 1102, Matilda was the daughter of King Henry I of England and the widow of Emperor Henry V of Germany (1111–25). She later married Geoffrey of Anjou. She contested the English crown with King Stephen but it was her son, Henry II, who succeeded Stephen in 1154. She died in 1167.

Michael Palaeologus A scion of a noble Byzantine family, Michael was sent to Italy by Emperor Manuel to regain former Byzantine holdings in Apulia on the Italian mainland. He died of natural causes during the fighting against King William I at Bari in 1155.

Octavian, Cardinal Octavian was a member of the powerful Tusculum family in Italy, which had long supported the German emperors. He was appointed Cardinal of Santa Cecilia in 1151. After the death of Pope Adrian in 1159 a minority of the cardinals elected him Antipope Victor IV, with the strong support of Emperor Frederick. He died in 1164.

Otto of Freising A German Cistercian and chronicler, Otto lived from 1114 to 1158. He was noble born, an uncle of Emperor Frederick Barbarossa and his biographer.

Otto of Wittelsbach Otto was one of Emperor Frederick's most loyal and leading knights. After Henry the Lion's fall from grace in 1180, Frederick appointed Otto the new Duke of Bavaria.

Rainald of Dassel Born around 1120 to the noble family of Dassel in Saxony, Rainald was a younger son who embarked on a career in the Church. Emperor Frederick appointed Rainald to be his chancellor in 1156. He always took a hard line in supporting Frederick.

Ramon Berenguer IV Born *c.* 1114, Ramon Berenguer ruled as the Count of Barcelona from 1131 to 1162. In 1158 he became the effective ruler of the union of Aragon and Catalonia. In the Iberian part of the Second Crusade he led his forces in the capture of Tortosa from the Moors in 1148. He died in 1162.

Richard d'Aubeney, Abbot
Abbot of St Albans 1097–1119, Richard was probably the abbot who rejected Breakspear's attempt to join St Albans monastery.

Robert de Gorham, Abbot
Abbot of St Albans 1151–66, Robert visited Pope Adrian at Benevento in 1155.

Robert Pullen
Robert was perhaps born in Poole in Dorset and lived from 1080 to 1146, becoming the first English cardinal around 1143. He had been a distinguished teacher of logic and theology in Paris, where one of his students was John of Salisbury.

Roger II, King of Sicily
Roger lived from 1095 to 1154; he was the son of Count Roger I of Sicily and the first Norman King of Sicily 1130–54. He bound the Norman conquests in Sicily and the southern Italian mainland into a strong, united kingdom.

Roland, Cardinal
Born in Sienna, and a teacher at Bologna's university, Roland was appointed Cardinal of SS Cosma e Damiano in 1150. He was papal chancellor to popes Eugenius, Anastasius and Adrian, and led the cardinals who opposed Emperor Frederick. In the schism of 1159 most of the cardinals elected him Pope Alexander III.

Stephen, King of England
Stephen was a grandson of William the Conqueror, and was King of England from 1135 to 1154. His reign was unsettled as he had to defend it against the Scots and the Welsh and to fight rival claimants Empress Matilda and her son, Henry of Anjou.

Sverker, King of Sweden
Sverker, nicknamed 'Clubfoot', was King of Sweden from 1125 until his murder on Christmas Day 1156.

**Sweyne III,
King of Denmark**

Sweyne was one of three competing kings in Denmark at the time of Breakspear's visit in 1154. Born in 1125, he reigned from 1146 until he was killed by a rival, King Valdemar, in 1157.

**Theobald of Bec,
Archbishop of
Canterbury**

Theobald of Bec, in Normandy, was chosen by King Stephen to be Archbishop of Canterbury from 1139 until 1161.

**Wibald of Stablo,
Abbot**

Born in 1098, William was a Benedictine and Abbot of Stablo in the Ardennes (in present-day Belgium). An influential member of Emperor Frederick's entourage, William was always eager to maintain good relations between Frederick and Adrian. He died in 1158.

**William I,
King of Sicily**

Born around 1120, the fourth son of King Roger II, William was crowned King of Sicily in 1151, three years before the death of his father. Unfairly nicknamed 'The Bad', he defeated attempts by disaffected Norman barons supported by Byzantine troops to seize his throne. He died in 1166.

PART ONE

Nicholas

ST ALBANS
Rejection at the Abbey

Breakspear, son to Robert [*sic*] Breakspear (a lay brother in the Abbey of St Albans) fetcht his name from Breakspear, a place in Middlesex, but was born at Abbots Langley.

Thomas Fuller
The History of the Worthies of England[1]

In the year 1100, Henry Beauclerc was crowned King of England following the death of his brother, the unmourned King William Rufus. No more than a few years later, in the tiny hamlet of Bedmond in densely wooded Hertfordshire, a boy was born and christened Nicholas. There were few records of births then and none at all for peasants. Nicholas himself probably did not know his exact year of birth. Birthdays were celebrated by their proximity to one of the many Christian feast days – never very distant in the twelfth century, when no fewer than fifty holy days were marked – but many would not know which birthday they were celebrating. Low-born people did not refer to years in *anno domini* form, such as 1110, but rather anchored past events by how long ago they had happened. If in 1110 someone asked when Henry had been crowned, they might reply, 'ten days before the Feast of the Assumption ten years ago'. Even members of the landed gentry might not know their exact age. Jury courts to establish 'proof of age' for the purposes of receiving inheritance or ending a wardship were not uncommon.[2]

The England into which this impoverished boy was born was different from the England we know today. A few of Henry's subjects who had fought for the

Anglo-Saxons or the Normans in 1066 would still be alive, a war less distant then than the 1982 Falklands War is today, but by the twelfth century the former antagonists were relatively settled, more than ready to enjoy the peace that the new King Henry and his Queen Matilda had brought.

We would not recognise the landscape, language, dress or customs of that time. The population of England was only about 2 million and most would have spoken Anglo-Saxon, or Old English, which, after the Danish conquest of the early eleventh century and the imposition of the Danelaw, had captured some Old Norse. The smaller governing classes would have spoken Norman French. This was when these two languages were starting to merge into the ancestor of modern English. The Victorian historian J.A. Froude remarked that perhaps the only twelfth-century sound we would recognise today is the pealing of church bells.[3]

Even the bounds of the English kingdom were far different from what they are today. Henry's authority included the Duchy of Normandy from 1106, and later the rule of Henry II (r.1154–89) extended beyond the English shores to cover much of France, including Brittany, Anjou, Touraine, Poitou and Aquitaine. Within the kingdom, London had been England's largest city since the ninth century, and by Henry's time its importance had supplanted Winchester, having become the capital city under William the Conqueror (r.1066–87). Forests stretched out almost everywhere from the north bank of the Thames to St Albans in Hertfordshire, with rivers flowing in wooded valleys. Not yet had medieval England's trees disappeared for building, agriculture and fuel.

While we may not know the exact date of Nicholas's birth, we know that his father was called Richard Breakspear, although there has been some confusion over this. Matthew Paris (*c.* 1200–59), a famous monk chronicler of St Albans, wrote:

> [Nicholas] was the son of a certain Robert de Camera who, living honourably in the world, moderately educated, received the habit of religion in the house of St Alban.[4]

Paris's misnomer continues to this day in St Albans Abbey. In 1979, during archaeological excavations, the remains of Nicholas's father, along with those of several medieval abbots, were relocated from 'the column of the Cloister' of St Albans and laid under the presbytery itself, in front of the high altar, where the commemoration stone bears the name 'Robert de Camera'. Better sources now agree that Nicholas's father's name was in fact Richard, and he is recorded in the Canterbury obituaries as 'Richard, priest and monk'.[5]

Although Nicholas's father's first name was wrongly recorded, it is possible that both surnames of Breakspear and de Camera could be correct. Camera was a known surname at this time, particularly in Devon, but it is more likely given here as a place name or a monastic office holder. In twelfth-century England it was not unusual for someone to be named after a place, or indeed by his occupation, rather than by his father's family name.

At Harefield, south-west of Watford, on the border of Hertfordshire and Middlesex, there is an ancient seat of a Breakspear family. A Victorian biographer of Nicholas, Alfred Tarleton, lived at Breakspear House in Harefield and it pleased him to record a direct link from his house to the English pope.[6] The surname Breakspear is unusual in England and this connection with Harefield is more than likely to be true.

Harefield, now a village in the borough of Hillingdon at the edge of the London sprawl, was then a small hamlet on the brow of a hill above the River Colne. The Domesday Book recorded it as a 'five plough' settlement. Just close by on the banks of the Colne was a preceptory named Moor Hall, also sometimes called by the Latin term '*camera*'. This was a small daughter house of St John's Priory in Clerkenwell. While growing up in Harefield, Richard Breakspear may have had a connection to this nearby chapel and this could explain the name that Paris gave to Nicholas's father. Richard had ambitions to enter Church life and it would have been quite natural for him to show a connection with a religious house near his original home.

There is another possible explanation. De Camera could have been a reference to Richard's later role at St Albans Abbey, being a term used for a particular clerk in the abbot's chamber. The *camerarius* was one of the officers of a medieval monastery and a relatively senior role, but it was not seen in records at St Albans until sometime later.*

Whether Richard Breakspear or Richard de Camera, or both, Nicholas's father was the second son in his family. He may well have wished to stay in Breakspear House in Harefield, but the rules of primogeniture meant that the family home would be inherited by his elder brother. By the time he was of age, Richard Breakspear would have to leave Harefield and make his own way in the world, which he did, but he did not go far. Perhaps inspired by his experiences at Moor Hall, he may already have had an ambition to join a monastery so he travelled 12 miles north towards St Albans. Living near a monastery, among the traders who supplied it, would have been an attractive

---

* Matthew Paris attributes the creation of the role *camera abbatis* to Abbot Ralph, 1146–51, and so too late to apply to Richard (*Gesta Abbatum*, vol. 1, p. 107).

proposition, whatever his intentions, and he settled down at Bedmond, a hamlet beside Abbots Langley. Richard stayed in Bedmond for a few years but failed to make a better living for himself. It is possible that it was here that Richard met Nicholas's mother and had Nicholas and his brother Ralph. If he was already a father by this time, the desire to provide for his family may have led him to improve his circumstances. Whatever the reason, sometime later he moved into nearby St Albans and became a serving brother at the monastery, although his actual status at the abbey is unclear. Richard eventually became the 'chamberlain', whose chief duties were concerned with the wardrobe of the monks. The chamberlain would examine their clothing and provide repairs or new garments when needed. He would also supervise the laundresses.[7] This was a necessary and vital role, but hardly the high office that other writers suggested for Richard.

William of Newburgh (1136–98), by contrast to the other chroniclers, was less than complimentary about Richard. William was an Augustinian canon from Bridlington in Yorkshire and a contemporary of Nicholas who carefully documented as much information as he could about the famous fellow Augustinian that Nicholas would become. He was not impressed by Richard Breakspear's position in life: 'He had a certain clerk of no great skill as his father.'[8] By calling Richard a 'clerk' of the abbey, William implies that he was ordained, albeit in minor orders. Richard probably started at the abbey only as a servant or lay brother, as Thomas Fuller recorded. Nevertheless, he would have shared a comfortable life with the other monks. Few then lived as well as the men in a monastery. Good sanitation, warm rooms and regular meals were luxuries to which few others could aspire.

While Richard was living comfortably in the monastery, it is not clear what happened to Nicholas, Ralph and their mother. We do not know if Richard ever married Nicholas's mother or what became of her. She may have died before Richard joined the monastery. Historical records of men are sparse, and there are hardly any at all for women. It would not have been unusual then for a minor cleric to be married; nor would it have been exceptional for a priest-monk to father a child after taking religious office, though it would carry a mark of shame. Paris does not suggest that Richard had any children out of wedlock, but even if it were the case he would not have wanted to sully the reputation of a fellow monk of St Albans. Whether true or not, rumours of Nicholas's illegitimacy persisted throughout his life.[9]

Paris tells us that Richard dwelt in the monastery for fifty years. This could be another example of Paris's lack of attention to detail. If he did live that long he would have outlived his son, which does not seem likely as, when pope, Nicholas never mentions his father. During Adrian's papacy a delegation from St Albans visited him in Italy and his father was not a part of it, and nor did the delegation carry any paternal greetings. John of Salisbury (*c.* 1115–80) was one of the most reliable chroniclers of these times, and a direct contemporary and friend of Nicholas, yet he makes no mention of a surviving father either.[10] We are left not knowing how long Richard dwelt in the monastery or when exactly he died.

Richard must have been a formative figure for the young Nicholas, but the absence of dates and Richard's move into the monastery means we cannot be certain how much contact there was between father and son. Nonetheless, bearing in mind St Francis Xavier's maxim, 'give me a child till he is seven years old and I will show you the man', Richard must deserve some credit for instilling in Nicholas a yearning for education, and his desire to play a role in the Church.

Richard Breakspear's religious life seemed to impact his second son, Ralph, who also entered the Church. He became a clerk in Feering in Essex, a church under the patronage of Westminster, and later he became an Augustinian canon at Missenden in Buckinghamshire.[11] Like his father, although he was in clerical orders, Ralph had at least one son who was also called Nicholas, presumably named for his uncle.

Boso (*c.* 1110–78), the first contemporary biographer of Nicholas, had served as an official in Church government, known as the Curia, since 1135 and became chancellor to Pope Eugenius (r. 1145–53). This Italian later became one of Nicholas's closest collaborators, for which Nicholas rewarded him first by appointing him as his *camerarius*, papal chamberlain, and in the following year by raising him to cardinal. Boso's *Vita Adriani IV* was written in the 1170s and, as he was both a close adviser and a friend, his biography can be regarded as reliable although sadly it tells us nothing of Nicholas's early life.[12] This may have been an agreed policy for official Church biographies of its leaders, born of caution following the unwelcome speculation about the parentage of an earlier pope, Gregory VII (1073–85).[13] It may also have reflected that, unlike today, little importance was placed on someone's early life.

English chroniclers tell us something of Nicholas's youth. Paris describes Nicholas as 'a handsome youth, fairly backward in clerical skills', while Thomas Fuller (1608–61) tells us that Nicholas grew up near Abbots Langley in Hertfordshire.[14]

Abbots Langley, a village dating far back into Saxon times, is close to St Albans and, as its name suggests, was owned by the abbey. Like all villages of the time it would have been self-sufficient. Nicholas would have been familiar with all the wooded paths to neighbouring villages, and the direct road to St Albans, 5 miles to the north-east. The Domesday Book was written around 1086, only thirty years or so before Nicholas was born, and the entry for Abbots Langley gives us a measure of what was then a tiny place:

> Households: 10 villagers. 5 smallholders. 2 slaves. 1 priest. 1 Frenchman.
> Ploughland: 15 ploughlands. 4 lord's plough teams. 1 lord's plough team possible. 10 men's plough teams.
> Other resources: 2.5 lord's lands. Meadow 5 ploughs. Woodland 300 pigs. 2 mills, value 1 pound.
> Annual value to lord: 10 pounds in 1086; 12 pounds when acquired by the 1086 owner; 15 pounds in 1066.[15]

Even the larger St Albans, a metropolis of its day, then had only ninety households. It would have been marvellous if the Domesday Book had given us names, but it does not. It was not a census as we now know it. Everybody in Abbots Langley and the adjoining hamlets would have known each other well and a couple of those Domesday Book villagers might still have been alive, in their fifties, when Nicholas was growing up. They could have known the young lad well. It is unlikely that the priest mentioned was Nicholas's father; however, it might have been the Frenchman who first aroused curiosity about France in young Nicholas. Might he have heard his first spoken French at home, long before he travelled to France?

One mile north of Abbots Langley, in Bedmond, about 2 miles northwest of the modern M1 and M25 crossing, there was a farmhouse called Breakspear's. It was demolished in the 1960s to make way for a small crescent of new houses and all that remains there now is a rather mean concrete plaque commemorating the site's historical significance. The farmhouse itself was undistinguished and of relatively modern brick. Parts of the inside were older, although unlikely to have been any earlier than Tudor, but it could well have been built on the site of the original home of Nicholas's family. At the end of the nineteenth century a watercolour painting of Breakspear's farmhouse was presented to Pope Leo XIII (1878–1903) and it is now somewhere in the Vatican, giving some weight to the authority that this was indeed Nicholas's home.

Bedmond is still tiny. Even though it is within commuting distance of London, its population today is less than 1,000. It boasts just one inn, a village hall and a single convenience store. Its church, the Church of the Ascension, was built in 1880 and is a rare example of a prefabricated corrugated-iron church. The road signs at the entries to Bedmond mark the village as the 'Birthplace of Pope Adrian IV' but those signs, and the concrete plaque at the site of the farmhouse, are the only mentions of a man who achieved such an exalted position. There is a further plaque in the church of St Lawrence in nearby Abbots Langley: 'About the date of the building of this present church was born Nicholas Breakspear.' This Norman church was built around 1150 and Nicholas may have been baptised in the Saxon church that lies beneath it.

Nicholas was most likely living in Bedmond when his father moved into the abbey at St Albans, although we do not know how old he was at this time. Unlike today, even young children would often have had to fend for themselves. He would not have been allowed to live with his father in the abbey, so he would have spent his early years in Bedmond with his brother, Ralph, and their mother, if she were still alive. By contrast to Richard, their lives would have been anything but comfortable.

Brickwork did not become widespread until the fourteenth century and rural houses and barns were built from local timber with some undressed stone. Rural dwellings consisted of a simple wooden frame covered with wattle and daub, or clay. The dimensions of the building would have been limited by the span of a tree trunk holding up the roof, no more than about 5 yards wide. There was plenty of space for houses in the small hamlets and so they would normally have had just one storey and be open right up to the roof. There were no individual rooms and screens were used to partition areas. Typically, one half of the house was for the family and the other half for stores and animals. Roofs would have been straw or thatch, fastened with branches. Thatching did not last long but was easy to replace.

Houses had windows but these were never glazed, instead having some cover such as oiled cloth or wooden shutters. The only heat came from an open hearth consisting of not much more than a ring of stones in the centre of the house. There were no chimneys; instead, smoke went through a hole in the roof. Wood for fuel was collected from the forests, no doubt a daily chore for the two boys, and lit by striking sparks with an iron on a flint. At night the only lighting was crude, such as rushes dipped in oil or fat. Tallow candles were a luxury the Breakspears could not have afforded and the boys' winter nights would have been dark and long.

Homes were bare. Furnishings were primitive, limited to beds, chests for what few clothes they had, a table and three-legged stools, which would stand more securely on the uneven earthen floors. Beds would have been at best rope or leather stringing on a wooden frame with rough cloth stuffed with straw to serve as a mattress. Simple pottery and wood would be used for bowls and pitchers. Everything that the two brothers would have had was basic, but resilient as all young children are, they would hardly have noticed their disadvantage.

Plumbing was non-existent. Only monasteries had running water. Water for a rural house would come from a nearby stream or from wells dug down to the water table and would have been collected in rough wooden buckets, another daily chore for Nicholas and Ralph. At first light every morning, they would dump their waste water on to the garden and walk to the well to fill their pails. Excrement was chucked on a midden and, once rotted, spread to fertilise the land. None of these modern indignities would have bothered Nicholas and Ralph; for them it was all part of the hard life of the rural poor. This was no idyllic childhood for the brothers but they would not have been unhappy.

The first thing we would notice if we were at Bedmond then would be the pervading smells; clothes and bodies were thick with the scents of cooking and smoke. As today, one's status in life would have been obvious from dress. There was no fashion or colour in the brothers' attire. Wool was the main textile, but clothes were also made from hemp or linen – textiles which rarely survive. Wool was tightly spun for hard wear, and so quite uncomfortable. These tough clothes would be passed down from one generation to the next and Nicholas would have spent his early years dressed in ill-fitting hand-me-downs. Shirts and underclothes were of linen, with a knee-length woollen tunic worn on top.

The brothers' diet would have been monotonous and seasonal as there were few ways to preserve food. Eggs, as likely to have come from ducks and geese as hens, and dairy foods from goats' and ewes' milk, not just from cows', were available for much of the year, although they were forbidden during Lent. The mainstay of a poor family's diet was potage, a soup made from grain, white peas, onions and leeks, all grown around the house. Most villages had a shared bread oven, baking with wheat, barley or oats when available. In scarce times, flour for bread was ground from acorns or hazelnuts.

The young Nicholas would rarely have tasted meat and is likely to have gone without potage on some days. Such was his hunger, and his determination to survive, that after his father joined the abbey he would trudge the 4 miles to St Albans most days and 'haunted the monastery for the sake of daily handouts'.[16] Despite his growling belly, Nicholas would have thought nothing of the 4-mile hike, and in summer he would have enjoyed his pleasant walk over rolling fields and through woods north from Bedmond to the abbey. Not so in the biting cold of winter, but still worth it for the chance of food. The M1 and M10 motorways now intersect this route, leaving it unrecognisable from

Nicholas's day, but the soaring red kites that Nicholas would have observed on his journey have now been reintroduced.

✠   ✠   ✠

It was thanks to the Romans that St Albans ever came to have a monastery for Nicholas's father to attend, and for Nicholas to haunt. Verulamium, as the Romans called St Albans, was the second largest town in their British province. As early as the first century, Roman traders and artisans had brought to England news of a new religion that came to be known as Christianity. Some English people converted to this new religion, but it took root only slowly. Christianity required the rejection of all other gods, which the polytheistic Roman authorities would not tolerate. Consequently, Christians were persecuted throughout the Roman Empire, which kept down the numbers of Christians until 313, when Emperor Constantine first permitted Christian worship.

St Albans was destined to become a Christian centre thanks to its eponymous saint, the first Englishman to be martyred for his faith in 305. Details of St Alban's martyrdom reach us through legend rather than archaeology. The story of a Roman soldier arrested for sheltering a Christian was passed through word of mouth until the Venerable Bede wrote it down in 731–32:

> The blessed Alban suffered death on 22 June near the city of Verulamium, which the English now call either Uerlamacaestir or Uaeclingaceastir. Here when peaceful Christian times returned, a church of wonderful workmanship was built, a worthy memorial of his martyrdom. To this day sick people are healed in this place and the working of frequent miracles continues to bring it renown.[17]

Bede tells us that when Alban was executed his severed head fell to the ground, and so immediately did the executioner's eyes. This miracle established the cult of St Alban and in the following centuries St Albans became a major pilgrimage destination as people sought atonement for sins or cures from illness. With such a steady flow of Christian worshippers, perhaps it is not surprising that St Albans claims to be the only place in England where there has been continuous Christian worship since Roman times. Colchester in Essex might challenge that: outside its city walls are the remains of a church which dates to 302.

As Christian worship grew in England, monasticism started to take off in the wider Church. Individual monks who had previously retreated from the world as hermits started to come to live together in communities. This practice developed in England too and marked the emergence of the first Celtic monasteries, although some of these 'monasteries' may have been no more than settlements of Christian families coming together for common security. Western monasticism developed further through St Benedict, who was born in Italy towards the end of the fifth century. His widely followed rule was severe but less harsh than the previous austerity of the hermit monks. Benedict's rule required moderation in all aspects of monastic life, but he did insist that members of his communities put aside personal preferences for the common good. Absolute obedience to the superior was non-negotiable. Today we struggle with such absence of any right to reply but then it was accepted.

The Rule of Benedict found its way from Italy into England only half a century after St Benedict's death, arriving with St Augustine of Canterbury, himself a Benedictine. Pope Gregory I, Gregory the Great (590–604), happened to see one day some captive Anglo-Saxons in the slave market at Rome and described them as 'not Angles but angels'. To make sure that these 'angels' would reach heaven, Pope Gregory sent Augustine as a missionary to Kent. The decision had significant effect:

> Never did a Pope resolve on an undertaking more big with consequences. Not only did the doctrine take root in Germanic Britain, but with it a veneration for Rome and the Holy See such as no other country had ever evinced.[18]

On arrival Augustine wasted no time in establishing the first English Benedictine monastery in Canterbury in 598, thus forging lasting links with Rome. After Augustine's time papal legates would visit England regularly, and English kings and nobles, including King Offa of Mercia (757–96), made pilgrimages to Rome. It was Offa who initiated the Church tax of 'Peter's Pence', called *Romefeoh*. This was a fee due to Rome that was widely paid in mainland Europe, and which Nicholas would later introduce into Scandinavia.

The importance of Rome to England was demonstrated when Alfred the Great went there as a child in the mid-ninth century. These English links with Rome became stronger still after the Battle of Hastings, William the Conqueror having invaded England under a papal banner. This may have caused the Roman pope to lose some popular sympathy among the Anglo-Saxon English, but any such resentment did not persist, and the Church retained its power and authority. People were true to the faith, living in an age when it was rarely questioned, and Nicholas was no exception. Still, the

Conqueror could never have imagined that within 100 years of Hastings an English peasant boy would become pope.

After Canterbury, other monasteries followed. The abbey at St Albans was one of many Benedictine foundations in England and tradition claims it was founded by Offa himself in 793 on the site of the tomb of St Alban. The new Benedictine abbey, holding the shrine of Britain's first martyr, gained steadily in prestige and throughout most of the medieval period it was England's premier abbey. Successive abbots of St Albans missed no opportunity to capitalise on their stewardship of the shrine. The old Saxon pilgrim route from London to St Albans, *Eldestrete*, meaning 'the old road', can still be followed snaking through Wembley and Radlett to St Albans.

Pilgrims were encouraged to visit the abbey shrine regularly. In accordance with Benedictine rules of hospitality, monks received guests kindly. It made sense: pilgrims' offerings were a vital source of their income. Learning flourished too, and the abbey's scriptorium was renowned for the high quality of its books. Nicholas knew from an early age that the abbey could sustain his hunger for food and his ambition for learning.

The abbey continued to flourish until late in the ninth century, when it was ravaged by the Vikings, and it was only towards the end of the tenth century that the Benedictines were able to re-establish themselves at St Albans. The constant flow of pilgrims soon provided the monks with enough riches to rebuild their abbey. This the Benedictines did in some style. Their vast new Romanesque church, larger even than Canterbury Cathedral, was started under their first Norman abbot, Paul of Caen, on the site of King Offa's old Anglo-Saxon church. The tower, built between 1077 and 1088, was particularly splendid and is now the oldest surviving cathedral tower in Britain. Unusually, the Norman builders used recycled brick and flint rather than stone, since bricks were readily available from the surrounding Roman ruins.

The church was completed by Paul's successor, Abbot Richard, and its dedication took place on 28 December 1115, the feast of the Holy Innocents (or, as they would have said, 'on the feast of the Holy Innocents in the sixteenth year of King Henry's reign'). King Henry and Queen Matilda held their Christmas Court at St Albans and all the great and the good of the day were invited for the lavish celebrations, led by Geoffrey, the Archbishop of Rouen, and including Richard, Bishop of London, Roger of Salisbury, Ralph of Durham and many abbots and earls, both English and Norman.[19] The procession to the new abbey church, led by the royal court and followed by the princes of the Church in all their pomp, provided once-in-a-lifetime excitement to the townsfolk.

Those attending the dedication of the new abbey were entitled to the 'indulgence' of an unspecified number of days' remission from penance, a valuable reward in medieval times. All the neighbouring villagers benefitted from the feasting laid on by the abbey. Nicholas, a young teenager by now, would have been excited by these parties, which lasted until Twelfth Night, 6 January 1116. These momentous events perhaps sowed the seed of his ambition in the Church, and that of his brother Ralph too.

The new abbey was stunning. It had taken thirty-eight years to complete and the Benedictines had achieved a remarkable result. The walls then were covered in gleaming white plaster to protect against the weather (today they are plain, but still impressive). The abbey sits on a hill in an idyllic landscape, nestled in the south-eastern corner of the massive Diocese of Lincoln and astride the Roman Watling Street. The journey from London took only one day, and the view for travellers approaching the abbey was outstanding:

> Its impressive physical position marking the highest site above sea level of any English Abbey and visible for miles in every direction.[20]

Modern development around the church, which only became a cathedral in 1877, has taken away some of the impact of the earlier distant view.

Monasticism in England peaked in the twelfth century. There were as many as 15,000 men in monastic orders from a population of 2 million, meaning that almost three out of every 200 men were monks.[21] Many more men were tied to the monasteries by employment. The monasteries dominated all aspects in the life of the nation. Monastic life brought regular work. The monks set the standards in education and were the only producers of books. They provided refuge for the sick. By the time of the Reformation the monasteries had come to own about a quarter of all agricultural land in England. They had become a power to be reckoned with.

The disciplined approach in a monastery demonstrated the belief that this was the way to Christian perfection. Nicholas knew from his father the set daily routine for a monk, the canonical hours, and it was strict: 'Seven times a day I praise thee'.* The day began soon after midnight with Matins, prayers and psalms held in the church. The second hour, Lauds, consisted of the early morning praises usually celebrated in song soon after Matins and before dawn. After Lauds the monks would return to bed. The third hour, Prime, was the early Mass at 6 or 7 a.m., meaning that the monks would have

---

* Psalms 119:164.

had about seven hours' sleep, albeit broken. This first Mass would usually be attended by the servants and lay staff of the monastery. After Prime, the monks would have said their private prayers and then studied in the cloister. There followed a simple breakfast of bread, baked in the monastery, with weak beer or wine, water not being clean enough to drink. The Chapter Mass would be celebrated at about 9 a.m. after which the daily Chapter, a meeting of all the monks, would be held behind closed doors to discuss the business of the day. Terce was the mid-morning hour, Sext the midday prayer and Nones the mid-afternoon prayer. The final prayer of daytime was Vespers, which took place around sunset, and the night prayer, Compline, was held at about 7 p.m. It was only in the fourteenth century that a day was divided into twenty-four equal hours. At this time the length of seasonal daylight was divided into twelve hours, meaning that hours raced by in wintertime and the prayers were shorter then than in summer.[22]

This regime sounds harsh, but Nicholas would not have thought so. In those austere times monastic life was an attractive option, and broken sleep and strict discipline was a small price to pay for it. Joining a monastic community brought security, companionship and comfortable accommodation, even if the cloisters were cold. Food was provided and a monk could rely on the monastery's hospital, if needed, and on care in old age. This attractive package explains why so many men chose the monastic life, although among those numbers there would have been some who felt a genuine divine calling to religious life.

Nicholas knew the abbey routine, but he was not part of it, much as he would have liked to have been. Instead, even as a youngster he would have had to play his part in the rural life of Bedmond. An exercise for schoolboys to translate into Latin gives a rare picture of the onerous duties of a plough boy around the time of the Norman Conquest:

'What say you ploughboy, how do you do your work?'

'Oh dear sir, I must work very hard. I go out at dawn, drive the oxen to the field, and yoke them to the plow. However hard the winter is, I dare not idle at home for fear of my master, and when I have yoked the oxen and fastened the ploughshare and coulter to the plough I must plough daily a whole acre or more.'

'Do you have a helper?'

'I have a boy who guides the oxen with a goad, and he also is hoarse with the cold and his shouting.'

'Do you do anything else during the day?'

'I have more to do than I have said, certainly. I must fill with hay the mangers of the oxen and give them water and carry their dung outside.'

'Oh, oh! Your tasks are heavy ones.'

'Yes, sir, they are heavy, for I am not a free man.'[23]

The teenage Nicholas would not have been too young to work the land and might have seen the abbey as his way out of a rural existence. Not for him a life following the plough. Whenever his chores allowed, he visited his father at the monastery to get food, standing outside the abbey waiting for handouts, dreaming of one day eating inside with the monks, never imagining the comforts he would enjoy as pope in years to come.

But it was not just food he craved: he also wanted a real education. Some basic schooling would have been offered in the village churches, but his family would not have had the money for it, and even if they had, it would never have been enough for him. He knew instinctively that he had the ability to learn, and ambition drove him. He knew that he had to become part of a Church establishment if he was to obtain the best education available.

Richard doubtless would have encouraged his son. He might have hoped that Nicholas could join him in the community, a reasonable ambition for a twelfth-century father. Paris tells us that Nicholas approached the abbot and asked to be accepted as a monk at St Albans, or possibly a cleric at one of the abbey's outlying churches. The abbot, Richard D'Aubeney (r. 1097–1119), did give Nicholas a trial, but he did not pass muster: 'Wait, my son, and work further at school, so that you may be better prepared.'[24]

Paris may have wanted to be kind to Nicholas in reporting his rejection as a gentle rebuff; other less kind reasons for Nicholas's rejection are recorded. Bale said he was turned down because he was a bastard; Trollope suggests he was refused because he was a 'bondman', meaning a tied, unpaid servant of the abbey.[25] Another possibility is that the abbey was only admitting young men who came with a 'dowry'. This was one of the ways that the monasteries raised funds and there was no way the Breakspears could have found such monies for Nicholas.

William of Newburgh suggests that Nicholas was turned away from the abbey by his father, rather than by the abbot:

Since he [Nicholas], on the threshold of adolescence, was not able to attend schools because of his poverty, he haunted the same monastery for the sake of daily handouts. His father was embarrassed because of this, reproaching his sloth with biting words; denied all solace, he went away indignantly.[26]

The suggestion that Nicholas was thrown out by his father is repeated in other accounts. Although William of Newburgh is regarded as reliable, it is doubtful that Nicholas left St Albans in anger: it does not fit the picture of the Nicholas that emerges after he leaves England. Nor is it likely that he was slothful as a youth. He might well have left at the shame of his rejection rather than being driven away by his father's anger. It is possible that William of Newburgh simply latched onto an easy explanation of how Nicholas might have come to leave England. William himself, writing later about Nicholas's election as pope, drops the idea that Nicholas had been slothful and suggests he remembered his father and St Albans kindly:

> With the concurrent wishes of all, Breakspear, taking the name of Adrian, assumed the pontificate. Not unmindful of his earlier instruction, and chiefly in memory of his father, he honoured the church of the blessed martyr, Alban, with donations, and distinguished it with lasting privileges.[27]

Rather than accept the plough, Nicholas decided to leave his family and sever his connection with St Albans. We can be quite certain that he never nursed a grudge because, as William told us, he favoured the abbey that rejected him many times during his papacy. He left because he would not take no for an answer. If he could not receive his education at St Albans he would look elsewhere. His had innate self-confidence and the prospect of long journeying into lands unknown to him was no deterrence.

PARIS

Searching for a School

When he was found upon examination to be inadequate, the abbot said to him courteously enough, 'Wait, my son, and work further at school, so that you may be better prepared.'

Matthew Paris
Gesta abbatum S. Albani[1]

Nicholas's ambition marked him out from other boys. Few in the twelfth century had the opportunity of an education, and there was little demand, since agricultural workers and peasants had no need of literacy. Even country priests in remote parishes would have had little learning. Nicholas was different, desperately wanting an education to unlock his future, and he knew that he would find the learning he craved only at a monastic establishment.

He was still young when he left St Albans. Now, we would not expect children to leave home any earlier than their late teens, but at that time boys as young as 10 could enter monasteries. Life was tough and for struggling families putting a son in a monastery would bring welcome financial relief.

In theory, there was plenty of choice for him: monasteries abounded in England and it would not have been at all unusual to look further afield. At this time, the Roman Church dominated life throughout western and central Europe. Latin was still the universal teaching language and once fluent an able student could seek his education and employment anywhere. Church learning was a passport to a career throughout Europe as two Italians, Lanfranc and Anselm, could testify. Thanks to their proficiency they both became

Archbishops of Canterbury. Englishmen also benefitted from this inter-nationalism and held the sees of Palermo and Messina in Sicily. People today might be surprised as to how widely travelled were certain twelfth-century people. Nicholas's friend in later life, John of Salisbury, followed the example of many compatriots and looked abroad for his education, studying in Paris and Chartres until about 1146 and becoming a clerk in the papal court sometime before 1147. It is not at all surprising then that Nicholas, like John, decided to travel to Europe to pursue his dream.

The obvious place for Nicholas to begin would be an English monastery that might then open the door for travel to Europe. Having been rejected at home, he had not made the best start. Despite that rejection, the Abbot of St Albans might have helped Nicholas with his next step. After all, the abbot had advised Nicholas to 'work further at school' and, being well aware of Nicholas's ambi-tions, it would have been natural for him to do what he could to assist.

It is generally accepted that Nicholas was born around 1100 but this might be no more than a convenient round date. Historian R.L. Poole argued that Nicholas did not move to France until sometime after 1130, which would mean he was not born until around 1115.[2] However, we know that Abbot Richard who rejected Nicholas at St Albans died in 1119, which means that Nicholas must have been born much nearer to 1100, perhaps around 1105.[3] Knowing the exact year of Nicholas's birth would help plot his early life against recorded events. Taking 1115 as a possible year of birth allowed Poole to explain his possible route out of England, suggesting that the Abbot of St Albans introduced Nicholas to the Augustinian school which emerged soon after 1120 at Merton Priory in Surrey, south of London.

The Augustinian Order takes its name not from St Augustine of Canterbury, who introduced the Benedictine Rule to England, but from St Augustine of Hippo, in Algeria, a Roman-African Christian philosopher who died in 430. The clergy of larger churches were called canons; since the eighth century, these canons formed communities and lived under the rule of St Augustine, thus becoming 'regular' canons. They were conventual and so attached to a particular monastic house, but unlike monks they were not confined within the precinct. Austin canons, also known as black canons because of the colour of the habits they wore, were permitted to live and work in the outside world. Individual regular canons often served outlying parishes associated with their mother house. Nonetheless, like the Benedictines and other monastic orders, the Augustinians observed the seven canonical hours in church, took vows of obedience, poverty and chastity, gave alms to the needy and provided hospital-ity to travellers.

Gilbert the Norman introduced the Augustinians to England. This Sheriff of Cambridgeshire and Huntingdonshire founded St Botolph's at Colchester in 1100. The ruined nave can still be seen just inside the city walls. This first Augustinian house then moved to Huntingdon in about 1106. Eight years later King Henry rewarded Gilbert with the gift of the *ville*, or farm, of Merton in Surrey where he was also sheriff 'for the building of a church in honour of the virgin Mary, and for the health of my soul' and 'to possess freely in hereditary right'.[4] Gilbert soon moved Merton Priory a short distance to a better site on the banks of the River Wandle, which powered its two water mills, providing a good income for the priory. By 1117 the black canons had settled in their new home and established a school. Merton Priory quickly became one of the largest and most flourishing of the English Augustinian houses, benefitting by its proximity to London and by royal patronage. Queen Matilda and her young son, William, visited Merton in 1118 and supported its development, but only for a brief time. Matilda died later that year and William, Henry's heir, died tragically in 1120. Other financial supporters stepped into the breach to help fund Merton's growth.

One way that monasteries of this era raised money was by providing a secure and comfortable standard of living in old age for those who could afford it. Some wealthier people would even enter the order and gain entitlement to burial in the monastery churchyard, and so benefit from the canons' continuing prayers and gain a surer pass to heaven. These 'corrodians' paid for the privilege by gift of land or money, and if they died relatively quickly then the canons would turn a good profit. Actuarial life tables, setting out expectation of life according to age, had not been invented in the twelfth century but had they been available Merton might have been safeguarded against one of its corrodians, who lived on after his deal for a further and expensive twenty-nine years.[5] Fortunately for the canons, such longevity at this time was unusual.

Merton's influence grew alongside its buildings. It did not take long to become a centre of power and it developed an early and close association with Canterbury. Merton was especially honoured when, on his death in Normandy in 1135 (famously from a surfeit of lampreys), Henry's body was brought back to lie in state in the church at Merton before his burial at Reading Abbey, which he had founded in 1121. Today the long-since ruined abbey is being searched for Henry's body, which is believed to lie below the site of the former Reading Prison. Likewise, little evidence of the once-proud Merton Priory remains today, although the foundations of the chapterhouse can still be seen underneath the A24 at Merantun Way by Merton Abbey Mills, a sixteenth-century textile factory later used by William Morris at the end of the nineteenth century.

The Abbot of St Albans would have known of this emerging Augustinian school and Poole concluded that Nicholas did study at Merton on the evidence of the last sentence of one of John of Salisbury's letters.[6] John wrote of conversations he had had with Nicholas about the Augustinian canons of Merton. In his letter he puts to Nicholas, after he had become pope, a petition of the canons of Merton. John's letter closed with:

> May it profit the brethren of Merton that, while you were in the church of
> St Ruf their good odour reached even to you, as your highness used to tell
> me, your servant, when we talked together.[7]

This is not convincing evidence, but if true it could have been difficult for Nicholas to find a better education than from the Augustinians. Their schooling was formal and taken very seriously. Thomas Becket attended Merton Priory school in about 1128 and a public information board near Morden Hall Park, the site of the old Merton Priory, claims that both Becket and Breakspear were old boys of the school, but there is little direct evidence in the case of Breakspear. How amazing it would have been had the two giants of the twelfth-century English Church been schooled together. The London borough of Merton must think it is true, since in 2012 it commissioned a bronze plaque for Queen Elizabeth II which shows King Henry III (1216–72) standing between Becket and Breakspear, 'both pupils at Merton Priory'. It was presented to the queen to mark the first English parliament held at Merton by King Henry III in 1235 and is now held in the royal collection. The Statute of Merton was the first law on England's statute book and its eleven chapters were a step in the post-Magna Carta struggle to limit the king's arbitrary powers; it was repealed only in 1953.

Believing that the Augustinians provided Nicholas with an education would help explain how he reached France. In 1132, the Bishop of Coutances asked Merton to establish a daughter house at St-Lô in Normandy, then controlled by Henry, who had become Duke of Normandy in 1106.[8] St-Lô had been an ancient monastery, traditionally founded in the fourth century by St Helena, the mother of Emperor Constantine the Great, but it had been destroyed twice since then, first by 'Northmen' in the eighth century and again by Vikings in 888.[9] The monastery was re-established in the ninth century and it became one of many collegiate churches in eleventh-century Normandy staffed by secular canons.

Attached to a cathedral or major church, the secular canons did not take vows of poverty, chastity and obedience, and by the twelfth century they were increasingly being criticised for their too-comfortable lifestyles. In 1128 William d'Evreux, the king's treasurer, decided that St-Lô should be converted to a house of regular canons to correct their scandalous behaviour. St-Lô looked to England for help and Merton accepted the challenge. Its Canon Theodoric became the first abbot of the re-established St-Lô and Poole suggests that Nicholas was a junior member of the band that Theodoric led to Normandy. However, there is no evidence to support this.

Nicholas was probably never at Merton, instead making his own way from St Albans around 1120, crossing to France from Dover. Such a journey, unsupported, would have been difficult but by no means impossible. As a young man with no means he would have cut a shabby figure, likely barefooted, as he travelled through Kent towards the Channel. The main route from London to Dover would take Nicholas through Rochester and Canterbury and he must have stopped to rest in churches as he passed, taking advantage of monastic hospitality whenever he could. Evidence indicates that he was a personable young man and the churches he passed were well used to assisting travellers and pilgrims. Even so, his food would have been meagre and his lodgings bare, but for Nicholas this was not so much different from his days at Bedmond.

We must guess how the penniless Nicholas managed to cross to France. He might have worked his passage but, as far as we know, he had no experience to offer. The English Channel would have been his first sight of the sea. The voyage across the Channel, about 30 miles, then took about twelve hours and it would not have been comfortable. We can see in the Bayeux Tapestry the types of boats then in use, weighing less than 30 tons, somewhat less than a modern container lorry. They had no deck protection, and with no rudder they would have been steered by an oar at the stern.

Crossing the Channel was also risky. At about the same time as Nicholas would have been sailing to France, a more illustrious group was crossing the other way from Normandy to England. On 25 November 1120, King Henry and William, his 17-year-old son and heir, were on their way back to England in good spirits, having defeated King Louis VI of France in battle. William had been married for just seventeen months. They set off from Barfleur at night in clear weather, prince and king travelling in separate ships, as was their usual practice. Thomas Fitzstephen, whose father had captained one of the ships that had brought William the Conqueror to Hastings in 1066, asked for the honour of taking Prince William in his brand-new ship *Blanche Nef*, the White Ship.

The weather that night was mild and the unnecessary tragedy happened when Fitzstephen's ship hit Quillebœuf, a submerged rock close by the Norman shore. The two ships may have been racing and therefore careless.

It may even have been gross negligence. The Benedictine chronicler Orderic Vitalis (1075–*c.* 1142) blamed the shipwreck on an excess of alcohol.[10] Prince William had loaded the ship with wine to continue the victory celebrations. Not many then survived a shipwreck as few people could swim. As the *Blanche Nef* sank, William managed to get into a small boat, but rather than row to safety he selflessly returned to the wreck to look for his half-sister Matilda and his half-brother Richard. William's small boat was swamped when other panicking survivors tried to board it and dragged it under. Only one person survived.* This tragedy had dire consequences for the country, which on Henry's death in 1135 descended into anarchy as a fierce struggle for the throne erupted between his daughter Matilda and his nephew Stephen, a grandson of the Conqueror.

Despite the dangers, Nicholas reached France safely, and he never returned to St Albans. Although he left at an early age, he never lost his affection for his first home. In conversation with John of Salisbury in later years, he expressed a wish that he had never left his native land of England.[11] Yet, if he had stayed at home the Church would have missed the service of a remarkable, self-made man.

---

* The tragedy is described graphically in Dante Gabriel Rossetti's 1880 ode 'The White Ship'.

PART TWO

BREAKSPEAR

3

PROVENCE
An Augustinian Canon

In the time of his adolescence, leaving both his land and his family, so that he could make progress in the study of letters, he came to Arles.

Cardinal Boso
Vita Adriani IV[1]

At this time, it was not unusual for family names that carried meanings to be translated, so once in Normandy Nicholas could have become known as *Briselance* (or *Hastafragus* in Latin). Matthew Paris wrote that in France he was also known as *Nicholaus de Langele*, meaning Nicholas from Langley.[2] Nicholas, probably in his late teens, was by this time already a young man and we shall now call him Breakspear.

The twelfth-century France in which Breakspear found himself was small, consisting of just five major cities – Paris, Melun, Étampes, Orléans and Sens – and the countryside around them. Travelling the 200 miles to Paris by foot was not an easy prospect. Ambush by lawless bands was not uncommon, although the young student Breakspear would hardly have offered any temptation to brigands. He would not have had the road to himself, probably walking in the company of pilgrims, constantly on the move around Europe. It is not clear when he reached Paris, nor how long it took or where he stayed. He had no profile to justify a mention in the few twelfth-century church and monastic records that have survived. Breakspear is still invisible at this stage in his life.

Paris was a good place for Breakspear to continue his education. Until the tenth century, the city had little significance but had now developed into an important religious and administrative centre with an estimated population of 30,000, more than London at that time. Notre-Dame would not appear until 1163, but the monasteries on the left bank of the Seine had already become the leading centre of learning in medieval France. This century was the dawn of universities throughout Europe and the University of Paris, one of the oldest in Europe, was recognised as early as 1150. Oxford University developed a little later than Paris but grew rapidly after 1167, when Henry II banned English students from attending the University of Paris. Until then studious Englishmen had favoured Paris, including Robert Pullen, who was later appointed the first English cardinal (1144–46), and John of Salisbury, who studied there in 1138, sometime later than Breakspear. John's friendship with him was not forged in Paris as by then Breakspear was already in Avignon.

Breakspear may somehow have carried a recommendation for one of the schools in Paris but we do not know which one. There was a particularly famous Church teacher in Paris, Suger (1081–1151), who in 1100 had sheltered Walter Tyrrell, the huntsman who had accidentally killed King William Rufus before fleeing into exile. Suger was the influential Abbot of St Denis, which held the relics of the third-century martyr and patron saint of France. Judging by the dates, it is possible that Breakspear studied under Suger but the records of St Denis contain no reference to the young Englishman. In later years, when he was pope, Breakspear did refer to a friendship with a teacher in Paris, an Irish monk called Marianus about whom we know nothing.[3]

Breakspear's accommodation in Paris was probably no more than a bare room attached to one of the churches, sharing with other students. We know that Thomas Becket also studied in Paris around 1136 but Breakspear had left the city by then. Student life in Paris was hard, but that was nothing new for Breakspear; he had known nothing else in his life so far. He would most likely spend the day odd-jobbing or begging for his food and drink, and and then study at night under oil lamps. Breakspear would have accepted all of this without complaint, knowing that it was what ambitious students had to do.

It is not clear how successful a student Breakspear was in Paris. William of Newburgh and the later writing of Matthew Paris provide only thin details of this part of his life and neither of them were writing from personal experience. They disagree as to whether Breakspear stayed long in Paris, leaving us us wildly differing accounts. William thought Breakspear achieved little there and had quickly moved on:

> But, left to his own devices and forced by necessity to take a risk, he went to the regions of Gaul, being embarrassed as a freeborn man, either to dig or

beg in England. And when he failed to prosper in France, going into remoter regions, he travelled across the Rhone to the region called Provence.[4]

Matthew Paris was more positive but once again he may have been writing deliberately kindly of a monk with connections to St Albans. He is adamant that Breakspear succeeded in Paris:

> Therefore the clerk, ashamed, considering such delay to be rejection, went away and, going to Paris, he became a most assiduous student and surpassed all his associates in learning.[5]

So, who was right? If Breakspear had proved to be an excellent scholar in Paris, why would he have quit such a renowned centre of learning after perhaps only two years? He would find nothing as prestigious anywhere else. It is more likely that someone with his talents and diligence would have succeeded in the French schools and his leaving was not simple wanderlust but a course plotted by his teachers in Paris to enrol at particular schools in the south and broaden his education. His move south might have been instigated by the well-connected Abbot Suger himself, who knew Provence well. Louis VI had sent Suger to the court of Pope Gelasius II at Maguelonne near Montpellier, where he lived from 1121 to 1122. Whatever drove him, Breakspear still wanted to be received into holy orders and knew that the more rounded his education, the better his chance of finding a house that would accept him.

The prospect of another long journey did not trouble Breakspear. Whether following a pre-arranged Augustinian plan or using connections made in Paris, he would have been given introductions for some hospitality along the route, and, as ever, his poverty was his best protection against footpads. The journey from Paris to his next stopping point, the schools at Arles, was 470 miles, half as far again as the distance he had trudged from St Albans to Paris. Walking direct to Arles would have taken at least a month.

We now have some details, albeit sparse, from Breakspear's biographer Boso. He tells us that 'in the time of his adolescence' Breakspear reached Arles, in lower Burgundy, which was not yet part of France.*[6] It had been a provincial Roman capital and still boasts impressive Roman monuments that are well worth seeing. The Romans first took the town in 123 BC and built a direct canal link down to the Mediterranean. The magnificent coliseum at Arles is still in use today, with bull fighting taking place there twice a year. In

---

* Arles did not become part of France until 1487.

Breakspear's day, the coliseum's impact was largely hidden by the houses and even a church built within the arena.

Arles had been less important than its rival neighbouring city Massalia, which we know as Marseilles, but in the war between Julius Caesar and Pompey, Arles sided with the victorious Caesar and came out on top, and much of Massalia's wealth was taken there. The Rhône forks into two branches just north of Arles and forms the Camargue delta. Arles remained an important port on the Rhône until the railways replaced river traffic and Marseilles regained its old ascendancy.

Christianity was introduced to Arles by the Romans. The first Christian emperor, Constantine, declared himself emperor in the west in 307 and expressed his love of the town, making Arles his capital. Constantine's son, the future Constantine II, was born there. After the Roman era Arles was ruled by independent kings but not always securely. Even this far south, so close to the Mediterranean, people were not safe from Viking raiders, who destroyed Arles in the seventh and eighth centuries. The territory of the medieval kingdom of Arles was not much smaller than France itself, stretching from the Mediterranean to the high Rhine in the north, roughly corresponding to the present-day French regions of Provence-Alpes-Côte d'Azur, Rhône-Alpes and Franche-Comté, as well as western Switzerland.

The rule of the independent kings continued until 1032, when Rudolph III died without any surviving heirs, and in accordance with a treaty of 1006 the kingdom passed to the German emperor, Conrad II. Arles was then incorporated into the Roman Empire but it still enjoyed considerable autonomy. Emperors held the title 'King of Arles' but few bothered to be crowned there. An exception was Emperor Frederick Barbarossa, a major player in Breakspear's later life, who was crowned King of Burgundy in the Cathedral of St Trophime in Arles in 1158. This impressive church on the market square was built between 1100 and 1150 and Breakspear would have seen it taking shape. St Augustine of Canterbury was Bishop of Arles in 597, and in 2001 the Archdiocese of Canterbury donated a stone baptismal font to the St Trophime to mark this English connection.

Some records suggest that, around the time when he was at Arles, Breakspear spent time with the new Norbertine order. This was a time when new monastic orders were spinning out of the Benedictines, and helpfully all these newcomers were colour-coded. The Carthusians, founded in 1084, wore black robes over a white habit; the Cistercians, founded in 1098, wore white robes; and the Tironensians, founded in 1106, wore grey. All three orders grew quickly, especially in France, England and Scotland. The newer Norbertines, distinguished by their white habits and known as 'white canons', came along in 1120 when some Augustinian canons at the Prémontré monastery near Reims in France signed up for a stricter rule of life. They were led by Norbert, a friend of the Cistercian St Bernard of Clairvaux (1090–1167). Bernard, a charismatic preacher, was defender-in-chief against all controversies and became the most influential voice in the Church in the first half of the twelfth century. Bernard's Cistercian spirituality had been a major influence on Norbert.

The Norbertines became better known as Premonstratensians. Like the Augustinians, they were not monks but regular canons. They followed the Augustinian Rule but with added austerity. In effect, they were to the Augustinians what the Cistercians were to the Benedictines. Breakspear may have studied with them briefly but information about this is sparse. A Norbertine abbot, Georg Lienhardt of Roggenburg (1717–83), wrote of Pope Adrian:

> That the blessed Adrian was once, at least for a time, an alumnus of our order he himself testifies in a Bull prefixed to our statutes, where he speaks thus in commendation of our white institute: 'Mindful how your institute and Order, of which we were once an alumnus, brilliant with abundant splendour of merits.'[7]

If he was an alumnus, Breakspear was an early customer of their hospitality. Their house, established in about 1130 within a former Benedictine monastery, was only 20 miles from Arles, halfway to Tarascon at Frigolet. Some Norbertines claim that Breakspear was professed as a Norbertine, but this is unlikely. The reference to him being an alumnus means no more than that he was briefly a pupil with them. Had he professed in religious orders at Frigolet he would have been included in their records, but he is not. He was still too young for ordination. We would also have seen more involvement by Breakspear with the Norbertines after he became pope.

It was probably in the early 1130s that Breakspear worked his way south across the Rhône to Arles and, if he were carrying good credentials from his teachers in Paris and the nearby Norbertines, he would have found it easy to be accepted at one of the schools there. Like Paris, Arles was a centre of learning, specialising in Roman law, which he studied briefly. Now in his early twenties, and well educated, he must have felt fully equipped for his real goal, to enter a monastic house, and he was ready to move on again.

Breakspear turned up next in a small parish church at Melgueil, close to Montpellier and about 30 miles west of Arles. Bernard Gui, a French Dominican born in 1261, was a papal inquisitor in the early part of the fourteenth century who was fictionalised in Umberto Eco's novel *The Name of the Rose*. He too wrote about Breakspear's life and tells us that 'at first, as a poor or very poor clerk, he was maintained in the church of St James in Melgueil in the diocese of Maguelonne'.[8]

This apparently insignificant role may have been why William of Newburgh assumed that Breakspear had not left Paris as a successful scholar. He was probably wrong, and it is more likely that Breakspear was given this poor clerkship as a trial. He may have already applied for admission to the monastery of St Ruf in nearby Avignon and been told that he would first need to serve an apprenticeship in one of their out-parishes, of which St James at Melgueil was one. The canons of St Ruf did not undertake parish work themselves, and regularly appointed unordained clerks to run their dependent churches. The Augustinians would likely want to see if Breakspear could apply his learning in a practical setting, earning his clerical spurs while they watched to see how he coped. If so, there can be no doubt that Breakspear passed the test at St James. The laconic Boso tells us that, after Arles, Breakspear went to the Augustinian monastery of St Ruf at Avignon. where at last he did 'receive the religious habit, after his canonical profession'.[9]

✠   ✠   ✠

Just as at both Merton Priory and St-Lô, regular canons were favoured by the Church and their houses were equal in status to the monasteries. Canons had long played a key role in Church reform, filling a gap between monks proper and the secular clergy. They had proved useful to successive popes, but just as we saw at St-Lô, their influence had waned by the eleventh century as they abandoned their close connection with the bishops. Their style of a common 'monastic' life lapsed and the canons had allowed themselves to live comfortably in the local town, even owning houses and other possessions. The lack of discipline in their canonical life became an issue and was raised at a synod of bishops at the Lateran in 1059, where they were warned to drop their worldly ways and return to a more spiritual life.[10] This reform was pushed through by the Archdeacon of Rome, Hildebrand, who was later elected Pope Gregory VII (1073–85). In an immediate response to the Lateran Synod, four canons of Avignon Cathedral, Kamalda, Odilo, Ponce and Durand, established an Augustinian community in the abandoned fourth-century church of St Ruf, which had previously been an important Augustinian house.[11] It lies 1 mile south of Avignon's city walls on part of what was the Via Agrippa, the Roman road from Arles to Avignon.

There is a lovely fourth-century legend matching the tale of *Beauty and the Beast* with a local dragon, the *Tarasque*, which had the head of a lion, the legs of a bear, the body of an ox covered with a turtle shell and a scaly tail with a scorpion's sting. It lived on a rock in the middle of the Rhône where it feasted on passers-by until St Martha, famous friend of Jesus in the New Testament, tamed it with her prayers and took it to the village now called Tarascon, some 15 miles south-west of Avignon. St Martha founded a church in Avignon and one Ruf was its first bishop. The Ruf, or Rufus, after which the abbey was named was believed to be the son of Simon of Cyrene, who carried Christ's cross to Calvary.

Avignon, about 25 miles north of Arles, is an impressive walled city sitting on a limestone bluff on the left bank of the Rhône, just above its confluence with the Durance. There has been a settlement there since Neolithic times. The Romans called it Avenio, and Emperor Hadrian, Breakspear's papal namesake,* stayed there from 121 to 122. In Breakspear's time, Avignon was part of the kingdom of Arles but it had changed hands many times, including in the eighth century when the Saracens fought their way east from Spain and took control. At the beginning of the fourteenth century it would become the temporary home of the popes in exile from Rome. Avignon did not become part of France until the revolution of 1789 to 1799. The skyline of Avignon is dominated by the Cathedral of Notre-Dame des Doms d'Avignon, standing 100ft above the Rhône. The present Romanesque building was largely built in the second half of the twelfth century and an imposing statue of Mary the Blessed Virgin was added to the bell tower in 1859. Breakspear would not have seen the new church or Avignon's eponymous twenty-two-arched Pont d'Avignon, which was not built until the latter part of the twelfth century.

The new community at St Ruf took root and its influence spread quickly throughout Provence. After Breakspear became pope, in 1156, he sanctioned the move of the abbey 80 miles north to Valence and it survived there for another 400 years until it was destroyed by Calvinists in 1562. Today the barred-off chancel and bell tower are all that remain to be seen of St Ruf in Avignon. Thankfully, all traces of the sewage plant built around these ruins, a nineteenth-century indignity, have gone. Now the only activity there is pétanque, played on the gravel in the shade of enormous plane trees.

The regime of the abbey Breakspear had joined was not, by monastic standards, severe. It was ruled by an abbot who was elected by the whole community. The canons lived in cloisters and dined in a common refectory where they

---

* The 'H' disappeared from about the thirteenth century.

were permitted both meat and wine, except during Lent. Their identical robes were of linen rather than wool and consisted of a white habit with a black sash across one shoulder, Scottish style. They grew beards and wore small black skullcaps. The canons left the abbey only on rare occasions, spending their time primarily saying the divine offices, writing and illuminating chronicles. They would also have run a school.

Breakspear spent more of his adult life in Avignon than anywhere else; it moulded him into the finished priest. Full of learning from Paris and Arles, he adapted well to community life, commending himself to his new brothers at St Ruf by whatever services he could. Here, William of Newburgh is at last willing to acknowledge Breakspear's strengths:

> He was handsome of body, smiling of face, prudent in words, and swift to carry out instructions, he pleased everyone.[12]

As a postulant, the monastic equivalent of an apprentice, Breakspear would have completed menial duties such as serving in the refectory, mending habits, cleaning and other domestic chores, just as his father had done at St Albans some twenty years earlier. Breakspear's obedience to the abbey's rules was exemplary, William of Newburgh describing him as the leading follower of the community's discipline and adding that by this stage he had made great strides in his learning.

How sweet was the prize for Breakspear. By sheer determination he had won through. Around 1130, about ten years and 500 miles away from rejection at St Albans, still in his early twenties, Breakspear had become an Augustinian canon of St Ruf. His travails had not been in vain, and although he would have far more travels to complete in his short life, never again would he need to endure the hardships of his road to Avignon. Breakspear's regular life in the Church had finally begun.

And it was only the start. Breakspear did not rest on his laurels as a canon at St Ruf. Boso writes of his hard work which, by around 1137, led to promotion:

> Then by God's will, advancing always from the good to the better, he first obtained the office of Prior in that house, and afterwards ascended to the pinnacle of the abbey by common desire of the brethren.[13]

The prior was second-in-charge to the abbot and appointed by him, usually after consultation with the canons. The prior had no official duties as such and performed tasks as the abbot directed. Several years later, Abbot Fulcher, who had appointed Breakspear to be his prior, died and the monks of St Ruf elected Breakspear as the tenth abbot. This was sometime soon after 1143, when Fulcher was known to be still in office, and before 1147, when Breakspear was addressed as Abbot of St Ruf in a letter from Pope Eugenius III dated 29 January 1147.[14] On becoming abbot he would have been in his early forties.

This second promotion was significant and gave Breakspear credibility and high-level access in Church circles. St Ruf was a small establishment but an important part of the medieval Church and its abbot had considerable prestige. However, things at St Ruf soon started to go wrong. William of Newburgh tells us that Breakspear's fellow canons soon regretted their choice of a foreigner as their abbot:

> When he had ruled them for some time, they became regretful and angry that they had raised a wayfarer over their heads, and they became thenceforth disloyal and rebellious.[15]

Although the regime at St Ruf was not strict, and in the twelfth century many monastic rules were followed only half-heartedly in any event, Breakspear proved to be too severe a taskmaster for his over-comfortable brothers. He had been a favourite when he arrived at St Ruf and the canons must not have realised that he would prove strict once he had responsibility for their discipline. Abbot Breakspear did not tolerate any relaxation from the Augustinian rules even at the cost of his popularity, and he may even have reintroduced rules that had fallen away. He had earned his position by his absolute obedience and he expected no less from others now that he was in command. Here was an early sign of a pope who would live faithfully by the rules.

His fellow canons tackled their abbot on his strictures but to no avail. Breakspear would not compromise – another sign of his steadfastness – and the mutterings continued. The canons could not un-elect him, a course that would lead to anarchy in a closed community. Removing an elected abbot would take more than another vote. Breakspear may have been slow to address their unhappiness and it was the canons, not Breakspear, who brought things to a head by complaining formally to the pope.

Pope Eugenius was exiled in France at the time and several of the canons stormed off to Paris to lay their grievances before him. Breakspear followed in order to defend himself personally, which he did effectively. The pope, himself a Cistercian monk, one of the strictest monastic orders, empathised with Breakspear and Eugenius found in his favour. Eugenius was a gentle man and he dismissed the canons' complaints in a kindly manner. He reconciled the abbot and canons and they returned together to St Ruf. It was during these exchanges in France that Pope Eugenius first formed his good opinion of the calm and measured young Englishman. He had earmarked Breakspear as a potential candidate for his papal team.

The reconciliation between canons and abbot proved temporary, lasting no more than a couple of years at most. For much of this time Breakspear was away, already working on the pope's behalf, first at the Council of Reims and subsequently in Catalonia. The cantankerous canons may have welcomed Breakspear's absences from the abbey, although the old wounds never healed:

> But ignorant malice was not peaceful for long and the storm rekindled thundered forth more loudly. The same venerable Pontiff was again approached and his ears were soon ringing with the whisperings and complaints of those brethren.[16]

For the second time the recalcitrant canons and their abbot went to see the pope. This time their complaints went beyond criticism of Breakspear's hard discipline. The abbot and canons may have fallen out over the controversy raging on the nature of the Trinity that had been stirred up by Gilbert, Bishop of Poitiers.[17] Gilbert argued that the pure God must be distinguished from the Trinity, which was contrary to the Church's teaching. By 1148 he had agreed to follow the official line. The canons may also have argued disingenuously that, since their first complaint, papal duties had kept Breakspear away from St Ruf for too long.

This time the meeting was in Italy but not in Rome, which in 1146 was still in the hands of Arnold of Brescia* who presided over the rebellious Republicans of Rome. These Republicans harked back to Rome's ancient past and, inflamed by Arnold, bitterly attacked the riches and wealth of the pope and cardinals. Canons and abbot met the pope either in Viterbo or in Siena. This time an exasperated Pope Eugenius acted decisively. He dismissed the canons' complaints out of hand and rebuked them, ordering them to go away and choose an abbot more to their liking. The pope's words of dismissal say it all:

> I know my brothers where Satan has his seat; I know what is raising up this storm among you. Go, elect yourselves a father with whom you will be able to have peace, or one who is more pleasing to you; for this man will no longer be a burden to you.[18]

---

* Brescia is a city in Lombardy.

We know not if the chastised canons did find a new abbot to their liking but their loss proved to be the Curia's gain. As Boso put it, 'Pope Eugenius of blessed memory kept [Breakspear] at his side'.[19]

Breakspear had always made a good first impression on people. His presence, his intelligence and not least his perseverance had helped him become abbot of a well-regarded Augustinian monastery. He had proved himself a good team player, which had led to his election, but once in authority perhaps he had been too severe on the canons, most of whom were older and more experienced than he was. It would be an easy mistake for a zealous new abbot to make. If so, it was a lesson he learnt, since as far as we know his people-management skills were never questioned thereafter.

For most an abbacy would have been career enough and he could have spent the rest of his time in and around Avignon. Instead, events had brought him to the attention of the pope. The English abbot and Pope Eugenius had been thrown together by chance and they now set about forging a close working relationship. Breakspear's life journey was set for more twists and turns.

4

CATALONIA
The Second Crusade in Spain

The more powerful and the nobles should vigorously gird themselves to oppose the multitude of the infidels who are now rejoicing in the victory they have gained over us, to defend in this way the eastern Church.

Pope Eugenius III
Quantum Praedecessores[1]

It is not surprising that Eugenius and Breakspear got on so well: they were kindred spirits. Eugenius saw in Breakspear a man of his own mettle. Eugenius had been dragged into the papacy from the Cistercian Abbey of Tre Fontane outside Rome by followers of St Bernard of Clairvaux, who saw Eugenius as a holy but simple man and someone whom they could easily control. Eugenius, who had not been a cardinal, was elected pope on 15 February 1145, the same day that Pope Lucius II had died after being hit by a stone while leading an attack against the rebels in Rome. Eugenius's election was a surprise even to Bernard, his mentor, who wrote disparagingly:

May God forgive you what you have done! ... What reason or counsel, when the supreme pontiff was dead, made you rush upon a mere rustic, lay hands on him in his refuge, wrest from his hands the axe, pick or hoe, and lift him to a throne?[2]

Eugenius was not a man to take offence and Bernard remained a spiritual force by his side throughout his papacy. Bernard was, in any event, mistaken:

Eugenius proved to be his own man and his record during his eight years as pope is marred only by his encouragement of the disastrous Second Crusade. As pope, Eugenius led with strong principles and was free from corruption, but he was too gentle a man to make a firm leader. He chose not to stand up to the rebellious citizens of Rome, quasi-Republicans who spurned the pope's authority, and he was forced to spend the majority of his papacy in exile. He was a modest man, and the first pope who routinely returned the splendid gifts given to him by kings and potentates. Eugenius had no need of wealth and his humility won him popular respect. Throughout his papacy this humble man continued to wear the coarse Cistercian habit beneath his papal robes.

The Second Crusade was prompted by the disastrous defeat at Edessa* on Christmas Day 1144. On a day that shook the west, thousands of Armenian Christians were slaughtered and their children taken into slavery. 'Edessa – which we cannot mention without great grief and lamentation,' groaned Otto of Freising.[3] Since the successful First Crusade in 1096–99, Edessa had been one of the four great cities in the Holy Land held by Christians, although it was always the most vulnerable to the Seljuks, Turko-Persian Muslims, as it was the most northerly and the only one east of the Euphrates. Edessa was of course a human tragedy but it was also an enormous blow to the Church's prestige. The pope had been obliged to respond and he did so within a year.

Eugenius issued the call to arms in December 1145, but the now elderly Bernard of Clairvaux was the driving force behind him. Together they were instrumental in promoting the Crusade and making preparations for what would prove to be an ill-fated venture. For the first time a crusade would be led by two reigning kings, Louis VII of France and Conrad III of Germany, and this had encouraged many of Europe's great barons to sign up. The Crusades were the first examples of European-wide military inter-vention and so the arrangements were somewhat clumsy; in fact, bickering between the various rulers would contribute to the failure of the campaign. King Stephen of England (1135–54) was fighting his own battles at home and could not have contemplated joining the Crusade but many English and Scottish knights did commit. They knew that in return they would gain an eternal reward for bearing arms for the Church, but it was still a tough choice. Not only did it carry great personal risk, but it would also take two years out of their lives, and going on a crusade was an expensive venture for a knight. Most had to raise loans to pay for the horses, saddles, swords, lances, mail shirts and helmets they would need. Eugenius did his bit to help by

---

*   Now Urfa in eastern Turkey.

releasing Christians taking part in the Crusade from paying interest on these loans while they were away.[4]

Ever since his tussle with the canons a year earlier Breakspear had been a member of Pope Eugenius's wider team and he was in France with the pope as plans were laid for the Crusade. By 1147, some two years after the debacle at Edessa, the preparations were almost complete. The formal launch came at Easter when Eugenius celebrated High Mass in the Abbey of St Denis in Paris and in front of the gathered high and mighty presented King Louis VII with his pilgrim's staff and wallet.[5] If Breakspear was in the pope's entourage in Paris that Easter, he would have been delighted to return to the city in rather finer circumstances than on his first visit. Breakspear was not a proud man, but he must have drawn human pleasure in returning to St Denis, perhaps his alma mater, no longer an impoverished student but as a well-regarded member of the papal retinue. His hard student days must have seemed to be a lifetime away.

Emperor Conrad and the German crusaders left Regensburg for the Holy Land at the end of May 1147, followed in June by King Louis leading the French army from Metz. Attention was focused on the east but the theatre was not limited to the Holy Land; Eugenius wrapped into the Crusade a holy war against the pagan Slavs in northern Europe which started in June 1147, waged by Danes, Swedes, Poles and Saxons. Bernard followed the pope's lead by extending crusader privileges to those fighting the Moors in the Iberian Peninsula. A fleet of over 160 ships carrying crusaders from England, Scotland, Flanders and the Rhineland had left Dartmouth as early as May 1147,[6] but after being forced by harsh weather to stop at Lisbon, they took the opportunity to support a siege of Lisbon from 1 July to 25 October, when the defending Moors surrendered.[7]

Lisbon marked the first battle of the Second Crusade. Rather than continue their journey to the Holy Land, many of these crusaders moved to support further fighting in southern Spain which would take place close to St Ruf's sphere of influence, and where Breakspear's local connections would prove helpful.

For the time being, Breakspear was still in France. In March 1148, and before the crusaders had even reached Jerusalem, he was in Reims with the pope. Eugenius had summonsed almost 1,000 Church leaders to a council to consider a number of Church regulations. Popes called councils to seek views and support for decisions they intended to make and there was usually a three-line whip for all bishops to attend. Open discussions continued for eleven days. One proposal that was not approved concerned clerical attire and banning the wearing of fur.[8] Bernard of Clairvaux had requested that Gilbert of Poitiers,

who had challenged Church teaching on the Trinity, be put on trial during
the council. Gilbert had previously taught John of Salisbury, who was also in
Reims as part of the pope's entourage. In the event, Gilbert was cleared of
heresy and allowed to return to his bishopric.

All bishops and abbots had been ordered to attend at Reims except the Italian
bishops who were excused due to the distance. King Stephen of England was
then at odds with the papacy and had forbidden the English bishops to attend,
although Archbishop Theobald of Canterbury defied him, hiring a small fishing
boat, surreptitiously evading the king's guards and arriving in France looking
more like a shipwreck survivor than a prelate. Theobald was desperate to attend
Reims to claim primacy for Canterbury over the Archdiocese of York, but in
the event Eugenius was not ready to make a ruling on this.[9] With hindsight
King Stephen would have been glad that Theobald was at Reims. On the final
day of the council Eugenius proposed the excommunication of King Stephen
for obstructing bishops in England, and Theobald rose and successfully begged
mercy for the English king.[10] The Bishop of Winchester, Stephen's brother,
was not so lucky: he was suspended for his absence, although the sentence was
deferred for six months, again due to Theobald's intervention, in order to give
the bishop time to appear before the pope to apologise.

These councils were a good opportunity to catch up with events from around
Europe and while in Reims John of Salisbury would have briefed Breakspear
on the latest news from England. It was not good. Breakspear would already
have been well aware of the troubles ever since Stephen followed Henry on
to the English throne. Henry had died in Normandy in December 1135 and
peace had died with him. Stephen, his nephew, had seized the crown but he
never held it securely. Right from the start of his reign, he had had to fight to
maintain control of the kingdom. He managed to defeat a native uprising in
Wales, but then an opportunistic King David of Scotland had attacked Carlisle
and Newcastle. Stephen's troubles then went from bad to worse. Empress
Matilda, Henry I's daughter and designated heir, claimed the throne for herself.
In 1139 she brought armed supporters to England and fighting followed. In a
series of fierce clashes the advantage ebbed and flowed between Matilda and
Stephen. Worcester was burnt down by Matilda's troops, and Stephen laid waste
to the countryside around castles held by Matilda's supporters.

During this anarchy the south-west was particularly badly hit; its livestock
levels did not return to normal until the mid-1150s. Many fled the area and
those who stayed starved when villages were plundered then burnt, and the
staple foods of corn, cheese and butter became unavailable. This was a time
when men in England wailed that 'Christ and his Saints slept'.[11] At last in 1153,

a compromise brought peace. Stephen would keep the throne, but he agreed to designate Matilda's son, Henry, as his heir. Henry had to wait only a year before Stephen died, bringing an end to a tortuous reign of nineteen years. Breakspear did well to miss this turmoil in England.

✠ ✠ ✠

The Second Crusade had set off to the Holy Land with high hopes but only four months after the Council of Reims the fighting was all over, and it could not have ended more badly for the Church. King Conrad's German army, some 35,000 strong, had been hit hard by a flood near Constantinople on the way out and then all but wiped out by a Turkish ambush before it even reached Jerusalem. King Louis VII of France had travelled out a little later than Conrad and with an even bigger army, arriving at Constantinople in October 1147. The combined forces were large but the two kings and their subordinates managed them badly and made awful strategic decisions. They did not even attempt to retake Edessa, perversely deciding to attack the better-defended Damascus. Had this gamble succeeded it would have been a decisive blow to the Muslim world. Instead, the attempt failed after only five days, and the main thrust of the Second Crusade collapsed with it. Nothing of the main objective was achieved and the reputation of the papacy was significantly diminished.

The second simultaneous part of the Second Crusade against the pagans of the Baltic areas fared no better. Once again, the combination of two armies proved not to add up to a stronger force, the Danish and Swedish fighters, completely unable to work together. Bernard of Clairvaux was humbled by the failures and felt it necessary to make an abject apology to Pope Eugenius for the utter waste of men and resources.

Breakspear played his role in a third part of the Crusade which was definitely not a failure for the Church. This fighting, the *Reconquista*, took place in Catalonia, in north-east Spain and not far west of Avignon. In the eighth century, Muslim armies had crossed from Morocco to Gibraltar and occupied most of southern Spain. For 200 years Muslims and Christians had lived alongside each other, mostly in peace, but by the end of the eleventh century religious differences hardened and there was regular fierce fighting between them. Since about 1114 the papacy had given equal weight and support to Christian campaigns against the Saracens in the Iberian Peninsula as in the Holy Land, and in 1123 the First Lateran Council ruled that Spanish Christian fighters should stay in Spain, fighting the Saracens at home rather than travelling to the Holy Land.

After the Council of Reims, in April 1148, Eugenius had asked Breakspear to go to Catalonia and join its crusaders.[12] The Abbot of St Ruf was an excellent choice to represent the pope in Spain since the prestige of the saint already extended beyond Provence and the abbey had extensive interests in Catalonia. There were strong cultural and commercial ties between Provence and Catalonia. Breakspear was already familiar with Catalonia, having accompanied papal legate Archbishop William of Arles to Barcelona in late 1139.[13] Furthermore, a former Abbot of St Ruf, Oleguer (1110–16), had been a leading instigator of an earlier Iberian campaign, wielding enormous influence in Catalonia; he had been planning a campaign in Spain since about 1113 until his death in 1137.[14] Oleguer was canonised in 1675. Breakspear would have been aware of his work and he was now able to help to realise his predecessor's dream.

Division among the Moors, the Muslim inhabitants of Iberia, held the key to the success of the crusaders in 1148 rather than their own superior forces. In both North Africa and Iberia, the Almoravid Empire was being undermined by the more fundamental Almohad sect, despite both sides being Berber Muslims. Only too willing to wage war on their fellow Moors, the Almohads had invaded Almoravid Iberia in 1146, and in 1147 they had captured the Almoravid capital, Marrakesh. This in-fighting did not give the Iberian crusaders an easy victory, though; they had to fight for it.

The campaign had started well. On 17 October 1147, Almeria, on the Mediterranean coast about 125 miles east of Málaga, had fallen to Emperor Alfonso VII of Castile, who was supported by Count Ramon Berenguer IV of Barcelona. Lisbon had fallen to Alfonso Henriques of Portugal one week later. The considerable number of English and Scottish crusaders who had supported Alfonso Henriques chose to remain on the peninsula following the action into Spain. As it turned out, they made the better choice: few returned from the Crusade in the east and those who did returned without success.

Breakspear arrived in Catalonia in early summer 1148 amid preparations for an attack on Tortosa, which is close to the mouth of the River Ebro, about 110 miles south-west of Barcelona. Following the run of Christian successes in Lisbon and Almeira, by the end of June 1148 an emboldened Count Ramon Berenguer was ready to lay siege to Tortosa, which had been in the hands of the Moors for most of the previous 400 years. The wily count wanted to enhance the power of his seat of Barcelona while he had the support of the international crusaders. The Genoese fleet that had forced the victory at Almeria had spent the previous winter in Barcelona, using the time to fell trees in the surrounding forests to be used for building wooden siege engines. On 1 July 1148 the fleet, carrying Breakspear and more Catalan forces, sailed to the River Ebro and embarked on a three-pronged attack on Tortosa. Half the Genoese army supplemented by Catalan knights camped outside the city walls to the south. Ramon Berenguer himself, with the rest of the Genoese and his own Catalan forces, camped on a hill above the city to the north-east. The English, Scottish and Flemish troops and the military orders of the Templars and the Hospitallers, some fresh from the victories in Portugal, camped by a river just north of the city.

Breakspear spent most time with Ramon Berenguer's group, also liaising with the English contingent and the military orders. He did not bear arms himself but worked tirelessly to encourage the Church's coalition, literally waving the papal flag, giving the fighters the visible moral support of the pope. Evidently it worked: Balluini de Carona, the leader of the Anglo-Norman contingent, was one who gave Ramon Berenguer his support.

Using two wooden siege towers, the Genoese successfully breached the outer wall from the south-east. Inside the city walls the defending Moors still held out in La Suda, the inner citadel of Tortosa which is still visible on its skyline. Ramon Berenguer's forces had an arduous task to fill a ravine some 40 yards wide and 30 yards deep before they could bring their siege engines up to the wall of the citadel. The defenders had their own engines and the fighting became a stone-throwing contest. One of the defenders seriously damaged one of the Genoese wooden towers by shooting 200lb stones at it, but it was soon repaired and strengthened with ropes.

Trouble struck for Ramon Berenguer when some of his knights deserted as they had not been paid for some time, so he agreed a deal with the defenders. There would be a forty-day truce and if the Moors of Valencia had not come to their aid within this time then they would surrender the city.[15] Such a deal seems strange now, but was then a standard part of siege etiquette.[16] The Moors sent envoys to nearby Valencia asking for relief, but Valencia was too worried about its own security and could not help. There were other forces of Moors to the south, but their leader had previously agreed a treaty with Ramon Berenguer and would not come to the aid of Tortosa either. The defenders were on their own, demoralised, and Tortosa surrendered to the count on 30 December 1148.

There had been minimal bloodshed and the act of surrender meant that no slaves or property were seized, and the Muslim and Jewish populations were permitted to remain in the city. Those English fighters who had fallen in the siege were buried in a cemetery at Santa Anna in Barcelona, run by Augustinian Canons of the Holy Sepulchre of Jerusalem, and so received the same spiritual benefits as if buried at the Holy Sepulchre itself and in this sense fulfilled their vows to go to Jerusalem.[17] The surviving English knights were rewarded with property in and around the city and many settled there permanently. In return for their critical help, the sea-faring Genoese were given the valuable port and its dockyards.

Count Ramon Berenguer had not finished yet. Without the support of the international fighters he took the battle to Lerida (now called Lleida), about 75 miles north of Tortosa, and the city surrendered to him in October 1149. The Almohads did recapture Almeria in 1157, having gained the upper hand over the Almoravids, but the Moors never recaptured Lisbon, Tortosa or Lerida. These towns formed a bridge between Aragon and Catalonia and provided a strong point for future Christian gains in Iberia. These successes in Iberia in 1148 balanced the losses the Church was suffering in the east; more territory was captured in Iberia than was later lost in the kingdom of Jerusalem.

Pope Eugenius was pleased with Breakspear's endeavours in Catalonia and his efforts also benefitted his own Augustinian house. He ensured that the Augustinian rules of the St Ruf community became accepted practice in Tortosa Cathedral.[18] Breakspear also takes the credit for St Ruf becoming instrumental in re-establishing the Church throughout the territory recovered from Saracen rule. The Bishop of Barcelona was particularly grateful to him and gave a local church to St Ruf in February 1149 while Breakspear was still there. Breakspear could not have known it but his Iberian service, supporting the fighters and reconstructing the churches, would stand him in good stead when tested later as pope.

Over the years Breakspear retained his interest in Catalonia. He had made a lasting friend in Ramon Berenguer. In 1150 the count renounced the shameful practice, common then in Europe, that on the death of a bishop the local noble could seize his assets. Before departing on a perilous journey, Ramon Berenguer commanded his bailiffs not to plunder goods in this way, but instead to safeguard anything found in the deceased bishop's house for his successor.[19] Breakspear naturally approved of Ramon Berenguer's action and, when pope, ordered a complete stop to this practice.

Ramon Berenguer pleased Breakspear further in 1151 by making good use of the land he captured from the Moors by founding a Cistercian monastery at Poblet at the foot of the Prades Mountains. This monastery still thrives today.

Not only did Breakspear help his friend during the Iberian Crusade but on other occasions as well. Ramon Berenguer exercised power in both Catalonia and Aragon but, despite what he had achieved for the Church, the union of these territories had not been legitimised by the pope and this failure would prejudice the succession when he died. In 1150 Ramon Berenguer married

Petronila, the daughter of Ramiro of Aragon, but the Church had never recognised Ramiro's kingship in Aragon or his marriage to Agnes of Poitou, Petronila's mother, because Ramiro was a professed monk. Kingship and marriage were taboo for a monk. However, Breakspear remembered his good friend and, ever seeking practical conclusions, as pope he formally ratified the union of Aragon and Catalonia on 24 June 1158.

In that same year, Ramon Berenguer was threatened by the resurgent Almohads and Breakspear came to his aid by ordering Templar Knights bound for the Holy Land to stay and help face down the local Moors. Breakspear went further, telling the Archbishops of Tarragona and Narbonne to excommunicate any Christian who gave support to the Moors. Only a few months after that, in January 1159, Breakspear headed off a proposed opportunistic incursion to Spain by Louis VII of France and Henry II of England, following the death of King Sancho III of Castile, leaving his infant son as heir. By supporting Ramon Berenguer, Breakspear arguably spared Spain much turmoil and the new crown of Aragon became a bastion of Christian power in the Mediterranean world.

Breakspear had made a friend of Ramon Berenguer but may unwittingly have made an enemy at the same time. His closeness with the count during the Tortosa campaign could not have helped his future relationship when pope with Frederick, the German Emperor. A few years earlier Frederick's predecessor, King Conrad, had been actively supporting 'the other side', namely the Count of Toulouse, in his armed struggle with Count Ramon Berenguer's father for control of Provence. This fighting took place around Melgueil and at the very time Breakspear was at the Church of St James there. The count's father had been killed in this fighting in 1144 but by 1147 Ramon Berenguer had re-entered Provence and regained control. It was only in 1161, after Breakspear's death, that the Holy Roman Empire and Catalonia were reconciled.

✠ ✠ ✠

This work in Catalonia earned Breakspear a yet more impressive promotion in the Church. By 1149 Eugenius had got to know his man much better and, following the advice of his cardinals, he had no hesitation in appointing him as Cardinal Bishop of Albano, a prince of the Church.

It was surprising that an abbot of a smallish monastery in Provence was promoted to such a high office and after a relatively brief time in the pope's service. Many Church careerists expecting advancement must have been left disappointed. Breakspear had always had a religious vocation, but others entered the Church seeking worldly advancement. For younger sons of the nobility the Church could provide a fast track to secure political roles and access to the royal courts. Such careerists had no intention of bothering with either parochial chores or missionary work.They wanted well-paid clerical offices, and to become diplomats, lawyers, statesmen and even soldiers.Throughout Europe, sovereigns selected a number of their senior staff from the ranks of clerics. In England they did so right up to the time of Henry VIII; indeed, many English lord chancellors were clerics. Breakspear, a humble churchman of low background, leap-frogged all these sycophants entirely on merit.

England's first cardinal, Robert Pullen, was a strong voice of approval among the cardinals who advised Eugenius to promote Breakspear.[20] Probably a man of Devon, Pullen was born around 1080 and became one of the first teachers in the nascent University of Oxford. Pullen was later a noted teacher in Paris and became a protégé of Bernard of Clairvaux. He is credited with developing the Church's theology of purgatory.[21] We can thank Cardinal Pullen for introducing his bright student John of Salisbury to the papal court, probably at Reims in 1148. Later, from 1154, John was employed at Canterbury by the archbishop, but he continued to make regular visits to Italy. John's writings tell us much of what we know about Breakspear's papacy.

Popes had long had access to a body of clergy to advise them, and these senior clerics became 'cardinals'.This term was taken from architecture, where it meant 'firmly inserted'. Until the late eleventh century cardinals had only liturgical roles but under the reforming popes, especially Pope Gregory VII (1073–85), the power of the Roman families had ebbed away and their place as principal advisers to the pope was assumed by the cardinals.They started to take a full part in the administration of papal government, becoming the Church's civil service, known as the Curia. In the early days of the Church, these cardinals, Bishops of Rome, had been appointed by the clergy and people of Rome, and only from among their own number.The Roman Emperor had played a shadowy role, exercising influence behind the scenes, but this was later abolished. In the twelfth century all cardinals were still resident in Rome, although often they were obliged to relocate temporarily to other Italian cities for their safety.[22]

Gregory I (590–604) was the first pope to give his cardinals titles as priests of the oldest Roman churches. Breakspear's see, Albano, was a small town in the cooler Alban hills, about 15 miles south of Rome along the Appian Way. The Diocese of Albano was one of seven 'suburbicarian' sees close to Rome, comprising seven towns in the province of Rome. Albano is rich in history, reputedly founded by the son of the Trojan warrior Aeneas.There had been a Christian church in Albano since the time of Emperor Constantine.

The titular bishops of these suburbicarian dioceses were the highest-ranking cardinals, called 'cardinal bishops'. There were two lower ranks, cardinal priest and cardinal deacon. Breakspear jumped straight into the top rank, immediately a member of the pope's inner circle. His last known act as Abbot of St Ruf was on 12 December 1149, when he received a letter from the pope about the abbey.[23] Although Breakspear retained his title as Abbot of St Ruf until then, it may have already been common knowledge that he was earmarked for the see, which had been vacant since 1145.[24]

It can be assumed that he was consecrated Cardinal Bishop of Albano on Saturday, 17 December, the last of the year's Ember Days, three-day penitential periods in the Church's calendar.[25] He would not have received the traditional red hat, the *galero*, which was only introduced for cardinals by Pope Innocent IV, 100 years later. Even so, here he was, in his mid-forties, and a high prince of the Church. Non-Roman cardinals were unusual but their value was acknowledged. Bernard of Clairvaux, writing to Pope Eugenius in about 1150, emphasised the importance of electing non-Romans to the College of Cardinals.

How ironic that a series of rejections resulted in so many promotions and to such high office. Rejected first at St Albans, Breakspear came to Paris, where he may have been rejected a second time, then Arles and so to Avignon. Rejected for a third time by St Ruf's cantankerous canons, he became a cardinal in Rome. Had they never complained he might have seen out his days happily at St Ruf; instead, the boy rejected as an Alban monk had become an Alban cardinal. The generous-hearted Breakspear never bore a grudge and always remained a loyal supporter of St Albans, and nor did he leave St Ruf in high dudgeon. As pope, in a letter of 17 April 1155, he acknowledged the 'special bond of affection' that tied him to St Ruf which had been 'a mother to him'.[26] In the following year, he asked the chapter of Pisa Cathedral to aid the brothers of St Ruf who were in Pisa sourcing stones and columns from Carrara, presumably for the building of St Ruf's new home when it moved from Avignon to Valence in 1158.

Cardinal Breakspear got stuck into his new responsibilities quickly. From 1150 he would have been busy with affairs at the Cathedral of St John the Baptist in Albano, and in regular contact with the pope. Around this time and while staying at nearby Ferentino, he was visited by his English friend John of Salisbury, who appeared then to be looking to the new cardinal for his own promotion. He later had occasion to remind Breakspear of 'the words which proceeded from your lips, when at Ferentino, you gave me your own ring and belt as a pledge of things to come'.[27] Events conspired against John's ambition, but nonetheless he would play a continuing role in Breakspear's life.

By 1151 Breakspear became more visible at the Lateran, the seat of papal administration in Rome, and he was a signatory to all papal bulls written between December 1151 and February 1152. A bull is a papal letter taking its name from *bulla*, the lead seal attached to it, although in the twelfth century most papal letters were called privileges or decretals rather than bulls. The original seal was a lump of clay moulded around a cord which ensured that any tampering of the letter would be obvious. Breakspear was busy, but Eugenius soon found a more important task for the Curia's new boy.

✠   ✠   ✠

The Second Crusade had been an abject failure. In 1150 its architect Bernard and Abbot Suger of St Denis tried to raise a new expedition but found no support.[28] However, Pope Eugenius was eager to bolster the authority that the Church already had in Europe. He wanted to draw the outlying provinces closer within the Curia's influence, concerned that in several European countries the Church was under the control of local rulers. In particular, the papacy deemed it essential that the Church alone be responsible for the appointment of archbishops and bishops, the structure of the parishes and have responsibility for disciplining of errant clergy.

In pursuit of this strategy, Pope Eugenius had decided to send a legation to Ireland in 1150 to be led by Cardinal John Paparo and with the objective of drawing the Irish Church closer to the Curia, and doubtless to encourage them to make financial contributions to Rome as well. Pope Gregory VII had started the practice of sending his representatives to address both routine and controversial business. He and following popes used *legati a latere*, meaning 'legates from the side of the pope', for general diplomatic purposes and for general oversight or reform. Legates had the authority to hold councils, call synods, visit monasteries and settle episcopal elections. A legate exercised all the administrative and judicial functions of the pope, often without the possibility of appeal.[29]

The Church in Ireland had been seeking its own province for some time. Ever since 1074, Dublin – and Waterford since 1096 – had professed obedience to the See of Canterbury even though in practice the Archbishop of Armagh exercised authority over the whole of Ireland. Irish subservience to Canterbury might seem odd, but until 1472 the Church in independent Scotland was governed by the Archdiocese of York.

King Stephen refused to grant Cardinal Paparo safe passage through England, and the fighting in England delayed Paparo's arrival in Ireland until 1152.

Immediately he held a synod at Kells in March at which the supremacy of Canterbury was abolished. Armagh was formally given control and made directly answerable to Rome.

As in Ireland, the local Church in Norway and Sweden had been petitioning Rome regularly for their own provinces with direct access to Rome, Norway being the more concerned of the two. Pope Gregory IV had created the new German See of Hamburg in 831 with the explicit purpose of overseeing the missions to Denmark, Sweden and Norway. Soon after, in 849, Hamburg was merged with the older See of Bremen. Not only was the Scandinavian Church under the supervision of the German Archbishop, but through him it was subject to the German Emperor, who in effect directed the German national Church.

The Danish Church had already won its independence from Germany, and Lund was established as the new centre for the Scandinavian Church in 1103. Lund is now in southern Sweden, across the Oresund Strait from Copenhagen, but until 1658 it was part of Denmark. Favouring Denmark of the three Scandinavian countries made sense since the Danish Church was the most established in Scandinavia, but that is not how the Bishops of Sweden and Norway saw it. For them, Lund was just as foreign as Hamburg-Bremen. The Swedes and Norwegians always resented subservience to pre-eminent Denmark and pressed for autonomy, even though this would bring closer control from Rome. Meanwhile, the Germans had been unhappy to lose their direct authority over the churches in Scandinavia.

Envious of the independence from Hamburg-Bremen that the Danes had already achieved, a joint mission of Norwegian and Swedish clergy travelled to Rome in 1148, the year before Breakspear became a cardinal, to plead for their independence from the Diocese of Lund. Eugenius was happy to oblige them and the mission returned home carrying a promise from the pope that he would do what he could. Just as his papal predecessors had, he welcomed any opportunity to increase the authority of the Curia, and so bring the remoter provinces closer to Rome. It was only 100 years since the eastern Church had broken away from Rome in the Great Schism of 1054. The Scandinavian Northmen had long traded with the merchants in the east, and the orthodox schism was well known to them. The last thing Eugenius would have wanted on his watch was another schism.

In 1151 Bishop Reddar of Nidaros in Norway visited Rome and Eugenius presented him with an archbishop's pallium, a lambswool ecclesiastical vestment bestowed by a pope on metropolitan archbishops and primates as a symbol of their jurisdiction. Sadly, Reddar died before he got home, so the

pope needed to think again. Although he saw Scandinavian requests for autonomy as entirely reasonable, he could see that making it happen was a more
daunting task than the one that Paparo had faced in Ireland in 1152. Unlike
Ireland, the monarchs in Norway and Sweden still wielded tight control of
their national churches. The Scandinavian kings had first brought Christianity
to Norway and Sweden and they were unlikely to surrender their ecclesiastical
authority readily. Nonetheless, the recent successful Irish mission convinced
Eugenius that a similar solution should work in Scandinavia and he now made
this his considered plan. He decided to send a representative to the north
to assess the situation on the ground and introduce whatever wider Church
reforms were appropriate. He needed another legate, and he knew exactly
who to ask.

Eugenius turned to Cardinal Breakspear, inviting him to lead the delegation to Scandinavia as his legate. It might seem strange that the pope entrusted
this vital and challenging work to such an inexperienced cardinal. The travelling itself would be arduous. Though lacking in ecclesiastical experience,
there were many reasons why Eugenius would have seen Breakspear as a good
practical choice. Breakspear was from a northern country and fluent in several
languages.[30] Eugenius was an Anglophile and had even spotted the English
sense of humour; in the words of John of Salisbury, he 'had the highest opinion
of the superior power and fitness of the English for work of any kind, when
they were not spoilt by levity'.[31] Eugenius recognised that Englishmen on the
Humber Estuary and the Wash had always maintained close commercial and
spiritual ties with their former aggressors from the north. Breakspear could
capitalise on these ties in Scandinavia.

As a Cistercian, Eugenius's choice may also have been influenced by the
strong English connections with the missionary Church in Scandinavia.
English Cistercian houses had done valuable work in establishing Christianity
in Norway and Sweden.[32] Ranolv, a Norwegian monk from the Cistercian
Abbey of Fountains near Ripon in North Yorkshire, led a group of his brothers to establish a monastery at Lyse in Norway in 1141, which became one of
the most important abbeys there.[33] There was also an 'Alban' connection for
Breakspear in that Norway's earliest monastery at Selje, built around 1100 and
now in ruins, was dedicated to England's St Alban.* There were good English
foundations laid already and Breakspear's good nature and appealing character
had the potential to build upon them.

---

*   In 2020 Pope Francis moved Abbot Erik Vardon from his Cistercian Abbey in Leicestershire
to become the new Bishop of Trondheim.

Breakspear's life was about to change again. By March 1152 he was once more preparing for a long mission and the hardest challenge that he had yet faced. He accepted this northern adventure willingly, seeing it not as an easy reward for a new cardinal but a stern test. Although there were good relations with England, Scandinavia was still a daunting place. Norway's wild history, emerging from the Middle Ages when everything seemed to have been settled by the axe, would have been familiar to him. The memories of Viking brutality in England since the eighth century were still fresh. William of Newburgh wrote, not totally unfairly, that the pope 'sent him as legate, with full power, to the wild people of Denmark and Norway'.[34]

Breakspear was embarking on yet another journey.

NORWAY

Reform of the Norwegian Church

After a little time having experienced his probity and prudence, he sent him as legate to the regions of Norway, so that he could preach the word of life in that province and apply himself to the winning of souls for Almighty God.

Cardinal Boso
Vita Adriani IV[1]

Willing though Cardinal Breakspear was, his 1,800-mile journey to Norway would have been arduous. We know that the cardinal travelled with a large retinue, and it is likely that Boso was among them since his name is not seen on any documents issued by the Curia during this period. The group may have included members of the 1148 Norwegian delegation returning from Rome. A Benedictine monk, Nicholas Saemudarsson, had probably been part of that delegation and before leaving Italy Breakspear may have been briefed by him on current Norwegian affairs. He may well have had a Norse language tutor in his travelling party. He was well versed in both French and Latin but there would have been no use in Norway for either language. He was not fluent in Old Norse, although there are some similarities between Old English and Old Norse and, with the help of his tutor, and having an aptitude for languages, he would have quickly managed the basics of the Norwegian tongue.

Equipped with an entourage and funds befitting his status as papal legate, Breakspear was ready to set off early in 1152. He had three different routes to Norway to choose from. The first option, the *Austrvegr*, was a long journey to the east, largely on water. From Rome this route would first take him overland to Constantinople and then by boat into the Black Sea via the Bosphorus. Using the rivers and lakes of Russia and the Baltic states, he could reach Visby on the Isle of Gotland. Such a journey would have taken around a year, and Breakspear was in too much of a hurry.

The *Vestvegr* was a straightforward route by sea, following the traditional pirate routes of the Vikings. From the west coast of Norway, they would sail past the Orkneys to the Bay of Biscay to reach Gibraltar and enter the Mediterranean, and so to Italy. The Northmen were not unused to travelling as far as the Mediterranean and the long trip would not have bothered them. The *Vestvegr* was a quicker journey but only the wealthy could afford to fit out a boat for the purpose.

It is most likely that Breakspear followed the overland route favoured by most pilgrims to Rome. The *Romavegr* would take him over the Alps into Germany and on into Denmark. This route was shorter but still no soft option. Indeed, Scandinavians would have regarded this overland route, so far away from their familiar sea, as a penance. Travelling at that time was always dangerous although most pilgrims carried 'passports' issued by local bishops which offered some protection.

Breakspear left Italy around March 1152, not much more than two years after becoming a cardinal. At that time, the Curia was exiled at Segni, a town in the hilltops about 40 miles south-west of Rome. Danish historian Saxo Grammaticus tells us that Breakspear took the opportunity to visit England en route, but this is most unlikely.[2] Reaching Norway via England would have meant travelling through London, and no details of what he might have done there have been recorded. We can be sure that he did not visit St Albans, as the monks there would have told us about such an important event. Furthermore, in 1152, England was riding out the unsettled dog days of King Stephen's rule. The Archbishop of Canterbury, Theobald, the pope's man, supported the other claimant to the throne, Henry of Anjou, the son of Empress Matilda. The kingdom was still locked in this power struggle between Henry and Stephen. Ever since the Council at Reims in 1148 the relationship between Pope Eugenius, a Cistercian, and Stephen's brother, the Cluniac Bishop Henry of Winchester, had been difficult. The papal legate would not have been welcome at Stephen's court, or even in London itself, which remained loyal to Stephen.

Adding to the instability in England was the fact that, even though many Englishmen had volunteered for the Second Crusade to avenge the 'disgrace' of the loss of Edessa, there were still more than enough to take their place in the fierce fighting of the civil war back at home.[3] The failure of that crusade had contributed to a grim national mood and the economy was depressed, not least by all those unsettled loans to crusaders who had never returned. This would not have been a suitable time for Breakspear to spend reminiscing with people in England. He would not have tarried in England in any event: Breakspear was a conscientious man and his obligations lay elsewhere. The route to Norway from England would have been by boat from Grimsby, in which case he could have landed at Bergen in Norway, only 224 miles east of the Shetlands. Breakspear actually landed further south, at Stavanger, on 18 July 1152, which suggests he sailed directly from the continent.[4]

Breakspear found himself in what was then a small village of fishermen and traders, sitting on a jagged coastline sheltered by offshore islands and in the most northern country of western Christendom. The first Bishop of Stavanger had been Rainald from Winchester, and its cathedral, built in 1125, is dedicated to St Swithun, the ninth-century Bishop of Winchester who was reputedly a tutor to Aethelwulf, father of Alfred the Great. Having the Gulf Stream running around Norway warms the climate by about 5°C more than would be expected at these latitudes. The country was not suited for crops, but Norway's coast, rivers and lakes abounded with fish and its forests and mountains had plenty of game. In the twelfth century, Norway's population was about 400,000, one-fifth the size of England's.

The type of village settlement that Breakspear was familiar with throughout England and continental Europe was not seen in Norway. Development in Norway took place around dispersed farmsteads, often shared by three or four families. Over time, local tribal leaders, working together, supplemented their agriculture with fighting forays. Archaeology shows that trading with Europe was taking place from the fifth century, although this early 'trade' was unpaid for, being the booty from seaborne attacks. The Vikings of legend were drawn from the whole of Scandinavia, not just Norway, their raiding taking place from the eighth to the eleventh centuries before the three separate countries had really emerged. The Vikings' horned helmet was always a myth, but their piratical expeditions were real enough and they caused absolute terror in neighbouring countries.

The first recorded Viking raid in England was at Lindisfarne in 793. Many of the raiders took root in England and from the ninth century onwards Viking settlements also emerged all around the North Sea, in Scotland, Normandy, Iceland and Greenland, reflecting their dominance of the seas. Viking ships were equipped with sails as well as oars and were the most advanced vessels of the time. Their maritime skills, especially navigation, meant that they did not need to hug the coasts as did ships from Europe. The Vikings knew more about the world than anyone else at that time. By the eleventh century, Viking raids had ceased as European rulers became stronger and the Scandinavians then harnessed their nautical skills for commerce rather than for war, even as far as Constantinople, where they traded for silks from the east. However, their notoriety as fearsome warriors had never diminished.

Cardinal Breakspear had no idea what reception he would receive from the Norwegians. He would have been warned that the kings in both Norway and Sweden were unlikely to welcome someone planning to reduce their hold on religious appointments and he would have been wary of their warlike reputations. He was at the furthest edge of Europe, far away from Rome and with no personal protection. His role as papal legate gave him considerable status and authority, but beyond the Church the Norwegians would have seen him as an unknown quantity, a foreign interloper. Although a man of northern Europe, Breakspear was no Northman.

Surprisingly, Archbishop Eskil of Lund was not in Norway to greet Breakspear, having left Denmark for France at about the same time as Breakspear arrived. Eskil might have waited to give the papal legate support, but instead he had gone to visit his ailing friend, Bernard of Clairvaux. As the archbishop responsible for Norway, Eskil must have been aware of Breakspear's impending visit but perhaps the date of his arrival was unexpected. It may also have been that Eskil was making a silent protest, being aware of the proposal to grant both Norway and Sweden independence from Denmark.

Also absent when Breakspear arrived was any royal representation. Breakspear's visit to Norway took place amid continuing struggles over the throne. Prince Eystein, one of three claimants, was away on a raiding expedition to Scotland and eastern England until the autumn of 1152. Perhaps Breakspear's arrival did take Norway by surprise.

Breakspear's mission in Norway was clear. He was there to reorganise the Church, to bring its practices into line with the rest of Europe, free of royal interference, and to give Norway its own metropolitan see. Breaking the jurisdiction of Lund in Denmark and upsetting its well-regarded Archbishop Eskil was a risk Pope Eugenius was willing to take, as he had a hidden agenda. The pope wanted to reduce the possibility of Hamburg-Bremen re-establishing control over Lund, which would increase German imperial power in the region. Eugenius did not want that, and Breakspear was expected to break the German link permanently. He was to free northern clerics from secular meddling and establish Peter's Pence, already operating in western Europe. This was the first time Breakspear had been given specific objectives, and onerous ones at that. Success was down to him alone and it could not be taken for granted.

Breakspear's first task, to separate Church from state, was not going to be easy because the two had been so thoroughly entwined from the very beginning of the Norwegian Church. Christian missionaries had struggled to reach Norway until late in the tenth century and prior to this the Northmen had long clung to pagan beliefs. They did believe in a hereafter, even to the extent of scorning death, and their fearsome reputation was well deserved. Their lifestyle was austere and their religion as wild as they were. They were animistic, worshipping not idols but rather gods of storms, fjords and mountains. Norwegians were isolated from Europe, cut off by rough seas, and during the tenth century almost always at war with Denmark and Sweden, whose borders were constantly changing.

Harald Halfdansson, known as Harald Fairhair, having a helpful nickname as did many Norwegian kings, reigned from 872 to 932 as the first king of a united Norway. He was succeeded by his son Eric Bloodaxe, but not for long: Eric went into exile, first to Orkney, in 934, and then to Cumbria in England, where he died in 952.

Only later that century did any national respect for the 'royal family' take root and just as Christianity was reaching Norway. Eric's successor, his half-brother Haakon I Haraldsson, known as Haakon the Good, introduced Christianity to Norway but it took until the end of the tenth century, when Olaf came to the throne in 995, for Christian momentum to gather. Olaf's defining moment had come a year earlier when he led a fleet of ninety-four Viking ships on a raid to England. He pillaged all over the south of England and was successful everywhere except in London. The English King Aethelred* sued for peace and paid Olaf an extremely high ransom of 16,000lb of silver.[5] This fortune gave Olaf the wherewithal to buy support from sufficient warriors to overthrow Earl Haakon of Lade, his rival for the Norwegian throne.

Aethelred had paid Olaf a ransom, but there was a string attached. As part of their deal, Olaf agreed to accept Christian baptism in Andover, with Aethelred becoming his godfather. In turn, Olaf demanded that his followers also accept the new religion. The Icelandic poet Hallfred Otterarson, poet to the Norwegian king, expressed his cool feelings about dropping the Nordic pagan gods:

It's the creed of the sovereign
of [Olaf Tryggvason] to ban sacrifices.

---

* Aethelred the Unready, who spent most of his reign in a state of war against Denmark's King Cnut.

We must renounce many a long-held decree of norns.*
All mankind casts Odin's words to the winds;
Now I am forced to forsake Freya's kin and pray to Christ.[6]

Hallfred accepted his Christianity reluctantly and Olaf struggled to convince many of his sterner compatriots, not least the well-established pagan priests, to do likewise. Rooting out the old religion was not easy as Norwegian paganism had neither shrines nor temples with anything tangible to attack. It was beliefs, not buildings, that the Christian missionaries had to challenge.

Olaf, who died in 1000, gets the credit for starting Christian conversion but a namesake drove it forward. His sainted successor, the warrior king Olaf II, imposed Christianity on Norway using the force of axes when necessary. This was a man who in 1014, the year before his coronation, had invaded England and destroyed the wooden London Bridge which had stood firm since Roman times.** Herein lay the root of the problem that Breakspear was being sent to correct. The kings themselves had been responsible for Norwegian Christianity and had naturally kept for themselves control of Church matters. It was the king, not the Church, who appointed laymen to sit in judgement on errant clerics. Unlike other European countries, Norwegians paid no tithes to the central Church, which meant that the clergy in Norway struggled for their livelihood and were often reduced to begging.

This intertwining of state and Church meant that Breakspear's mission was as much diplomatic as ecclesiastical. Any opposition would come from the kings themselves. The Norwegian Church would not be a problem as he was there at its request and its bishops would likely agree anything in return for release from Danish control, even though that foreign control had largely been observed in the breach.

Throughout the eleventh century Scandinavian kings had generally ignored the then primate, the Archbishop of Bremen, instead recruiting their own bishops from countries such as England and Poland. The Church had grown through the efforts of these 'missionary bishops',*** who had no established sees and taught their own versions of Christianity rather than adhering to the strict teachings of the Church. Adam of Bremen, writing in the 1070s, described them:

---

*   Norns were Norse gods responsible for the fate of men.

**   This is one possible origin of the nursery rhyme 'London Bridge is Falling Down'.

*** Sturlason in *Heimskringla* calls them 'common' bishops.

I think the reason is that, with Christianity in a rude state, none of the bishops was as yet assigned to a fixed see, but that as each of them pushed out
into the farther regions in the effort to establish Christianity, he would strive
to preach the Word of God alike to his own and to the others' people. This
even now seems to be the practice beyond Denmark, throughout Norway
and Sweden.[7]

It was during the twelfth century that most of Norway's famous 'stave
churches' were built. These striking wooden buildings were supported by
posts, or staves, which were driven into the ground and carried the load
of the steeply angled roofs. Typically, the main door was deliberately low,
and the portals on either side of the door were elaborately carved with
images of furious beasts. The Norwegians had not forgotten their pagan
past and they did this to scare away from the church the old gods, and
in particular *Midgardsormen*, the serpent of middle earth that encircled the
world ready to gobble up any ships that sailed too close to the edge. There
were once over 1,000 stave churches in Norway but only twenty-eight
remain standing today.

✠ ✠ ✠

Breakspear's mission to separate Church from state was further complicated
by the fact that there was no single monarch to address. King Harald IV
Magnusson had been murdered in 1136 and, ever since, three of his sons had
been fighting to succeed him. The rules of succession in Norway were vague
and favoured agnatic descendants, where a king's brothers took precedence
over the king's own sons, whether born in wedlock or not. When there was
more than one candidate, which was often the case, the contenders had to fight
for the throne. Formal rules of succession were only introduced in Norway by
the law of succession in 1163/64. Thanks to Breakspear's endeavours, this law
included a degree of election in that it prescribed an electoral court comprised
mostly of bishops.

Harald's throne was first seized by Sigurd Slembe, called Noisy Sigurd, who
had claimed to be a half-brother to Harald and who was probably involved in
his murder. Sturlason thought so and gives a graphic tale of how Sigurd carried
out the crime. Two of his accomplices dined with King Harald and pretended
to have had a wager with each other for a stake of a pot of honey. One of them
cheekily asked Harald:

I say that you will sleep this night with your Queen Ingrid; and he says that you will sleep with Thora, Guthorm's daughter.

The king answered laughing, and without suspecting in the least that there lay treachery under the question, that he who had asked lost his bet.[8]

Unwittingly, the king had revealed where he would be later that night, and Sigurd slew him in his bed. Sigurd did not enjoy his ill-gotten throne for long. Three years later he was convicted of regicide and suffered an awful death:

They broke his shin bones and arms with an axe-hammer. Then they stripped him, and would flay him alive: but when they tried to take off the skin, they could not do it for the gush of blood. They took leather whips and flogged him so long, that the skin was as much taken off as if he had been flayed. Then they stuck a piece of wood in his back until it broke, dragged him to a tree and hanged him; then cut off his head.[9]

With Sigurd dead, the Norwegian barons recognised both of Harald's sons, Inge, aged 8, and Eystein, or Augustine, aged 11, as successors to the throne. The contest became more crowded in 1142 when another Sigurd appeared from Scotland, also claiming to be a son of Harald. Sigurd was as vicious as his father Harald had been and, although at first he co-operated with his half-brothers Inge and Eystein, he soon turned against them. This Sigurd did not win the support of the barons and Norwegians rallied to Inge, even though he did not fit the model of Norwegian kings, being disabled: 'His stature was small; and he had difficulty in walking alone, because he had one foot withered, and he had a hump both on his back and his breast.'[10] Inge's calm patience found favour, and this forced Sigurd into an uneasy alliance with Eystein. Just as Breakspear entered the scene the two conspirators were preparing an attack on Inge and his supporters.

This was déjà vu. The royal mess was not dissimilar to that in England. Breakspear knew that he had to address this internecine royal feud before he could embark on his ecclesiastical agenda. He would make no progress for the Church until the three princes reached some compromise among themselves, and peace was restored. This was never part of his brief, but he had to deal with it.

In one way, the squabble between the princes might have helped Breakspear in as much as the royal influence which dominated control of the Church was diluted.

The royal family was divided, and in a lesser way so too was the Norwegian Church. Its subservience to the Danish Archbishop of Lund was resented by some Church leaders who turned for support to the more-distant Archbishop Hartwig of Hamburg-Bremen. This group saw it as convenient that Hartwig was much further away and less likely to bother them. Nonetheless, Hartwig was a surprising ally for them since his sister was married to the Danish King Eric, but Hartwig too resented the Lund archbishopric and hoped to regain control of the Norwegian Church. He went as far as to petition Rome in 1149 for the restoration of Bremen's previous authority over all the northern churches. He argued that the rumblings within the Church in Norway and Sweden demonstrated that giving control to Lund had been a failure and that Bremen's authority over all three Scandinavian countries should be reinstated. Archbishop Eskil would not have tolerated such a thought and nor was the pope going to agree to such a backward step. Independence is hard won and harder still to cede.

Breakspear had two challenges on his hands. First, to wrestle authority in the Church away from the monarchs and, second, to straighten out the doctrine. Before he could do either, though, he had to ease political tensions and he took this in his stride, dealing first with the quarrelling princes. He must have met them, but the meetings are not recorded. We know that he took a liking to Inge and Sturlason tells us that he found fault with both Sigurd and Eystein:

> The Cardinal had taken offence at the brothers Sigurd and Eystein, and they were obliged to come to a reconciliation with him; but, on the other hand, he stood on the most affectionate terms with King Inge, whom he called his son.[11]

We do not know why Breakspear had taken umbrage, but he would not have been pleased to learn that Sigurd had fathered a child by his first cousin, Kristin Sigurdsdottir.[12] Whatever it was, it is amazing that a newly arrived foreigner managed to get the aggressive Sigurd and Eystein to accept penance for their offences and make peace with Inge. This is an elegant testament to Breakspear's diplomatic skills.

Although the quarrelling brothers had laid down their arms, there remained the important matter of which prince was to be the first among equals, the single King of Norway. There had to be one and Breakspear, an outsider, took an enormous risk by taking sides. If he had made the wrong decision his stay in Norway would have been short.

The prize went to Inge, and for the first time Norway had a king who could neither mount a horse nor swing an axe. By preferring Inge, it was clear that Breakspear was not bothered by appearances. He was a good reader of men and saw Inge's inherent qualities and his superior wisdom. His favouring of Inge had not dealt with all of Norway's civic problems, but he had established a calmer atmosphere in which he could tackle his real purpose. Breakspear backed the right man and his work for the Church in Norway could begin in earnest.

Breakspear convened a synod 310 miles north of Oslo at what was then the capital of Norway. Nidaros, the settlement's original name, means the mouth of the River Nidelva but in the later Middle Ages people started to call it Trondheim after its fjord. The river used to be deep enough for most boats to pass through until an avalanche of mud and stones in the mid-seventeenth century made it less navigable. We can tell from rock carvings found there that people had been living in the region for thousands of years. The settlement itself was established in 997 as a trading post and it remained the capital of Norway until 1217. It was frequently used as the seat of the king during the Middle Ages, and again after independence was restored in 1814. Nidaros Cathedral remains the coronation church of Norwegian kings.

The cathedral is next to the archbishop's palace, in the centre of the city, and was one of the most important Christian sites in medieval northern Europe. Pilgrimage routes led to Nidaros from Oslo in southern Norway. It is the northernmost medieval cathedral in the world, and the second largest in Scandinavia.* The famous Lewis chessmen, chess pieces carved from walrus ivory found in the Hebrides and now at the British Museum, are believed to have been made in Nidaros in the 1150s, around the time Breakspear was there. Walrus ivory was a vital export from Greenland, where expatriate Northmen had settled.

Despite the importance of the event, the Council of Nidaros is not well documented. Some timings suggest that it was held in the middle of winter 1152–53, when the weather in the north made all journeys difficult and there were only four hours of daylight each day, though it is possible that the council took place in kinder weather in spring 1153. Ambiguities on the year it took place might exist because it was around this time that the start of the new year was moved from Christmas Day, 25 December, to Lady Day, 25 March.

There is some documentation on the attendees of the synod. Sees with bishops had been established in Norway in the early part of the twelfth century and by the time Breakspear arrived there were four: Nidaros, Bergen, Oslo and Stavanger. The Diocese of Nidaros covered territories outside Norway, including Iceland, Greenland, the Faroes, the Orkneys, the Shetlands, the Hebrides,

---

* It earns two stars in Simon Jenkins's *Europe's 100 Best Cathedrals* (Viking, 2021).

the Isle of Man and even Piel Island in far-off Morecambe Bay. The British islands had been snatched from the See of York and were only returned some 200 years later. Three dioceses sent their bishops to the synod: Jon Birgensson of Stavanger, Sigurd of Bergen and Viljalm of Oslo, each with twelve supporters. The See of Nidaros itself was vacant. Breakspear would have wanted the three princes to be present and it is likely they were at Nidaros.

Breakspear was an efficient manager and ensured that this was a successful synod. The most weighty decision was the creation of the long-awaited Norwegian metropolitan see. To achieve a metropolitan see to manage all of the four existing ones Breakspear needed to identify a first Archbishop of Norway, and he had an ideal candidate. His choice fell on the Bishop of Stavanger, Jon Birgensson, who had impressed Breakspear when he landed at Stavanger in July the previous year.

Breakspear took care to ensure that all three princes were content with his choice. He did not need their support: after all he was here to give the Church control of the appointment of bishops and he would not have wanted the princes to think they had any right of sanction on the appointments. Nonetheless, the collegiate monk in him was eager to keep them on side. With royal authority divided three ways, the three would not have had the courage to oppose the pope's legate and the three princes did concur.

Breakspear also persuaded the council to agree to set up canonical courts which would elect new bishops in the future. This proved not to be the end of the story and the loss of royal authority over appointments of bishops would lead to furious disputes between the king and the Archbishop of Nidaros after the death of Breakspear.

Breakspear granted the new Archbishop Birgensson authority over the other three dioceses of Norway and over the two suffragan (assistant) bishops in Iceland and Greenland which were in effect Norwegian colonies. Choosing the location for his new archbishopric was obvious. It would be Nidaros itself, whose cathedral was the resting place of King Olaf II, who was killed at the Battle of Stiklestad in 1030 and was immediately venerated as a martyr and sainted by the local bishop. His previous occupation as a Viking warrior was no bar to his being declared the patron saint of Norway and he was formally canonised by Pope Alexander in 1164. Sturlason elaborates the gory details of a miracle that Saint Olaf had worked just before Breakspear arrived:

A man called Haldor fell into the hands of the Vinland people, who took him and mutilated him, cut open his neck, took out his tongue through the opening, and cut out his tongue root. He afterwards sought out the holy

King Olaf, fixed his mind entirely on the holy man, and weeping besought King Olaf to restore his speech and health. Thereupon he immediately recovered his speech by the good King's compassion. This miracle took place a fortnight before the last Olafmas,* upon the day that Cardinal Breakspear set foot on the land of Norway.[13]

Having established the new archbishopric, Breakspear commissioned the building for the cathedral of a new cloister which still stands today. The cathedral itself was rebuilt later in the twelfth century by Jon Birgensson's successor, Archbishop Eystein. Close to the archbishop's palace, just by the river, is 'Hadrian's Plass', a fountain with a bronze plaque to the still well-remembered Breakspear.

The Norwegian Church had won their greatest wish, their own metropolitan see, with its archbishop now the leader of the Church in Norway. The Norwegians were in thrall to Breakspear and he was regarded as the most powerful man in Norway at that time. On this solid base, he could press on with the rest of his agenda and expect support. He created a fifth diocese at Hamar, which lies on the shore of Mjøsa, Norway's largest lake, some 80 miles north of Oslo. It became the only see not on the coast and, as its first bishop, Breakspear chose Bishop Arnoldur of Greenland.

Just as in the rest of Europe, regular clerical orders had become popular and both Augustinians and Premonstratensians followed the Cistercians to Norway. Breakspear ordered the building of an Augustinian monastery and a cathedral at Hamar and later, when pope, he sent English architects to help complete this building work. Hamar Cathedral was sacked in the sixteenth century and is preserved as a ruin.

Breakspear next introduced reforms to bring the Norwegian Church more closely into line with wider Church practice. He himself was a stickler for the rules, as was demonstrated at the Abbey of St Ruf, and he wanted to ensure that all aspects of canon law were clear and applied in Norway in the same way that they were applied by the wider Church. Ever since King Olaf's day, this control had been in secular hands and this was now to cease. The council had already confirmed the reduced royal influence over the Church, in particular the appointment of its bishops, and Breakspear insisted that parish clerics too must be appointed by the bishops, not by local barons.

Breakspear addressed practical issues too. A Church without resources could not thrive, so he turned to money matters. Norwegian clergy had a tough time,

---

* The feast day of St Olaf, 29 July.

dependent on handouts from pilgrims and begging for their living. Breakspear was determined to improve their lot. In theory, Church tithes had been in place since about 1100 but payment was rarely observed and to ensure that the clergy would have regular incomes Breakspear persuaded Norwegians to give voluntarily for the maintenance of their priests. This happened, albeit slowly. It was not until several decades later that Haakon the Old (1217–63) established a formal annual tithe of income and a once-in-lifetime tithe of possessions, at last providing Norwegian clergy with some sort of financial security.[14]

Breakspear also wanted Norway to contribute to the papal Curia by paying Peter's Pence. There is no doubt that Breakspear was successful in introducing these payments to Rome, but they took time to become routine.

Finally, Breakspear used the council to raise the thorny issue of priestly celibacy. In the wider European Church celibacy was required, although clearly not always observed. It seems not to have been required at all in Norway. This may seem surprising but perhaps not if we consider the links between Norwegian traders and Constantinople, where the Orthodox Church had no objection to married priests. In 1132 Pope Innocent II had sent a Bernardine monk, Martin Cibo, to enforce priestly celibacy in Denmark but perhaps to little effect. Several years after Breakspear's visit, Archbishop Birgensson's successor at Nidaros, Archbishop Eystein, formalised the rule of celibacy at a synod in Bergen in 1164. This was doubtless the culmination of Breakspear's entreaties, but it was a hard rule to enforce and it had only limited success. Repeated efforts were made to enforce it. In 1193 Pope Celestine III sent yet another legate, Censius, to Norway to ensure that the faithful kept to the regulations laid down by 'Adrian of blessed memory'.[15]

Even as late as 1237 Pope Gregory IX expressed surprise that Norwegian priests continued to be married.[16] He also suggested that, contrary to what had been recorded elsewhere, 'Adrian – then Bishop of Albano – acted as a legate in those lands permitted this [clerical marriages] to be done'.[17] Breakspear was known to have been opposed to clerical marriages. His own family circumstances may have left a scar, his father perhaps having been a married monk. He was also a pragmatic man and he knew that throughout Europe many clerics still took a wife, so it is possible that he had tolerated local practices in the north. Writing at the start of the twentieth century, Mackie believed that Breakspear's appeal for clerical celibacy had achieved nothing.[18]

Breakspear earned further credits in Norway. It seems that he acquired some Norse during his two-year stay, and it is claimed that he wrote the first Norwegian catechism.[19] If it is true, no trace of his catechism remains. Breakspear could hardly have had the time to do all this work personally, since his time in Norway was limited, but he could have completed it after his return. He is also credited with the banning of bearing arms in market towns, except for the king's bodyguards, who were not to exceed twelve in number.[20] This edict was welcomed by the local people, who felt much less intimidated when they went into the towns.

✠ ✠ ✠

Breakspear had worked hard in Norway. This is the first time we can judge how successful he was against the precise objectives that he had been set. The Church certainly approved the establishment of the new metropolitan see at Nidaros and, just before he died in November 1154, Pope Anastasius IV, the successor to Eugenius, confirmed this decision. The new archdiocese also brought knock-on benefits for the Norwegian monarchy. Incorporating the western islands as well as the Hebrides into the See of Nidaros gave Norway the impetus to add them to its kingdom too. As a coastal nation, the islands in the North Sea and the Atlantic were a natural area for territorial expansion. It also made sense because the inhabitants were largely descended from Norwegian emigrants and spoke the same language. As Christianity strengthened in Norway, greater centralisation of the state followed. Norwegian historian Trond Noren Isaksen has no doubt: '[Breakspear's] assignment was something far more than an administrative reform – it could almost be compared to the founding of a new nation or at least international recognition of the kingdom.'[21]

Breakspear's success in separating sovereign and ecclesiastical powers in Norway is not clear cut. He was just one player in this long-running drama; in several European countries the Church had come under the control of sovereigns and this had been a running sore for some time, and at least since 1076 when there was a fierce power struggle between Pope Gregory VII and Emperor Henry IV. Gregory was the first of the reforming popes to attack the customary right of kings to appoint bishops, abbots and senior clerics. This conflict between Church and state became known as the 'Investiture Controversy', the issue being whether pope or sovereign should 'invest' bishops. Pope Paschal II and King Henry I of England fought their own Investiture Controversy from 1103 to 1107.

In all of these conflicts the papacy was adamant that it alone should be responsible for the appointment of archbishops and bishops, and the structure of parishes. However, a temporal sovereign could not easily accept that papal sovereignty should limit his own authority. The issue was supposed to have been settled in 1122 when Pope Callixtus II and Emperor Henry V agreed the Concordat of Worms, which drew the lines between royal and ecclesiastical powers. The outcome at Worms was largely a papal victory, but the emperor still retained a limited role in selecting bishops, and in reality, the matter of papal supremacy remained unresolved. The continuing Investiture Controversy would dog Breakspear's own papacy.

While he was in Norway, Breakspear did succeed in separating sovereign and ecclesiastical powers but, soon after he left, King Inge went back to his old habits, interfering in senior Church appointments. As pope, Breakspear reiterated the need for obedience to the decrees on this matter set down in the Lateran Council of 1139 but the king did not listen. In 1161, after Breakspear had died, King Inge defiantly appointed his own chaplain as Archbishop of Nidaros, finally winning the upper hand and letting his old friend down. Sometime later, King Sverre, who reigned in Norway from 1184 to 1202, had a go at further undermining Breakspear's initial successful separation of Church and state by arguing disingenuously that the election of Archbishop Birgensson back in 1153 had been but a temporary expedient because of the inability of the three princes to agree on one man. Pope Celestine III then intervened, as he did about clerical marriages, and insisted that the election of bishops was reserved for the Church alone.

The Norwegian state interfered in more than the election of bishops. At first, the canonical courts established by Breakspear in 1153 to administer Church laws held, but some forty years later disciplinary cases were still being brought before secular judges. Celestine yet again exhorted the Norwegians to stay true to Breakspear's reforms:

> That the canonical constitutions of Adrian 'of happy memory' should be thus suffered to fall into neglect. Had they then forgotten all the innumerable labours and hardships and sufferings endured by the legate, for the reforming of their Church? If not how could they tolerate such a condition of things? And by the present authority we distinctly forbid that any lay person in your diocese should exercise ecclesiastical jurisdiction, or hear or define cases which appertain to ecclesiastical judgement alone.[22]

Sturlason, writing around 1230, paid an enormous tribute to Breakspear:

> He improved many of the customs of the Northmen while he was in the country. There never came a foreigner to Norway whom all men respected so highly, or who could govern the people so well as he did. After some time

he returned to the South with many friendly presents and declared ever afterwards that he was the greatest friend of the people of Norway.[23]

The final verdict on his Norwegian work may rest with Torfaeus, an Icelandic historian who wrote a comprehensive history of Norway in 1711. Even though Torfaeus was writing after the Norwegian Church had broken away from Rome, he had only good things to write about Cardinal Breakspear. He went one better than Sturlason, saying that Breakspear:

> Was a man full of piety ... no one had possessed such authority in Norway until this day ... our writers number him with the saints.[24]

The twelfth century was a heroic age for the Scandinavian Church, and Breakspear can claim part of the credit for this. His achievements largely stood the test of time. Breakspear and Norway had proved good for each other.

6

SWEDEN
The Swedish Church

Since the Swedes and the Goths were unable to agree on a city and personage suitable for such an important function and contended for the privilege, he denied them this honour.

Saxo Grammaticus
History of the Danes[1]

There could be no rest for Breakspear. He had similar work to do in Sweden, so from Nidaros he moved south to Hamar in late spring 1153 and on to Oslo, making the brief hop over to Sweden that summer. Although not far, the difficult terrain meant that it was still an arduous journey, taking several days. He could possibly have returned to the Norwegian coast and sailed to Sweden and this would have been a shorter trip.

Sweden, like Norway, is a land of snow-capped mountains, lakes, rivers and thick forests. Its settlements too were mostly on the coast and roads inland were few and far between. This Scandinavian kingdom, along with neighbouring Denmark, had also converted to Christianity, and both rather earlier than Norway. Notably, throughout Scandinavia, people had chosen to convert rather than having Christianity forced upon them. With their new religion came increasing trade with the continent, Scandinavians having realised that adopting Christianity created a beneficial bond with Europe. Just like the Norwegians, by the time of the eleventh century the Swedish successors of their warring ancestors were making their journeys into mainland Europe as traders and pilgrims.

Sweden's population was about 300,000, rather less than that of Norway. Militarily, Sweden was the weakest of the Scandinavian countries, and had but one naval port, Skagerrack, compared with at least six in Denmark and Norway. Denmark, Norway and Sweden are closely related by culture and by geography but in the twelfth century they were constantly at war with each other, their borders ever fluid.

By contrast to his Norwegian counterpart, Sweden's King Sverker was ready and waiting to greet the cardinal, thanks to the good word sent ahead of him by the friends he made in Norway. These were turbulent times but Sverker himself was a peaceful man, a good supporter of the Church, and ready to help Breakspear make a quick start.

Breakspear had reason to feel optimistic about his mission in Sweden, where he had the support of the king and there was a longer history of Christianity. Surprisingly, it would be more difficult and prove less successful. His primary mission, as in Norway, was to establish a metropolitan see in Sweden and so give the Swedish Church independence from Lund in Denmark and direct access to Rome. In Sweden there were five sees: Skara, Uppsala, Lynkoping, Strangnas and Vasteras. Like Norway, paganism was still practised but, unlike Norway where there were few visible signs of it, Sweden had many pagan altars, including the central sanctuary of Odin at Uppsala which was not destroyed until 1168.

Wasting no time, Breakspear called a national assembly at Lynkoping, the royal base of King Sverker. Its bishop, Gislo, was the effective leader of the Church in Sweden. Gislo had been at the Synod of Lund in 1139, and in Lund again in 1145 for the consecration of Archbishop Eskil's new cathedral. Lynkoping (now spelt Linköping) is some 125 miles south-west of Stockholm, and the spire of its cathedral still dominates the skyline. After the cold of Nidaros, Breakspear welcomed its mild and humid summer climate.

Sweden, unlike Norway, enjoyed internal peace in the sense that there was no fighting, but there were bitter rivalries between the Swedes 'proper' in the north and the Gotlanders in the south. The one thing they did agree on was mutual hatred of the Church authority in Lund.

Breakspear was ready to hear the opinions of both groups but could not have been surprised to find that there was no common cause between them. Breakspear had been able to bring the disputing brother princes in Norway together but they were of one blood; reconciling the two distinct Swedish tribes was a challenge of a different order. Despite his efforts to knock heads together, the Swedes and the Gotlanders could not agree on the location for a new archbishopric. Naturally, the Swedes insisted that only Uppsala, in their territory, could possibly serve as the base for the new archbishop, whereas the Gotlanders insisted on Skara in Gotland.[2] Breakspear could see that the only solution that would be acceptable to all Swedes was to establish two archbishoprics, one in the south and one in the north, but that was not part of his plan.

Breakspear had to close the synod without any agreement on the archbishopric and in that regard his mission to Sweden failed. The negotiating skills that had served him well in Norway had not proved sufficient to unite the two Swedish tribes. Some chroniclers have suggested that Breakspear was not unhappy with the failure and had deliberately left Sweden under the control of Denmark's Archbishop Eskil as a favour to Eskil. Breakspear and Eskil did become friends but it is unlikely that Breakspear would have been swayed by such a request. He had not baulked at taking Norway out of Eskil's authority. There is also a suggestion that it was Eskil who was to blame for the failure to reach an agreement at Lynkoping and that while Breakspear had been busy in Norway, Eskil had been just as busy creating dissent in Sweden. If so, surely Breakspear would have known, and had Eskil really behaved like that it would have prejudiced their ongoing friendship.

Nor would Breakspear have thought it sensible to place the Swedish Church under the control of the new Norwegian archbishop in Nidaros. That would have added insult to Sweden's injury. In the circumstances Breakspear's decision to leave Lund in control was the only sensible conclusion that he could have reached.

Breakspear had to break the news to the Swedes that they would remain subject to the Archbishop of Lund but, good tactician that he was, he delayed announcing his decision until he had put in place his other reforms to the Swedish Church. First, he installed a fellow Englishman named Henry in the vacant See of Uppsala. As in Norway, and throughout his life, Breakspear had shown himself to be a fine judge of character and now was no different. Henry was probably a member of Breakspear's travelling entourage and Breakspear would have got to know him well. Henry later became better known in Finland, just emerging as its own country, where he was murdered in 1156 and venerated as a martyr for the Church.

Breakspear repeated in Sweden the Church reforms that he had made in Norway: enforcing the celibacy of the clergy; the remittance of Peter's Pence to Rome; and the freeing of the Church from secular control. This last change was only possible because Breakspear had kept close to King Sverker, with whom he had a good relationship, and in turn because Sverker had confidence in Henry, the new Bishop of Uppsala. Once all these reforms were agreed,

Breakspear told the disappointed Swedes of his decision to leave Sweden within the Archdiocese of Lund, doubtless explaining that this was only a short-term expedient.

Less was achieved in Sweden than in Norway, but these changes were still positive for Sweden's Church and Breakspear's groundwork had a lasting effect. As he had assured the Swedes, their archbishop was not long in coming. Breakspear's successor pope, Alexander III, sent a papal mission to Scandinavia in 1163–64, led by Stephen of Orvieto, who established the Swedish archbishopric in Uppsala. The Swedes did not, however, have quite the same direct access to Rome that the Norwegians enjoyed: Breakspear had left the Archbishop of Lund with supremacy over the Swedish Church, and even after 1164 Lund retained this privilege. This supremacy of the Danish Church remained in place until the Reformation in the sixteenth century.

Sadly, that consecration of the first Swedish archbishop could not take place in Sweden. King Valdemar I of Denmark and Archbishop Hartwig of Hamburg-Bremen had sided with Pope Alexander's rival, the Antipope Victor IV, who had been elected in opposition to Alexander in 1159, and Sweden was not a safe place for foreign visitors. Instead, the consecration took place at Sens in France when Stephen, a Cistercian monk, was consecrated Archbishop of Uppsala in the presence of Eskil of Lund and Thomas Becket, Archbishop of Canterbury.

It was the same Archbishop Stephen who probably drafted the coronation oath for King Magnus Erlingsson (1161–84), the first occasion when a Norwegian king was crowned by the Archbishop of Nidaros. This oath paid tribute to Breakspear's Scandinavian work, setting out the relationship between Church and state and emphasising the importance of royal obedience to the Church:

> I, King Magnus, swear by the Father, the Son, and the Holy Ghost, and on these holy relics: that I shall be faithful and obedient to the holy Roman church and to the highest pontiff lord Alexander, and his Catholic successors; that I shall observe those things which Lord Pope Adrian instituted when he was a legate in Norway, about the Peter's Pence and the affairs of the kingdom and the church, and that I will make others observe them to the best of my ability.[3]

Having completed all that he could do in Sweden, Breakspear set off to his final Scandinavian destination.

7

DENMARK
A Futile Plea for Peace

After looking at the appearance of the season and thinking how dangerous and frightening it could be to sail back over the ocean in winter, he concluded that the route via Denmark would be the most appropriate one for his return journey.

Saxo Grammaticus
History of the Danes[1]

The distance from Lynkoping in Sweden to Lund in Denmark is only 250 miles, and Breakspear could have made this journey either by road or sea, likely arriving early in 1154. Denmark is low lying and the best suited of the Scandinavian countries for agriculture, and Lund sits in the heart of its farming district. Today's Danish capital, Copenhagen, 40 miles to the west, is visible from the low hill to the north of Lund. In the twelfth century, Denmark's population was about half that of England, somewhere below 1 million, and greater than the combined population of Sweden and Norway.

Of the three kingdoms, Denmark was the strongest and the most developed, its armies regularly raiding the Prussians on the Baltic coast as well the Swedes and the Norwegians. Only a century before, the Danish Prince Cnut had even brought England to its knees, becoming its king in 1016. He became King of Denmark two years later, forging a personal union of the two countries. After Cnut's death in 1035 Denmark became less influential but remained the leading power in the region, forming a Danish North Sea empire with Norway and England. Norway regained its independence in 1046, although that ended at the start of the fourteenth century when it was joined to Sweden.

Saxo Grammaticus (1160–1220), a Danish historian and theologian who was probably a canon at Lund Cathedral, suggests that Breakspear's visit to Denmark might just have been expedient while he waited for better weather for sea travel. Nonetheless, it gave Breakspear an opportunity to 'offer a soothing benefaction to allay the offence caused by his advancement of Norway'.[2]

The Church in Denmark was better established than in either Norway or Sweden and there was no need for Breakspear to interfere. Christianity arrived in 826 when King Harald 'Bluetooth' was baptised by German missionaries. There had been bishops with Danish sees as early as 948 but it is thought that these were no more than suffragan bishops of the Archbishop of Hamburg-Bremen, who in all likelihood never left Germany. Even though the German archbishops never visited their sees, it helped the Danish Church that there had been regular contact with Rome since King Cnut made a pilgrimage there in 1027 and founded a hospice for Danish pilgrims. In 1104, Denmark's first archbishop, Asger, had received from the legate Alberic his pallium, the badge of office of archbishops. In 1137 Asger had been succeeded by his nephew Eskil, who had been appointed apostolic vicar of all Scandinavia at the synod in 1139. Lund is still dominated by its towering cathedral which was completed only nine years before Breakspear's arrival.

In Archbishop Eskil the Danish Church had a good and faithful leader. As a close friend of the Cistercian St Bernard of Clairvaux, Eskil actively promoted the Cistercians, also Pope Eugenius's order, in Scandinavia. It is believed that Eskil had missed Breakspear's arrival in Norway in 1152 because he had gone to Clairvaux to seek Bernard's permission for him to become a fellow Cistercian but Bernard discouraged him on the grounds that he could better serve the Church as a bishop.

Had Breakspear not visited Denmark, both Eskil and King Sweyne, who controlled the eastern part of Denmark including Lund, would have been disappointed. A visit from a papal legate was an important event and Breakspear knew that a personal visit from him would do much to win Eskil's acceptance of his changes in Norway. He had to tread carefully, knowing that any clerical challenge to the decisions that he had made in Norway would come only from the Danish Church, proud of its own autonomy yet more than happy to hang on to its control of the Church in Norway. Fortunately, Breakspear already knew Eskil, having met him on several occasions before, including in Italy. He recognised that Eskil was a good and pious man, but he also knew that he was a prickly character. Despite this, once again a reassuring Breakspear persuaded

Eskil to accept his decision. That Breakspear had granted Lund primacy over Sweden softened the blow somewhat. According to Grammaticus, Eskil was more than content with Breakspear's decision:

> So approaching Eskil, by means of envoys, he [Breakspear] promised to award him new, greater authority than he had previously lost, explaining that he would compensate for the deprivation of Norway, now it had been snatched away from him, by the gift of the Swedish primacy. Eskil leapt at the proposal and eagerly entreated the legate to give him an interview.[3]

Breakspear left with Eskil the pallium that he had intended for a new Swedish archbishop and granted Eskil and his successors the authority to consecrate future Swedish archbishops. In this Breakspear exceeded his brief, but when pope he confirmed his own decision in a letter to Eskil on 15 January 1157.[4] The privilege was later confirmed by Pope Innocent III in 1198.

As with Norway, Breakspear had found a confusion of kings in Denmark. Thrones were being contested at this time throughout the north and there were three competing Danish monarchs: Sweyne, his cousin Valdemar, and Cnut, a son of King Magnus I of Sweden. The three had been contesting the throne ever since King Eric III had abdicated in 1146. In 1154 each controlled separate provinces in uneasy agreement.

Unlike in Norway, Breakspear did not get involved in any reconciliation, spending his time only with King Sweyne. However, he did act as a temporary peacemaker between Sweden and Denmark.

Jon, the son of Sweden's King Sverker, was a wild youth who had insulted the wife of his elder brother and her sister, both of whom were Danish princesses. Denmark's King Sweyne was outraged by this and opened hostilities against Sweden. It was clear, though, that Jon's offence was no more than a convenient excuse, as Sweyne had long nursed a yearning to possess Sweden. He reckoned that the elderly King Sverker was unfit for fighting and that there was no better time to extend his realm. Breakspear became aware of Sweyne's plans and intervened to convince his host of the futility of war, especially over such a trivial matter. He showed the king that he was being 'seduced by a pointless campaign, draining himself of strength in his greed for petty returns'. Breakspear made a droll comparison to the spider:

> Sweyne was trying to imitate a spider; after it had spun the strands of its web by voiding its entrails at the risk of its own life, what did it catch? – nothing but stinking beetles and other worthless creatures.[5]

King Sweyne appeared to accept his advice and agreed to desist. In the summer of 1154, he politely escorted Breakspear to the border on his way back to Italy. However, as soon as Breakspear's back was turned Sweyne reneged on his promise and marched his armies into Sweden. He was so confident of success that he started gifting Swedish territory to his Danish warriors before the campaign had even got under way. In response to this invasion, the elderly Swedish king first tried to sue for peace and when that failed, rather than prepare to engage the stronger Danish invaders, he cleverly withdrew to the far cold regions of what is now Finland. King Sweyne chased after him, thinking the winter cold would freeze the marshland and make his progress northwards easier. He could not have been more wrong. Grammaticus described the awful scene:

> But now mountainous drifts of snow had invested almost all the countryside and the ferocity of the cold was such that, when women put their babies to their breasts, the infants' limbs were so numbed by the icy temperature that they expired even while they sucked the nourishing milk; the mothers, not far from suffering a similar fate themselves, would fondle the corpses of their offspring in a dying embrace. As the Danes, too, were persecuted by the merciless climate, they did not spend their nights in camp or observe sentry duty, fears were not due to the violence of weapons but of the weather, seeing that everyone shunned the elements more than the enemy.[6]

The Danes were routed. King Sweyne should have heeded Breakspear and remained true to his promise. Sweyne was killed in a battle with Valdemar in 1157, leaving Valdemar with the Danish throne to himself until he died in 1182. King Sverker did not outlive Sweyne, being assassinated by a servant on Christmas Day 1156.

Breakspear was remembered throughout Scandinavia as 'Breakspear the good cardinal and now considered a saint'. Less pleased with what he had done was the See of Hamburg-Bremen. It would never again have jurisdiction over the Scandinavian churches. Breakspear was never canonised by the Church but Sturlason, writing in about 1230, regarded him as a saint:

> According to the report of men who went to Rome in his days, he never had any business, however important, to settle with other people, but he would break it off to speak with the Northmen who desired to see him. He was not long pope and is now considered a saint.[7]

Breakspear had faced difficulties at every stage of his two-year mission to Scandinavia and dealt with them all well. Breakspear's work in the north benefitted both his Church that had sent him there and Scandinavia itself. In all three countries his good political instincts and strong self-confidence brought him deserved success, using his initiative to calm fractious kings before embarking on his agenda for Church reforms. A lesser man might have stepped aside from the civic chaos and clumsily, and less effectively, discussed Church reforms only with the bishops. Pope Eugenius had chosen the right man as his legate and Breakspear did not have to wait long for his unsought reward.

PART THREE

DRIAN

ROME
The Throne of St Peter

When he came south to Rome the former pope died suddenly, and all the people of Rome would have Cardinal Nicholas for pope, and he was consecrated under the name of Adrian.

Snorri Sturlason
Heimskringla[1]

Breakspear left his Scandinavian friends in late summer 1154, returning to Rome by the quickest route, overland through Germany and over the Alps. He had no time for a last visit to still-unsettled England and he would not have wanted to visit Archbishop Hartwig of Hamburg-Bremen, where he would hardly have been welcome. He was never to return to Scandinavia, but he had left behind in all three countries men on whom he and the Church could rely: his own two appointees, Jon Birgensson in Norway and Henry in Sweden, and Eskil in Denmark. Eskil had accepted graciously his loss of authority over Norway and he and Breakspear had parted as friends.

Breakspear travelled home with the jaunt in his step of a mission fulfilled but saddened that his mentor had died while he was away. Eugenius had been a good pope, if not a strong one (over 700 years later, he was beatified by Pope Pius IX; as he had always been seen as humble and pious, it is a mystery why the Church took so long to honour him). Eugenius had been replaced seemingly by a stopgap, Pope Anastasius IV. The oldest of the cardinals, at the age of 80, he was elected on 12 July 1153, four days after Eugenius's death. He, like Adrian, was an Augustinian canon and the former abbot of another Abbey of

St Rufus, this one in Orléans. Given his age, it appeared as if the cardinals had
chosen Anastasius to keep the Throne of St Peter warm for someone else. That
could only be one person.

In late November 1154 Breakspear was warmly welcomed back to
Italy by the new pope and the cardinals, who could not wait to hear
first-hand news of his two-year mission. They were delighted by everything that Breakspear had accomplished, especially in Norway. Anastasius
wasted no time in endorsing his decisions. First, he wrote encouragingly to
Jon Birgensson, stressing the dignity of his new office as archbishop and
that his life should be an example to his people. Next, Anastasius sent a kind
letter to King Sverker in Sweden, commending Breakspear's reforms and
sharing his disappointment that Sweden did not yet have its own metropolitan see. He was confident that the setback was only temporary (as it
proved to be).[2]

No sooner than he had done that, on 3 December 1154 Pope Anastasius
died of old age after a papacy that had lasted only seventeen months. The
Throne of St Peter was once again *sede vacante*, a vacant seat. That Anastasius
died so soon proved timely for Breakspear: his stock with his fellow cardinals
could not have been higher. The general admiration for his courage in visiting
the remote northern lands was genuine, and the cardinals saw the reforms that
he had instigated as essential to the development of the Scandinavian Church.
Breakspear was the standout candidate.

Preparations for choosing a new pope were made quickly. The rules for
the election had been revised quite recently and only the cardinals now
had a vote. Since 1059 the consent of the Roman people to new popes had
been reduced to a formality, although until Pope Eugenius III was elected
in 1145 the bishops and deacons of Rome were still expected to endorse
the winner. By 1154 the cardinals had become the sole papal electors and a
simple majority sufficed.

Papal elections normally took place in the Lateran papal church, built in
the fourth century by Emperor Constantine on land confiscated from the
Laterani family and which had evolved into the cathedral of the Diocese of
Rome. However, at the time of Breakspear's election the centre of Rome was
a dangerous place. By the twelfth century, its population had dropped to about
30,000, having been well over 1 million in the classical era. Rome's prosperous
days were long behind it and someone had to be blamed. A rebel 'Commune
of Rome' had been established in 1144 to protest the increasing powers of the
pope and the entrenched powers of the wealthy Roman families. This rebellion was still in full flow ten years on. The Romans harked back to former

glory days, believing that a government of Rome rebuilt in the style of the classical Roman Republic, reinstating a Senate of the People, a second SPQR,* would restore their fortunes. These rebels, known as Republicans, made access to Rome difficult and unsafe and for this reason the 1154 papal election took place in St Peter's Basilica in the Leonine City.

It was not until the thirteenth century that the election gathering of the cardinals was called a conclave, as it is known today. The election of 1274 was the first time that the cardinals were locked in, *cum clave*, with a key, until they reached their decision. When Pope Clement IV died in 1268 political in-fighting between the cardinals and Rome's influential families delayed the election of the new pope, Gregory X, until 1271. Gregory immediately intro-duced new rules which prevented outside interference. However, in 1154, the cardinals were not locked in but simply gathered together.

This was Breakspear's first papal election, and it would be his last. He was elected unanimously by all sixteen members of the College of Cardinals on Saturday, 4 December 1154 in the first vote. The white-smoke, black-smoke procedure we are familiar with today was initiated in the twentieth century, but only white smoke would have appeared had the practice existed in Breakspear's day. That the vote for Breakspear was speedy and unanimous, despite his being a foreigner and lacking the patronage of any of the noble Roman families, underlined the success of his two years in Scandinavia.[3] His immediate election, when he was still a young man, was a literal vote of confidence by his peers.

At first Breakspear refused to accept, awed by the responsibility that came his way. After further thought, however, he relented and accepted the papacy.[4] Such modesty on election is the mark of most popes but Breakspear's reluc-tance was surely genuine. His humble beginnings had given him much to be modest about. As John of Salisbury wrote wryly, 'Who would have the ambi-tion to be the servant of all?'[5]

Boso, not then a cardinal and so not one of the voters, captured the qualities of the new English pope:

> For he was very kind, mild, and patient; accomplished in English and Latin, fluent in speech, polished in eloquence, an outstanding singer, and an excel-lent preacher; slow to anger and swift to forgive; a cheerful giver, lavish in alms, distinguished in every aspect of his character.[6]

---

* *Senatus Populusque Romanus*, the government of the ancient Roman Republic.

This seems over-effusive, but Boso was not always uncritical. It is in marked contrast to his writing on other popes and he was much less flattering about Breakspear's successor, Pope Alexander III. Tarleton, writing in the late nineteenth century, commented on the astonishing election of an Englishman:

> At last the humble Englishman, the poor student, the modest monk, abbot, bishop, Cardinal and missionary was called to occupy the position of the greatest and most fearful responsibility upon the earth of those days. What a moment! What a life.[7]

Somewhat hastily, and contrary to the papal constitution, Breakspear's election had been on the day after the death of Anastasius IV. In 607 the Synod of Rome had ruled that the papal election should not begin until the third day after a pope's burial. That rule did not seem to trouble the cardinals. The relatively small group knew that they were of one mind and had seen no reason to wait.

The formalities now happened apace. Unlike several predecessors, Breakspear did not need to be consecrated on election as he was already an ordained bishop. He was acknowledged as pope the following day in St Peter's and immediately clothed by the cardinals in the purple mantle, a relic of Roman imperial insignia.

In *The History of the Worthies of England*, published in 1662, Thomas Fuller wondered why the pope changed his name to Adrian IV rather than taking Nicholas III.[8] Popes had not always chosen a new name on election; this practice seems to have started in 983 when Peter Canepanova, Bishop of Pavia, chose to be called John XIV.[9] Doubtless humility was the reason for his not wanting to be called Pope Peter II. Curiously, the first and only pope after him to keep his baptismal name as his papal name was the only Dutch pope, Adrian VI, who was elected in 1459.

Why Breakspear chose to be called Adrian is not clear. There are several possibilities. He is unlikely to have chosen to be named after the previous Pope Adrian III, who served from May 884 for less than one year and was undistinguished, at least outside of Italy. It might have been in honour of the first Saint Adrian, a Roman soldier who was martyred at Nicomedia, now in Turkey, at the end of the reign of Emperor Maximinian in 306. This 28-year-old Adrian was head of the praetorium, the imperial guard, and, while presiding over the torture of some Christians, he asked them what reward they expected to receive from God. They replied:

Eye hath not seen, nor ear heard, neither have entered into the heart of man, the things which God hath prepared for them that love him.*

He was so amazed by their courage that he publicly confessed his faith even though he had not yet been baptised. He was immediately imprisoned and executed. St Adrian was second only to St George as a military saint in northern Europe, and was especially revered in Flanders, Germany and northern France. The Abbey of St Ruf had a particular affection for St Adrian and, if this was the reason for his papal name, it shows that Pope Adrian retained affection for his former brothers at St Ruf despite their differences.

More likely perhaps is that Breakspear's choice of Adrian was in recognition of the impressive Pope Adrian I, who reigned from 772 to 795 (only four other popes have had a longer reign) and who had first endowed St Albans Abbey with its privileges. Whatever the reason, Adrian was a good choice of name. He chose as his personal motto *oculi mei semper ad Dominum*, 'my eyes are always on the Lord'.

As the 168th successor to St Peter, Adrian was entering a relatively wealthy and powerful papacy, in an age of change. The Renaissance of the High Middle Ages was in full flow. Historian Kenneth Clark believed that Europe's first great age of civilisation began in the eleventh century and continued during the twelfth century when monumental abbeys and cathedrals appeared, decorated with sculptures, hangings, mosaics and works of art, and providing 'stark contrast to the monotonous and cramped conditions of ordinary living'.[10] Nobody could have been more conscious of this contrast than the humble lad from Hertfordshire.

Trade began to flourish too, and the Hanseatic League of northern cities, an early European trading union, was formed. The era of the crusades had opened up the luxuries of the Byzantine Empire for the first time and Genoa and Venice became significant maritime trading powers. Hellenic and Islamic tracts were translated and shared, Aristotle was rediscovered, and universities began to emerge. Technological innovation arrived. Paper was manufactured in Europe for the first time. The magnetic compass was discovered, and the astrolabe arrived from Islamic Spain. Stern-mounted rudders were also used for the first time, improving sailing performance. All these technological advances led to improving lifestyles and not just for the wealthy.

✠ ✠ ✠

---

* 1 Corinthians 2:9.

During the twelfth century the Church's civil service, its Curia, was taking shape in a style that mimicked the administration of the leading European countries. These countries were attached to the papacy in the sense that they all looked to the pope to defend Christian values and to fight abuses. Sovereigns, nobles, bishops and the powerful would all seek the pope's assistance on political issues and financial affairs as well as on liturgical matters. People complained to the pope about their rulers, and rulers complained to him about fellow rulers. Appeals could be made direct to the Curia by anyone who considered themselves oppressed. Innocent III (1198–1216) later justified the Church's authority in political matters succinctly: 'Christ left to Peter, not only the whole Church but also the whole world, to govern.'[11] In the person of the pope, the Church was the ultimate judge and the pope's authority in the twelfth century can hardly be exaggerated.

This papal authority now rested with a modest Englishman. He, though, would enjoy no rest: he had his work cut out. First, he had to become familiar with the workings of the Curia, not having been part of it for half the time he had been a cardinal. He needed to establish his authority among the cardinals whom he did not know that well. He had also lost the benefit of the papacy's most energetic supporter and defender of orthodoxy, Bernard of Clairvaux. Bernard had long been frail, his body wracked by prolonged periods of excessive fasting, and he had died in August 1153 while Adrian was away in the north.

With the miserable failure of the Second Crusade, Church morale was low. There were also physical forces at home and abroad that threatened the Church. The cardinals were conscious of all these challenges when they elected Adrian. He had dealt firmly with kings in Scandinavia and they would now find out if their young and energetic leader was up to the same task on a grander stage. The cardinals had chosen wisely but, had Adrian himself been able to choose the time of his papacy, he might not have opted for the troubled times of 1154. He described the Chair of St Peter as 'a chair full of thorns'.[12]

Politics rather than spiritual matters would dominate Adrian's papacy, and he would struggle for control of Rome throughout his reign. The fighting in the 1080s between King Henry IV of Germany and Pope Gregory VII during the Investiture Controversy, as to who had authority to appoint bishops, had devastated Rome and tension between its citizens and the papacy had persisted ever since. These issues with the people of Rome were not finally resolved until some thirty years after Adrian's time, when Pope Clement III made a final treaty with the Roman Senate. If the situation in Rome itself were not demanding enough, Adrian also had to face up to threats against the

Patrimony, the papal lands surrounding Rome and straddling the centre of Italy. These regions were insecure, with many wealthy families and local barons enjoying effective independence. To cap that, there were no fewer than three external powers eyeing up Italy's not inconsiderable wealth.

With threats at home and abroad, it made sense for Adrian to start in Rome with his first adversaries, the people of Rome, led by Arnold of Brescia. Today we would see Arnold as a religious reformer but contemporary chroniclers, including John of Salisbury and Otto of Freising, a German churchman, considered him to be a dangerous political agitator. In an age when the Church was the power in the state, any attack on the Church was a challenge to the state. Arnold and the Republicans in Rome were seen to be a real threat to the pope, and Adrian wasted no time in challenging them.

Arnold ruled the roost in Rome. This religious firebrand had studied in Paris under Abelard, a renowned theologian but also remembered for his disgraceful pursuit of Eloise, twenty years his junior. They had a son, curiously named Astrolabe, but they never married. Abelard's teaching fuelled Arnold's burning hatred of the temporal power of the Church. It is possible that Arnold's and Adrian's paths first crossed in the schools of Paris but, whether they had met before or not, they were now in direct opposition. Arnold's view was that the lay state should reign independently of the Church and that the papacy should drop all its worldly pomp, causes that are easily accepted today.

Arnold was an eloquent man and had first set his native Lombardy aflame with sedition. He had been challenged by the bishops and nobles alike, who resented any threat to the natural order. After the Lateran Council of 1139 in which he was exiled from Italy, he fled to France, but with no let-up in his inflammatory preaching. His views were not tolerated by Pope Eugenius's champion, Bernard of Clairvaux, who regarded Arnold an honest man but sorely mistaken. Arnold ignored Bernard's entreaties to support the teachings of the Orthodox Church and his teacher, Abelard, challenged Bernard to a public debate at the 1140 Synod of Sens, in France. Before that debate took place, wily Bernard privately beseeched the assembled bishops to condemn Abelard's teachings out of hand as heretical, which they did.

Bernard had won convincingly and, after a failed appeal to the pope, Abelard accepted defeat and confinement to the Abbey of Cluny where he died of scurvy in 1142. His disciple Arnold, disparagingly called 'Goliath's armour-bearer' by Bernard,[13] would not accept Abelard's defeat and continued peddling his inflammatory views. The pope ordered him to be confined in a convent, but Arnold had been forewarned and took flight. He escaped to Zurich in Swabia, now Switzerland, where its freer-thinking people gave him refuge.

Two years after the Synod of Sens, the Republicans invited Arnold to join
them in Rome. They saw Arnold as their potential saviour and believed that
they could harness his spiritual exhortations to promote their own ambitions. Arnold accepted their invitation and both he and the citizens begged
King Conrad III of Germany (1138–52) to come to Rome and rule directly
as emperor, as his predecessors once had. These early aspirations to reinstate
an imperial regime soon disappeared, and the emphasis of the Roman citizens
changed to an independent republic for Rome. Pope Lucius II (1144–45) was
told by the Romans that his authority was now to be only spiritual, and his
income restricted to Church tithes and voluntary offerings. Lucius refused all
this and led his soldiers in an attack on the Capitol in Rome. It ended badly
for the pope when he was killed by a stone.

This was the mess in Rome that Pope Eugenius inherited in 1145. The
humble Eugenius was a man of gentle demeanour and had some sympathy
for Arnold's views. This allowed Arnold to gain the upper hand in Rome,
forcing Eugenius to withdraw to France. Arnold was in the ascendant; his
silver tongue won him popular support and in 1147 he became the leader of
political reform in the quasi-Roman Republic. Tribunes of the people were
reinstated, and both German Emperor and pope were marginalised in Rome.

Pope Eugenius returned to Italy from France by summer 1148 and excommunicated Arnold, but that did not deter Arnold in the slightest. In 1149
Eugenius used Sicilian troops to mount an attack on Rome but that too
failed.[14] There was an uneasy truce, but it was not until 1152 that Eugenius felt
that he could re-enter Rome safely and only then by caving in and acknowledging the authority of the Roman Senate. This accommodation with Arnold
ran until Eugenius's death in 1153. In his book on the duties of the pope,
De Consideratione, written in 1150, Eugenius's mentor, Bernard of Clairvaux,
slated the Romans as 'detested by heaven and earth', people who would only
obey when forced.[15] John of Salisbury delivered his own judgement on Arnold:

> Arnold himself was frequently heard on the Capitol and in various assemblies
> of the people. He had already publicly denounced the cardinals, maintaining
> that their college, beset as it was with pride, avarice, hypocrisy and shame,
> was not the Church of God but a house of commerce[*] and a den of thieves,
> men who took the place of the scribes and Pharisees among Christian peo-
> ples. Even the pope himself was other than what he professed: rather than
> an apostolic shepherd of souls, he was a man of blood who maintained his

---

* John 2:16.

authority by fire and the sword, a tormentor of churches and oppressor of the innocent, whose only actions were for the gratification of his lust and for the emptying of other men's coffers in order that his own might be filled.[16]

Arnold and the Republicans thought they had won control in Rome, but they reckoned without Adrian, the forceful English pope. Adrian did try to make a conciliatory start with the Republicans and, as soon as he was elected, gifted money to the citizens of Rome in the traditional spirit of celebration. This failed to win them over and they temporarily confined Adrian to St Peter's Basilica and the Leonine City, now called the Vatican. This small hill on the opposite side of the River Tiber from the seven hills of Rome had been encircled by a 2-mile wall built by Pope Leo IV in the ninth century, immediately after the sack of the city by the Saracens, and it was named for Leo. St Peter's Basilica was built there because it was believed to have been the burial site of St Peter. For now Adrian was safe but, besieged, he was determined to get into Rome itself and his patience was wearing thin.

In a final outrage, some of Arnold's followers attacked and wounded almost to death one of the cardinals, Guido, as he walked through Rome on his way to the Leonine City. This was too much. Adrian was not going to tolerate criminal behaviour and he ordered Arnold to leave Rome immediately. When that order was ignored, he reached for his ultimate sanction and placed Rome under an interdict. Excommunication of individuals from the Church and its sacraments was not unusual but cutting off a whole town, diocese or country was a rare and dramatic event. This was the first time Rome had been placed under an interdict.

Some fifty years later, Pope Innocent III placed England under an interdict for six years, between March 1208 and May 1213, after King John refused to accept the pope's appointee Stephen Langton as Archbishop of Canterbury. Some 400 years later, in 1570, a second interdict of England was issued by Pope Pius V against Elizabeth I for having earlier declared England to be a Protestant state.

The interdict on Rome was an amazingly courageous step for a new pope, especially a foreign one, to take. Adrian had little popular support in Rome at this point yet at a stroke he closed all its churches. No masses could be said, or marriages solemnised, and nor could the dead be buried in consecrated ground. The only exceptions to this denial of the Church to Rome were private baptisms and the anointing of the dying. A papal legate proclaimed the interdict from the steps of the church's high altar at midnight, and the crucifixes and other sacred images were veiled.[17]

It is hard now to appreciate that this would have been so effective, but twelfth-century life was dominated by the Church, which baptised, married and buried almost everyone throughout the land. It was cataclysmic. The timing made it worse still. The interdict was announced on Palm Sunday, the Sunday before Easter, and in the coming Easter festival Rome would be denied its usual flow of pilgrims, which provided its principal source of income. The Romans could not contemplate an Easter without religious services. In panic, the citizens forced the Republicans to negotiate with the pope, who by now had withdrawn to Viterbo, 50 miles north of Rome.

Adrian dug his heels in. He sensed victory and refused to negotiate, and by Wednesday of Holy Week the Republicans caved in. All the pope's demands were agreed, and Arnold and his close followers were expelled from Rome. Arnold fled to Otrielo, where he was taken prisoner by Cardinal Gerhard, but then rescued by the Count of Campagnatico, who owed Arnold a favour. The count had benefitted when the Republicans of Rome had granted him an estate which properly belonged to the pope. Arnold continued preaching his heresies, but he was not to remain at liberty for long.

Boso trumpeted Adrian's victory in Rome:

> Then the aforesaid senators, compelled by the clergy and people of Rome, came into the presence of the pontiff and at his command swore on the Holy Gospels that they would without delay expel the said heretic and the rest of his followers from the whole city of Rome, unless they returned to the command and obedience of the said pope. And thus when they had been ejected and the City had been absolved from interdict, all were filled with great joy, praising and blessing the Lord.[18]

Adrian had won and was able to enter his See of Rome for the first time on Maundy Thursday 1155. He led his cardinals and bishops in a glorious procession from the Leonine City through rejoicing crowds.[19] Some four months after his election Adrian could now be formally 'introduced' as pope. Tradition required that this had to be at the Lateran, the centre of the pope's operations in his capacity as Lord Bishop of Rome, Christ's governor on earth and supreme apostolic judge.

The ceremonies that followed are the most elaborate in the Church's liturgy. Access to Rome had been hard won and Adrian was determined to make the most of the occasion. The commemoration of Maundy Thursday, the Mass of the Last Supper, at the Lateran Basilica was a special service. Immediately after the *credo* the wooden outer structure of the high altar was removed to a side chapel where it remained until the Easter Sunday Mass. The pope then approached the bare altar stone alone to complete the Maundy Mass.

Several explanations for this procedure have emerged. It was claimed that the wooden structure was the same portable altar used by St Peter and his successors up to the fourth century. A later explanation was that inside the altar lay precious relics including loaves from the Last Supper, the cloth Jesus used to wash the feet of the apostles, the cloth used by Veronica to wipe the face of Jesus on his way to Calvary, the blood and water that flowed from the side of Christ at the Crucifixion and the Ark of the Covenant itself.

The ritual was also a re-enactment of the Hebrew rite performed on the day of atonement, making a blood sacrifice to atone for the sins of mankind:

> The High Priest alone enters the second tabernacle once a year, not without blood, which he offers for his own sins and those of the people.[*]

From the basilica, the action moved to the adjoining Lateran Palace, which was no less grand. It was also replete with more relics including Christ's sandals, his circumcised foreskin, his umbilical cord and the heads of both St Peter and St Paul, all housed in the pope's private chapel there, which was dedicated to St Lorenzo.

There is no surviving account of Adrian's installation at the palace, a ceremony called the *introductio*, but we do know what the procedure would have entailed.[20] Adrian would have been led to a seat located in front of the palace known as the *sedes stercorata*. This translates as the 'dung chair' and had a keyhole shape cut into it and open to the front, rather like a commode. Legend relates it to the mythical Pope Joan of the ninth century, saying it was used to test the sex of newly installed popes. The reality is more prosaic. The *sedes stercorata* had, like so much else, been carried over from the Roman Empire when wealthy Romans had used a chair with a hole to let bath water drain away.[21]

Seated, the new pope would have said in Latin:

> He raises the poor from the dust, he lifts the needy from the dunghill to give them a place among princes and to assign them a seat of honour.[**]

Rising from the seat, Adrian would have thrown money to the crowd with words attributed to St Peter:

---

[*] Hebrews 9:7.

[**] 1 Samuel 2:8.

Silver and gold are not precious to me, what I have I give to you.*

Once inside the palace, in the chapel dedicated to St Sylvester, the pope during Constantine's imperial reign, Adrian would have sat in the right-hand of two stone seats, representing the authority of Peter and Paul, to receive the *ferula*, an episcopal staff which was the sign of guiding and correcting, and the keys of the basilica. Alumni of Jesuit schools will remember the *ferula* less fondly: for them, it was a stiff leather strap used for corporal punishment. On an arch above the two seats was a figure of Christ, a scene signifying Peter's authority and Paul's ministry, both under the presidency of Christ.

The pope was then presented with the keys, as a reminder of Christ giving Peter, the first pope, the power to forgive sins:

> I will give you the keys of the kingdom of heaven; whatever you bind on earth will be bound in heaven, and whatever you loose on earth will be loosed in heaven.**

Adrian would then have moved to the seat on the left to receive the obeisance of the palace officials. He would have been presented with a red silk belt from which hung a purple purse holding twelve precious stones and some musk. The belt signified chastity, and the purse represented his obligations to use papal wealth to nourish and protect the poor. The people of Rome expected nothing less and it was an important part of their income. A pope was expected to make gifts to them to win their support, a practice that Bernard of Clairvaux had condemned. Adrian's friend John of Salisbury also said that these handouts were resented by the wider Church. Nonetheless, Adrian was reported to have spent 11,000 talents on the Romans after his election, a significant sum.[22]

Adrian took delight in celebrating his Easter Sunday Mass, the highlight of the liturgical year, in his own Lateran Basilica. There was intense rivalry between the clergy of St Peter's and the clergy of the Lateran as to which church had primacy and in the twelfth century the Lateran began to supersede St Peter's as the site for papal events, even including burials.

After Adrian's Easter Mass there was a feast which re-enacted the Last Supper. The pope represented Christ and the eleven apostles were represented by ten cardinals and the *primicerius*, the high official of the Lateran Palace. The fare at this feast, marking the end of the forty days' fasting during Lent, would

---

* Acts 3:6.
** Matthew 16:19.

have been a world away from both the Last Supper and the potage Adrian had depended upon as a youth in Bedmond.

The next day, Easter Monday, Adrian marked his coronation in a procession to St Peter's Basilica on the other side of the Tiber, wearing his papal crown for the first time. This *adventus* procession was another carry-over from the days of the Roman Empire, when an emperor was ceremoniously welcomed into a city either during a celebration or after a successful military campaign, and now used as an evocation of Christ's entry into Jerusalem on Palm Sunday. Midway between the Lateran and St Peter's the procession paused at the Jewish ghetto, the *Parrione*, where, by tradition, a welcome was performed in the presence of the scrolls of the Torah.[23] By doing so the new pope was acknowledging the importance of the Hebrew prophets.

The papal tiara had not yet taken its triple-tiered form, which only emerged in the fourteenth century. In Adrian's time, the papal crown was a more modest Phrygian-style cap, a white linen conical cap with a circle of bejewelled gold. It signified the pope's temporal authority and would be worn on eighteen high feast days during the year including Christmas, the Epiphany, Easter Day, Ascension Day, Whitsun and, most importantly, the feast of Saints Peter and Paul on 29 June. The pope would also wear it whenever in procession with a crowned secular ruler. Such ostentation is frowned upon now, and even in those days not all were in favour. Saint Bernard rebuked Adrian's predecessor, Pope Eugenius, for this showy behaviour in 1150:

Peter is not known ever to have gone in procession adorned in jewels and silks, nor crowned with gold, nor mounted on a white horse, nor surrounded by knights, nor encircled by clamouring servants … In these respects you are the heir not of Peter but of Constantine.[24]

In a period when popes and antipopes were competing for authority, such as between Pope Innocent II and Antipope Anacletus II in the 1130s, it is perhaps not surprising that the insignia of papal office was flaunted. Much of the pomp has now been confined to history; the famous tiara was last used by Pope Paul VI in 1963 and then only once, for his coronation.

BEYOND ROME

Surrounded by Threats

Rome, therefore, against which a Teutonic host was about to advance, was not only in a state of internal tumult; it was in constant dread of a rear attack from the Sicilian King.

J.D. Mackie
The Lothian Essay, 1907[1]

Adrian had unequivocally shown his control and authority in Rome, and with the lavish celebrations over he now had to ensure his authority was also recognised abroad. There was no time to pause, and immediately he had to face up to several brewing international tensions. Adrian would be dealing with giants of twelfth-century Europe who were much better resourced than he was, and he would need all his wits.

Frederick I was the first and greatest of the three external powers set on Italy's wealth. He had become King of Germany on 4 March 1152 and was by far the most powerful leader in Europe. He was nicknamed Barbarossa, meaning 'Redbeard' in Italian, but he was not called this during his lifetime. He was actually fair-haired, and Redbeard would not have been a complimentary term, but rather a reflection of his fiery temper. It was perhaps this temper which made him such a formidable soldier: he was one of only a few rulers who had emerged from the disastrous Second Crusade with his reputation intact.

Frederick had not been destined to be king and emperor. The King of the Germans was elected by a college of princes and not necessarily by hereditary succession. He followed his paternal uncle King Conrad III on to the throne when he was 29, becoming the ninety-fourth prospective emperor in line from Augustus.[2] Conrad's elder son Henry had died suddenly in 1150, though it is unclear why the younger son, also called Frederick, was bypassed in the election process. True, he was only 6 years old, but minors had previously been chosen. Conrad himself was the younger of two sons in his family. His older brother Frederick, Duke of Swabia, had lost an eye during a battle which made him ineligible to become king so his eldest son, Frederick Barbarossa, could therefore be considered the rightful heir rather than Conrad's son. It may be that Frederick Barbarossa had intimidated the electors when he arrived at the election in Frankfurt with 3,000 armed knights.

Frederick was duly elected, and then crowned with undue haste only five days later, a speed which also led to suspicion of underhand activity. Henry I had done just the same in England, rushing for his crown after the death of his brother King William Rufus in 1100. Frederick himself always claimed that Conrad had designated him as his successor and this is plausible: by doing so Conrad ensured that the crown remained securely in his family.

Since Frederick had not been expected to assume the German throne he had not been prepared with the full education that an heir would normally be given. He was never taught Latin, which was the language used for all diplomatic exchanges, instead relying on translators throughout his life.[3] This shortcoming had profound consequences when in 1157 an ambiguous translation of a letter written in Latin from Adrian to Frederick resulted in a furious row.

On his deathbed Conrad was reported to have advised his nephew Frederick to maintain his alliance with the Byzantine Emperor, Manuel Comnenus; but, if this was true, his words were not heeded. Within barely a year, in 1153, Frederick made a pact with Pope Eugenius. This Treaty of Constance, which in the event proved a shaky alliance, required the German Emperor to prevent Manuel, disparagingly called King of the Greeks in the treaty, from re-establishing his Byzantine Empire in the south-east of Italy. If Manuel were to invade the peninsula, the treaty required both pope and emperor to work together and expel him. The emperor promised to assist the pope to re-establish control over the rebellious Commune of Rome. Frederick also agreed not to make a pact with 'Roger of Sicily', disdainfully shorn of his kingly title in the text for having been crowned without the consent of the pope. In return Pope Eugenius agreed to honour Frederick and crown him as emperor in Rome. Only after a coronation in Rome would the King of Germany become the Roman Emperor. Eugenius also agreed to help Frederick to maintain and increase his realm, although it was never clear whether this extended to southern Italy.

While the pope agreed not to concede any land in Italy to the Byzantine Emperor, he made no similar commitment regarding Roger of Sicily. Neither did Eugenius explicitly agree not to make a pact with Roger, and this later became a bone of contention. Surprisingly, the Treaty of Constance appeared to be weighted heavily in favour of the pope and the fact that Frederick made the commitments that he did reflected uncharacteristic passivity on his part. He signed it soon after he received his crown in unusual circumstances, which suggests that his main concern at the time was to secure his own position at home. Frederick was worried that he would be challenged within Germany and all that really mattered to him was to consolidate his authority with a prestigious imperial coronation by the pope. He valued this sufficiently to concede other matters even if it made him more vulnerable.

As part of his attempts to secure support for his kingship in Germany, Frederick had surrendered Swabia to his cousin, also named Frederick, who thus became the Duke of Swabia. Having lost this land and its income, Frederick looked for compensating funds from the imperial Italian territories. He saw himself as the new Charlemagne and his mission to be the restoration of the Roman Empire to its previous glory. He already controlled the Rhine and the Danube and wanted the Tiber as well. If Frederick were to do that, he would have to face up to the other two challengers: Roger, the Norman King of Sicily, and Manuel, the Byzantine Emperor, both of whom also had greedy eyes on southern Italy.

Frederick's ambition was hardly a surprise. German emperors had always wished to increase their power in Italy but in doing so they had always tried to stay on the right side of the pope, concealing their avarice behind a façade of defending the Church. Adrian could not know if Frederick would follow this pattern. Even with the benefit of the Treaty of Constance that he had inherited from Eugenius, Adrian was not sure if he could trust the German king. Frederick was a pious man and throughout his reign he attended Mass every morning. However, his piety did not translate into respect for the pope and relations between Frederick and Adrian were soon tested.

Charlemagne had conquered Pavia, the seat of the Lombard kings, in 774 and annexed most of northern and central Italy into the Roman Empire. The German Emperor was by right King of Lombardy and so claimed most of northern and central Italy apart from Venice. Frederick's ambitions in Italy were made more difficult by the neglect of previous Roman emperors. Distracted by Investiture Controversies with the pope, those emperors had lost full authority over Italian cities which had grown used to their effective independence from the German Empire, making the most of imperial neglect. The disparate Italian independent city-states in the middle of the twelfth century were not a single power base, but they played an active role in the struggles between the main powers. They were ruled by consuls, nominally chosen from all citizens but in practice they were appointed by their wealthy families. These consuls, who usually changed every year, were the visible leaders and recognised as such by everyone in the surrounding territory.[4]

The city-states had become wealthy through trade and had no qualms about granting knighthoods to successful men regardless of status and occupation and this practice provided the city with the manpower it needed to overcome any threats from their neighbours.[5] If Frederick were able to re-establish control of these cities his coffers would benefit enormously. That they were not under the empire's full control benefitted the popes who used them as buffer to maintain equilibrium in Italy. Adrian continued this practice during his papacy and would play these city-states against the power of the Germans.

✠ ✠ ✠

William I, the still-new Norman King of Sicily, was the second power Adrian faced and there was bad blood between Sicily and the papacy. Pope Honorius's death in February 1130 had triggered a damaging split among the cardinals. Innocent II was one of two popes elected and he had the support of most European countries. Unfortunately for him, the rival antipope, Anacletus II, a member of Rome's famous Pierleoni family, had possession of St Peter's. At first most cardinals had sided with Anacletus, but support for him faded when his use of Pierleoni wealth to buy influence backfired. Innocent, having been banished from Rome by Anacletus, had taken refuge in France and was thus better placed than Anacletus to garner international support, and it was the support of one man in particular that led to Innocent gaining the ascendancy. The wrath of Bernard of Clairvaux fell upon Anacletus, objecting among other things to the antipope's ancestry. Anacletus's great-grandfather had converted from Judaism to Christianity in the middle of the previous century. This was an issue for Bernard, antisemitism being rife then in France. Voltaire reinforced this antisemitic view later when he referred to Anacletus as the 'Jewish pope'.[6] Nevertheless, whether Anacletus had Jewish ancestry or not, there could not be two popes. Something had to be done to resolve the stalemate.

Louis VI took the matter in hand and convened a national council of the French bishops at Étampes, where the well-regarded Bernard was chosen to adjudicate between the rival popes. Unsurprisingly, he found in favour of Innocent II. By the end of 1131, France, England, Germany, Portugal, Castile and Aragon had all lined up behind Innocent.

Anacletus had to seek support wherever he could find it and he turned to Roger of Sicily, who agreed to support Anacletus's claim in exchange for Anacletus's endorsement of his Sicilian crown. The Normans, themselves the descendants of Vikings, had wrested control of Sicily and southern Italy from the Saracens in the eleventh century. On Christmas Day 1130, Roger de Hauteville was, with the blessing of Anacletus, crowned the first king of Norman Sicily by Archbishop Hugh of Palermo (confusingly, he was styled King Roger II even though his father was never crowned Roger I, instead styling himself as Roger, Great Count of Sicily).

King Roger had taken a risk by signing up to Anacletus, who also had gambled. His coronation of Roger was guaranteed to set the German King Lothair III (1125–37) against him. Anacletus cannot have been surprised when Lothair promised to lead Innocent back to Rome at the head of a powerful German army. For his part, Roger knew that if Lothair did invade there would be little to stop him pressing on beyond Rome to threaten his own lands in southern Italy. Roger could not even count on the support of his own Norman barons in the Italian towns on the mainland. The barons had always resented his father's rule, and he feared that they might well prefer to be subject to a distant emperor on the other side of the Alps rather than to a rival Norman in neighbouring Sicily.

Lothair did carry out his threat and he entered Lombardy with his army in 1132. Just as Frederick was now trying to do, Lothair wanted to prop up his support back in Germany by having himself crowned emperor by the pope. He reached Rome by June 1134 but could not persuade Anacletus to resign the Leonine City. Rather than attack Anacletus, Lothair left him holed up there. Anacletus was simply ignored. Pope Innocent had to be installed at the Lateran rather than at St Peter's, and in turn Innocent crowned Lothair as Emperor of the West.

Fortunately for Roger, and just as would happen again in 1154, the newly crowned emperor had no appetite to continue his Italian campaign. His knights could not be persuaded to continue their mission in the unforgiving heat of Apulia – modern-day Puglia, the heel of Italy's boot – and rather than challenge Roger, the imperial army headed back to Germany. Shorn of their imperial support, Roger overcame his rebellious barons and by the summer of 1134 he too was back home, in Palermo. His throne was secure, and everything settled down.

Roger's security did not last long. Lothair returned to Italy in 1137 with a stronger army. With Roger stuck in his Palermo stronghold, Lothair was able to wrest control over the mainland of southern Italy. He achieved his final victory when Salerno, Roger's mainland capital, surrendered. Roger's commander in Salerno was Robert of Selby, one of several Englishmen who served in Roger's government. Together, Lothair and Pope Innocent drove Roger out of Apulia. Lothair returned to Germany satisfied with his successes in southern Italy but in reality the kingdom of Sicily had not been defeated, only damaged.

It not only survived but prospered and enjoyed its independence. Roger ruled with tolerance. His many Greek and Arab subjects had complete freedom to practise their religions, many filling high offices under his administration. As a Christian kingdom, it remained technically part of the Patrimony but Roger's relations with the papacy had been difficult. On 8 April 1137, Innocent renewed his excommunication of Roger, his sons and all the bishops appointed by Antipope Anacletus, who died the following year. Lothair had returned to Germany and Roger was able to wrest back the territory that he had lost on the mainland.

In June 1138, and even without the support of Lothair's army, Pope Innocent and Robert of Capua felt capable to tackle Roger on their own. Rather foolishly, they led a much smaller papal army, 1,000 knights at most, to face Roger at San Germano. It was hardly surprising that the papal coalition was outnumbered. At least Innocent had the good sense to recognise this and, rather than fight, he sought terms from Roger, who now had the upper hand. Nothing was agreed and the two armies backed off for a while. They confronted each other again the following year at Gallucio, where the papal army was routed. Pope Innocent and his cardinals were taken prisoner by Roger.

Even as a prisoner Pope Innocent had to be respected. Roger did not take undue advantage of his triumph and in the following Treaty of Mignano he re-established friendly relations with the Church. Roger recognised the pope's suzerainty over mainland Italy in the south and performed homage to Innocent for his territories of Sicily, Apulia and Calabria. In return Innocent finally recognised Roger's kingship.

Roger kept good control of Calabria on the southern mainland but enforcing control in Apulia was more difficult. The Norman barons, who controlled cities on the south-eastern coast under their fiefs from the king, remained unsettled but bided their time. By 1152 the growing power of Roger's Sicilian kingdom had also alarmed the incoming German King Frederick, not yet the emperor. In that year, Robert of Capua and other Norman nobles from Apulia appealed to Frederick to restore to them their estates which Roger had seized.

For his own reasons Frederick was happy to oblige. He promised to cross the Alps within two years to help them do just that.[7]

The suzerainty of land within Italy had long been disputed. A decree known as the 'Donation of Constantine' claimed that, before departing to his new capital in the east, Constantine transferred to Pope Sylvester the city of Rome, imperial authority in the west and, in particular, certain districts of Italy. The document only appeared in the eighth century, and it was 700 years before it was proved to be a fake. Until then, the forgery would cause substantial damage in relations between popes and emperors and was even a contributing factor in the split of the western and eastern Churches, the Great Schism of 1054. The authenticity of the document had been questioned since 1001, though it took until 1439 for Renaissance humanist Lorenzo Valla to demonstrate that the language used in it was not authentic fourth-century Latin. The 'Donation of Constantine' had always been a lie. More than a century before Valla's textual proof, Dante Alighieri mocked the deceit in the *Divine Comedy*:

> Ah, Constantine, how much evil was born,
> not from your conversion
> but from that donation
> that the first wealthy Pope received from you![8]

Nonetheless, the document was considered to be genuine in the twelfth century and medieval popes relied upon it, none more so than Adrian.

Adrian was just as worried by Sicily as Eugenius had been before him. The papacy had always insisted that the 'Donation of Constantine' had included Sicily, and Eugenius had objected to Roger's coronation of his son William in 1151. It was not unusual for a king to crown his successor before his own death, especially by the Capetian kings of France; Henry II of England would do the same in 1170. In this way a king would hope to avoid disputes over the succession when he died – and yet Roger had crowned William without leave from the pope. Roger died in 1154 and, as he intended, the throne passed to William, whose three older brothers had all predeceased their father. The barons of Apulia saw the installation of the new and inexperienced King William I as the right time to flex their muscles and strengthen their own positions.

King William was powerfully built and a good military tactician, more than the equal to his father. After his death, he became known as William the Bad, but it is not clear that he fully deserved this epithet. He did lack the political skills of his father, but his nickname can probably be blamed on his contemporary biographer Hugo Falcandus, who never had a good word to say about him.[9] William's lack of acumen is perhaps not surprising. As the fourth son, he had never been expected to inherit the Sicilian throne and he had never been educated in the art of kingship, spending his youth on pleasure, not politics. His lifestyle was more like that of a sultan than a king, paying more attention to mistresses than his wife and the four sons that she bore him.[10] William was slow to reach decisions but, once made, he carried them out with determination.

One of Eugenius's last acts at Constance in 1153 had been to wring from Frederick a promise of imperial help to oust Roger, but the papal view of Sicily's growing power was more nuanced than Frederick's. The papacy wanted Sicily controlled but also saw that a friendly power in the south could prove a useful counterweight to the German Emperor if at any stage relations with him were to take a turn for the worse. Adrian knew he would need allies of substance to protect his Church and he also knew that as an Englishman in Italy he would have to work harder to secure that support. Ideally, he wanted to be able to ask for help from both the neighbouring and traditional supporters of the papacy, Germany and Sicily, even though they themselves were at loggerheads with each other. If the King of Sicily could be contained, Adrian might secure a second strong supporter for the papacy.

✠ ✠ ✠

If all this were not enough to make Adrian's life difficult, the situation in Italy was complicated by a third competing power in the person of Manuel Comnenus. By 1154 he was well established as the Byzantine Emperor, having inherited his throne on the unexpected and early death of his father John II Comnenus in 1143. Manuel was John's fourth son and, like Frederick and William, had not been expected to succeed. However, when Manuel distinguished himself in the war against the Turks, his father rewarded him by making him his heir in preference to his elder surviving brother.

Manuel proved to be an astute ruler and successfully managed delicate relations with the German and French armies when they crossed his territory during the Second Crusade. Although he saw Conrad, the Emperor of the West, as a mere usurper of the true Byzantine Empire, Manuel had formed an unlikely bond with him during that crusade. In a marriage made for convenience, Manuel had married Bertha of Sulzbach, Conrad's sister-in-law. Together, these two otherwise competing emperors had the capacity to overthrow Roger of Sicily, an objective their predecessors, John and Lothair, had shared but never managed to achieve.

Manuel, like Frederick, was an emperor on a mission. Both were good soldiers, ruthless, intent on re-establishing their authority in Italy, Frederick in the north and Manuel in the south. Manuel was in no doubt that southern Italy was rightfully part of the Byzantine Empire but his ambition to regain it was as much about security as gaining land. The Norman occupation of the Italian coast was a constant threat to Byzantine control of the Balkans on the other side of the Adriatic Sea. Manuel knew he could only get what he wanted by fighting and he had started direct campaigns against Sicily in 1148 without waiting for German help. It was perhaps not surprising that on his own he achieved little other than the recapture of the island of Corfu.

Both emperors spotted the same opportunity that the Apulian barons had seen after Roger II's death: a chance to challenge the new and inexperienced William. Conveniently, Manuel had become free of threats to his empire from the north, having imposed peace on Hungary in the winter of 1154–55, just as Adrian became pope. He was now ready for a fresh campaign in the west and had the funds for it.[11]

Manuel knew that the Norman barons of south-eastern Italy resented rule from Sicily and were likely to give him support. More importantly, Manuel was hoping to enjoy the same cordial relationship with the new German Emperor, Frederick, that he had with his uncle, Conrad. Manuel had good reason to believe that he and Frederick could together deal with Norman Sicily once and for all. Pope Adrian was not close to the Byzantine Greeks and would not have wanted Sicily to fall, but he would welcome the emperors' help in containing King William. Manuel was less of a threat to papal interests in Italy than the Sicilians since he controlled no part of the mainland, and Adrian would see Manuel as another potential counterweight to the mighty German Empire.

✠ ✠ ✠

There was another emperor in Europe in all but name, but he did not pose any territorial challenge for Adrian. Henry II was crowned King of England in 1154 at the tender age of 21, in the same month that Adrian became pope. Henry, a true redhead, ruled not just England but also much of north-west France, known as the Angevin Empire. Adrian would have dealings with the English king, but they never had any need to form a military alliance. One of Henry's first actions as king was to appoint Thomas Becket as his chancellor, the best-paid position in the royal household, but there is no record of direct interaction between Breakspear and Becket. Since Becket was still a layman at this point, he would have had no cause to have dealings with the pope.

Papal reigns in the twelfth century were generally short. From 1200 to 1599 the median age of popes at election was 60 and the median length of papacy was six and a half years.[12] Adrian was about 54, relatively young, and so his could have been the start of a long papacy. Health was always an issue, though, and the Roman climate bred infectious diseases. Life there was uncomfortable and illnesses did away with many visitors. Adrian was young, as popes go, and the rulers with whom he would now deal were younger still: when Adrian entered the stage in 1154, Manuel Comnenus was 35, William 34, Frederick 32 and Henry just 21. The leading players on the European stage could be dealing with each other for many years to come.

Not only were the leaders that Adrian faced young but, with the exception of Manuel, they were untested too. The inexperience of the nearest two, Frederick and William, could lead to all manner of strife within Italy. Adrian had good reason to fear that they might have little respect for the papacy. To the north the ambitious Frederick was intent on restoring the western Roman Empire to its former greatness, a clear threat to Rome. To the south, William's forces were now stronger than Roger's had been when he had defeated Pope Innocent only fifteen years earlier. For his part, William had his own problems. Sicily was still seen by its neighbours as an upstart, a parvenu. It was William's misfortune that his reign coincided with the reigns of two emperors of outstanding ability and the pontificates of the two greatest popes of the twelfth century. By contrast, it was William's good fortune that his principal enemies, Frederick and Manuel, who united would have been invincible, mistrusted each other even more than they feared and hated him, a fact which ultimately spared him annihilation.[13] Taken together, the volatile mix in Italy did not augur well for the new pope.

Communication between rulers was unavoidably slow, but it was just as important as it is today. Soon after his election Adrian both received and dispatched deputations. King William of Sicily had sent a deputation to Rome seeking a treaty of peace as soon as he had heard of the pope's election. Adrian ignored his entreaties, mindful of the 1153 Treaty of Constance that Eugenius had made with Frederick only eighteen months earlier. Any blatant partnership with William at this stage could only infuriate the more powerful Frederick. In addition, the Curia was still smarting from William's perceived insolence in assuming his crown without permission from the papacy. Nonetheless, Adrian might have been wiser to have at least acknowledged William's overture. That he did not was probably because he heard that Frederick had travelled from Germany to Italy and was already on his doorstep. He wanted to keep his options open until he was better informed about the German Emperor's plans.

Frederick's prime reason for marching into Italy was to be crowned Holy Roman Emperor by the pope, as had been agreed at the Treaty of Constance in 1153. Adrian knew that Frederick would also take the opportunity to re-establish German authority in northern Italy, but exactly what this would involve was a major concern for the pope. The immediate prompt for Frederick's Italian foray was an event that had occurred at Constance at the time of the treaty. Two citizens from the small town of Lodi had entered Frederick's court and thrown themselves at his feet, breaching etiquette by carrying heavy crosses on their shoulders, which had enabled their entry without prior permission. The ultimate Christian symbol could not be turned away. They complained bitterly that their powerful neighbour Milan had prevented them from holding their traditional market in Lodi. Frederick took their complaint at its word and, without giving Milan a hearing, agreed to support them. He had sent an envoy, Sicher, to Milan with his directive. When Sicher reached Milan, the Milanese tore up Frederick's directive and trampled on his royal seal and Sicher was forced to flee for his life. Frederick was livid when Sicher reported back and could not ignore the gross insult to him. He immediately started preparations to invade Lombardy.[14] The issue over little Lodi's market had grave consequences.

Frederick was already on his way to Lombardy when Adrian was elected. Two months earlier, in October 1154, he had set out from Augsburg with his army and crossed the Alps on his way to northern Italy, ready to avenge Milan and fulfilling the promise to free the Norman barons in Apulia from William's control. Adrian was kept well informed of Frederick's brutal passage through north Italy but could not yet know if Frederick was coming as friend or foe of the Church. It could be either. Adrian had, within a month of his election, sent three of his cardinals – Cencius of Porto, Bernard of St Clement and Octavian of St Cecilia – to Frederick but we know nothing of their specific intentions. The cardinals would have alerted Frederick to Adrian's twin worries about the Normans in the south and the rebels in Rome.[15] Adrian was asking for help, but more importantly he wanted to meet Frederick to be best placed to pass judgement on where lay the papacy's best interests.

The cardinals had known what they were doing when they elected Adrian. His diplomatic skills, learnt in Catalonia and honed in Scandinavia, were about to be tested.

SUTRI

Pope and German King Face Off

It was the custom of the German kings to go to Rome to take the crown, since none of them possessed the great imperial name, till consecrated hands had offered it. Desiring to respect this custom, Frederick moved to go where the high priest held the crown.

Barbarossa in Italy[1]

Adrian had brought the people of Rome back to obedience, but he still did not feel secure there. How ironic it was that Rome was the least safe place for the pope. In May 1155 Adrian withdrew from the Leonine City, moving his court to Sutri, an ancient town about 30 miles north of Rome. It lies on a narrow hill surrounded by ravines, one of many natural fortresses in Italy, and it had been given to Pope Gregory II for the Patrimony by the Lombard king in 728. Over the years it proved to be a popular sanctuary for threatened popes. Pope Gregory VI abdicated at Sutri in 1046. Like Adrian, Pope Eugenius had also taken refuge there to shelter from the Roman Republicans in 1146. Sutri is best known today for the important hoard of seventh-century jewellery known as the Sutri Treasure that was found near the town in the nineteenth century and is now in the British Museum.

Ever since Adrian's election, Frederick's presence in Italy had dominated his thoughts. Frederick and his army had taken the well-trodden route over the Brenner Pass. This popular path is the lowest Alpine pass but it is still a difficult route, even in summer. The distance from Augsburg to Brixen in northern Italy is about 150 miles, with only a few towns in between, and Frederick's soldiers had to carry their own provisions. There were few places to stop and rest, making this an exhausting journey. Some pack animals were used but the narrow road was far too difficult for wheeled carts to navigate. Frederick's men soon ran short of food and they resorted to raiding some monasteries and churches along their route. This angered Frederick, a God-fearing man, and he forced his soldiers to right this wrong by making reimbursements. He did not want to incur the wrath of the Church at the very start of his Italian venture.

To Adrian, Frederick was like a latter-day Hannibal advancing over the Alps towards him. Frederick might not be travelling with elephants, but Adrian still felt that he had the capacity to threaten Rome. Adrian was naturally fearful, but at this stage he would not have known that Frederick had not brought his full army. He had about 1,800 knights led by his cousin, Henry the Lion, Duke of Saxony, a powerful man in Germany (Henry's father and Frederick's mother were siblings). Together with foot soldiers the force probably numbered around 6,000 men. This was a small army compared with earlier German forays into Italy and Frederick was relying on bolstering his numbers with local Italian forces. As a new king whose election may not have been totally secure, Frederick had been forced to leave some of his troops back in Germany to cover his back.

Frederick and his army had reached Italy by November, one month before Adrian's election. He was not yet the Roman Emperor, just King of the Germans, but he had jumped the gun by already using the title emperor.[2] He wanted international recognition of his rule to strengthen his position within Germany and to be seen to be the undisputed leader of Europe.

The German root of Frederick means 'rich in peace', but would it prove a misnomer? Pippin (or Pepin), the first Carolingan King of the Franks, and the father of the first German Roman Emperor, Charlemagne, promised Pope Zachary in 751 that he would protect the papacy. However, it was never clear whether the Patrimony was a separate state ruled by the pope or whether the Roman Emperor ruled Christendom on behalf of the pope with the pope retaining all spiritual matters but direct control only of Rome. Some 400 years later this ambiguity would dominate Adrian's reign. Frederick could hardly sever the links between Catholic Germany and the papacy, but from the start he wanted to assert full independence from the pope. Control of northern Italy was the key to this ambition.

The Apulian barons and the bullied citizens of Lodi had asked Frederick to come to Italy but, as far as the Church was concerned, he was an uninvited guest. He regarded his coronation by the pope as his entitlement and expected the pope to crown him, just as Pope Leo III had crowned Charlemagne on

Christmas Day in 800. Unlike his predecessors, Frederick had not formally requested his papal coronation and this impoliteness would have been seen by the Curia as aggressive. If he were in Italy with a hidden agenda which could harm the papacy's interests, Adrian had not the physical means to defend Rome. Diplomacy was his only weapon.

Adrian was willing to believe that his relationship with Frederick could start well. The pact that Pope Eugenius and Frederick had made at Constance in 1153 had not died with Eugenius, at least in the view of the papacy. If this treaty could be relied on, Adrian would have had less to be concerned about, but he was aware that Frederick, like any twelfth-century ruler, could easily change his mind. It is possible that Frederick was having second thoughts about the obligations that he had signed up to in 1153. His biographer Otto, always careful not to offend his nephew Frederick, never mentions the treaty in his writing, which suggests that Frederick came to regret it. Adrian was right to be on his guard.

While Frederick's main motive for entering Italy was for his coronation, he also wanted to re-establish the empire's authority in northern Italy. Instead of rushing to Rome, he travelled west on a tour of Italy's north-western cities including Verona, Brescia, Bergamo and Cremona. Pavia welcomed Frederick, as did Count Guido of Biandrate, who controlled Novara, 30 miles west of Milan. Other northern Italian cities submitted to him a little less readily, but not all did. On 28 November Frederick reached little Lodi, which had sought and received his offer of help in 1153, but it had gone cool on the emperor. The citizens were worried about what might happen to them once Frederick was no longer around. Lodi had complained to Frederick about the bullying Milanese, but it was nonetheless a client town of Milan. Its citizens were reluctant to pledge allegiance to Frederick without the permission of Milan, which in the event was given.

Some of the townspeople in northern Italy refused to pay taxes to Frederick. He was in no mood to compromise, and their homes were burnt down in punishment. Leaving this destruction in his wake, Frederick moved his camp to the plain of Roncaglia, near Piacenza, a city situated on the road from Milan to Bologna and over 300 miles north of Rome. This traditional marshalling point for imperial armies had been where the Council of Piacenza had launched the First Crusade back in 1095. Frederick held his assembly there from 30 November to 6 December and the leaders of the various cities attended. He wanted to establish effective control of Lombardy and so protect his rear before he proceeded south to Rome, but this was not proving easy. Over the recent years of imperial neglect, a spirit of independence had taken root in the cities. Frederick's predecessor, King Conrad, had never even visited Italy during his reign. By contrast, Frederick would spend thirteen of his thirty-eight years on the throne in Italy, and most of these in Lombardy.

Independent though the Italian cities considered themselves to be, their leaders had no choice but to turn up at Roncaglia. Absent bishops risked losing their thrones, and any vassal baron who dared to ignore Frederick's summons would have his fief cancelled. To tighten controls that in recent years had become loose, Frederick reinforced the rule prohibiting the transfer of any fief without the permission of the vassal's lord, himself. Any attempt to do so would be invalid and the notary who drew up such a transfer would lose his hand in punishment. Eager to win his goodwill, the Genoese envoys presented gifts to Frederick at Roncaglia. Bizarrely, these gifts included lions, ostriches and parrots that had been captured in Almeria and Tortosa at the start of the Second Crusade.[3] One can only wonder what happened to the poor creatures.

Frederick closed the Roncaglia assembly and sent envoys ahead of his army to collect the traditional hospitality payments, called *fodrum*, which his vassal towns were obliged to provide to a travelling emperor. Payment exempted their men from serving in Frederick's army and in return they were entitled to Frederick's protection. Adrian sought to limit these payments, and Milan opposed them most vehemently. Frederick's response to towns refusing to pay was ruthless. By the start of 1155 he had reached Chieri, south-east of Milan, whose citizens had been insolent to Frederick's envoy. He spent a few days there, pillaging the town before destroying its buildings and walls. Nearby Asti, about 20 miles east of Chieri, suffered a similar fate on 1 February.

Fortunately for the rebellious Milanese, Frederick did not feel strong enough to attack the city itself, although he did ravage its suburbs. On 13 February, the frustrated Frederick then vented his anger on the smaller town of Tortona, south-west of Pavia, which had refused to renounce its friendship treaty with Milan. An anonymous poet of the twelfth century recounted the event:

Courageous Frederick built machines of war.
Machines to destroy towers and the walls;
Machines to repel defenders from the ramparts;
Machines to subjugate that proud Tortona.
A ram and catapults were soon constructed.
Now watch the missiles break the walls apart
And shatter houses, while frightened peasants run.[4]

If Frederick thought that he had chosen an easy target, he was mistaken. Even with all his war machines he needed sixty days, from 13 February to 20 April, to subdue Tortona, which shows how relatively weak his forces were. Tortona was small but it was a precipitous citadel with only one side accessible, and that only with great difficulty. Frederick ordered tunnels to be dug on this side with the intention of bringing down its sixth-century tower, named *Rubea*. The defenders learnt of the plan and succeeded in collapsing the tunnel and suffocating the attackers inside.

The anonymous poet was disingenuous. Frederick did use mangonels, large wooden catapults, but still he failed to bring down the walls. The defenders were vulnerable because their only water supply was a spring just outside the citadel. This required them to launch sallies to the spring which they did successfully. Seeing an opportunity, Frederick poisoned the spring with dead animals and sulphur, leaving the defenders without access to clean water. All Frederick had to do then was wait.

After their capitulation Frederick spared the citizens but destroyed Tortona's defences, the usual fate for a defeated town. At this time city walls came down regularly and were put up again just as often. Tortona did not have to wait long for theirs to be restored; on 1 May the Milanese reoccupied Tortona and rebuilt the shattered walls of its ally.

At the end of April 1155 Frederick reached Pavia, which had remained true to the empire. He was, for now, among friends. Here, just as Adrian was celebrating the Easter services in the Lateran Basilica, Frederick received the iron crown of Lombardy. This was one of the oldest royal insignias of Christendom: made in the early Middle Ages, it was an iron band covered in silver and jewels. Tradition holds that the iron was beaten out of a nail of Christ's cross and the crown can still be seen in the cathedral at Monza. Frederick spent a few weeks enjoying his welcome before moving on again.

By 15 May Frederick's slow progress had brought him to Bologna, a city of learning. Its university, the oldest in Europe, had been founded in 1088. Cardinal Roland, who was one of Adrian's most ardent supporters throughout his reign and who would succeed him as Pope Alexander III, had been both a pupil and a master at Bologna until 1150, when Pope Eugenius brought him to Rome and made him a cardinal. Scholars from all over Europe travelled there to study law, especially Church and Roman law. These students had freedom of movement but no legal protection, which meant that foreign students were held collectively responsible for any debts run up by their compatriots. Frederick was impressed by the warm welcome he received from both teachers and students so, when he heard of their grievances, he was well disposed to do something for them. By a decree, *Authentica Habita*, he gave students the same freedoms as those held by clergy, including the right to travel for the purposes of study and the right to be tried by the university or the Church rather than by local civil courts. This precedent for academic freedom caught on and was adopted at other medieval universities.

✠   ✠   ✠

Frederick did not have Adrian's undivided attention. While one king was stirring things in northern Italy, Adrian was troubled by the growing danger in the south: King William was on the move. Adrian was fearful that if Frederick and William joined forces they had the means to carve up the whole of the Patrimony between them. The Treaty of Constance had allied pope and emperor to defend it against William, but Adrian was still doubting Frederick's real intentions. His best hope was that the threat that William faced from Frederick's mere presence in Italy might persuade the Sicilian king to recognise papal authority and restore to the papacy mainland territory that had been seized by his father, Roger.

Unfortunately for Adrian, nothing was further from William's mind. He knew full well that the two emperors, Frederick and Manuel, were plotting to remove him from Italy and saw the opportunity to make the first move and so belie his reputation for indecision. During Lent 1155 William moved his army into Italy proper, spending Easter at his mainland headquarters of Salerno on Italy's west coast, about 170 miles south-east of Rome. This was a distance that a marching army could cover in about nine days. As soon as Adrian heard of this, he dispatched Cardinal Henry of St Nereus to William with his peaceful greetings, doubtless regretting that he had ignored William's friendly overtures to him in December 1154.

It was now William's turn to rebuff the pope. He refused to see the cardinal, not just because his own earlier entreaties in Rome had been ignored but also having taken offence at the letters that the cardinal carried, which were addressed to him as William, Lord of Sicily and not to him as king. Adrian was making the point that, in a breach of the treaty between William's father, Roger, and Pope Innocent II, William had been crowned in Palermo in February 1154 without first seeking the permission of the pope. The elderly Pope Anastasius had done nothing about this at the time, but Adrian was a pope of stronger mettle. With hindsight, Adrian would rue not having been more tactful in writing this letter.

For now, it was too late. As soon as he had dismissed the cardinal, William laid plans to invade papal territory, first attacking Benevento in a significant challenge to the Church. However, its citizens resisted strongly – even murdering the Archbishop of Benevento, who was a supporter of William – and the city was saved.[5] Benevento's success came at some cost to the surrounding towns, which were less well defended. Its suburbs were ravaged.[6] Adrian responded by immediately excommunicating William both for his invasion and his earlier offence to Cardinal Henry.[7] Evidently the excommunication did not seem to have unduly bothered William who, satisfied with his forays in Apulia, had already returned to Sicily. William's army remained behind on the mainland, now led by his chancellor, Anscotinus, who continued the fighting.

Adrian's focus on the north meant that he had done nothing to protect his lands to the south, not that there was much he could have done. Ceprano in Campagna, on the border between the Patrimony and the Sicilian kingdom, was burnt down on 30 May 1155, and only two days later the Sicilian army entered the Patrimony itself. The *castrum* of Bauco, 10 miles north of Ceprano, was razed to the ground. The Sicilian army was now within four days' march of Rome. Apart from Benevento, their attacks on the Patrimony had largely succeeded, but fortunately for Adrian, the Sicilian army pressed no further towards Rome, not wanting to goad Frederick's army which by then was closing in on the city from the north.

✠　✠　✠

This Sicilian reticence gave Adrian time to refocus on the far bigger threat posed by Frederick. Adrian was annoyed that Frederick had not faced up to the Roman Commune or help defend the Patrimony from the Normans in the south. Instead, Frederick was busy wreaking destruction in the north. He should not have wasted time at Tortona, although the difficulty with which he had taken the small town should have made Adrian realise just how ill-equipped Frederick was to take on William in the south. Frederick continued his slow circulation, although he had probably not intended to do this. He would have been taken aback by the determination of the northern cities to maintain their independence and he felt that he needed to make a show of his imperial strength. By now the other northern cities were well aware of what had happened to recalcitrant Tortona.

From Bologna, Frederick crossed the Apennines into Tuscany and to Pisa on the west coast, where he ordered the city to prepare ships for battle against King William. Frederick had so far shown no other sign of taking the fight to William, but clearly he had not completely forgotten his commitment at Constance to attack the Normans. Adrian, getting regular reports of Frederick's actions, at last took some comfort from news of this naval mobilisation. For the first time it augured well for taking the fight to the Sicilians.

Although not all dissent in Lombardy had been quelled, Frederick felt secure enough to move to Rome and he upped his pace. He needed to: time was getting short. He had been in Italy six months already and his army was suffering inevitable fatigue. He was also anxious to receive his imperial crown before the height of the summer heat of Rome. Having been worried about Frederick's slow progress, this sudden burst of speed, although perhaps welcomed by some, now caused some concern in the Curia. Boso remarked that his speed was more akin to that of an enemy than to that of a defender.[8]

Adrian and Frederick were getting close to each other at last. Since 16 May Adrian had been based in Sutri, preparing carefully for his coming meeting with Frederick. Adrian was a team player and always consulted the cardinals on major matters. It was important for him to do this now. Adrian was still an unknown quantity to several of the cardinals and he needed to make sure that he and they were as one in setting a strategy for dealing with Frederick. He also took counsel from Oddone Frangipane, an Italian military leader in the service of the papacy, and Peter, the Prefect of Rome. The prefect was the holder of an ancient office and combined the roles of chief of police and judge in criminal cases. An ordained priest was not permitted to take judicial decisions which involved bloodshed and so could not be an effective prefect. The prefect was funded by the pope and, in theory, responsible to him, but was appointed by the Roman citizens.[9] Peter was also Commandant of Castel Sant'Angelo, built by Emperor Hadrian to serve as his mausoleum but later used by the popes as a fortress.

Pope, cardinals and advisers all agreed that the next step was to send a delegation to Frederick to prepare the ground for the crucial first meeting of the two leaders. Adrian was still unsure whether he was facing friend or foe, and wanted a formal declaration from the emperor that his intentions for the papacy were peaceful. At the small hill town of San Quirico an embassy of three cardinals was met with courtesy by Frederick. He too wanted the coming meeting with Adrian to go well, as only the pope could perform his imperial coronation. As a sign of good faith, the cardinals first asked Frederick to hand over to papal officials the rebel leader Arnold of Brescia, who was still being held by one of Frederick's supporting barons. This was a deliberate test of the emperor's support for the pope, or otherwise.

While his delegation was away, Adrian, ever cautious, quietly left Sutri for Orvieto, a strong town on the northern edge of the Patrimony which he deemed to be safer. However, the imperial army was moving south too quickly for him to reach his destination and instead he took sanctuary in the Civita Castellana, a fortified castle to the north of Nepi and 15 miles east of Sutri. Both sides were as watchful as players hunched over a chessboard. Adrian waited anxiously at Civita Castellana for the return of his delegation.

At about the same time, Frederick dispatched his own embassy to the pope, sending the Archbishops of Ravenna and Cologne to start discussions on the papal coronation. It was not unusual for sovereigns to use senior churchmen as their close advisers, and they would have good knowledge of the emperor's intentions. If push came to shove, they could be relied on to take Frederick's part rather than that of their own Church leaders. Frederick played a waiting game, wanting to hear from his returning archbishops before answering the pope's cardinals in any detail. Farcically, the two delegations crossed again on the chessboard without either of them realising. Frederick's archbishops had struggled to find the peripatetic pope, but eventually caught up with him at Civita Castellana. Now it was Adrian who prevaricated. He was just as reluctant to make a decisive move, telling the archbishops that 'unless I have first received my brothers, the cardinals, whom I have sent the king, I shall not give you a reply'.[10]

Cardinals and archbishops returned to their respective masters, having achieved little. Both sides were palpably nervous. However, there was one positive outcome for Adrian. While the cardinals could not confirm Frederick's intentions, they were able to tell him that Frederick did consider Arnold to be his enemy as well as the pope's. This was good news, and Adrian read into it that Frederick regarded the pope as the supreme authority in Rome, and a clear sign that he had decided not to support the Republicans there. Frederick arranged for Arnold to be delivered to the cardinals and he was taken back to Rome in chains. It may have been Frederick's intention for him to be held there until his later arrival so that he could have him tried. However, in June, without waiting, Peter, the Prefect of Rome, had Arnold hanged in secret. Arnold walked calmly to the scaffold, and as he knelt to make his last confession his executioners could not restrain their tears.[11] Arnold's body was then burnt, and his ashes were scattered on the Tiber lest his grave became a shrine for the Republicans.

While alive, Arnold had been a continuing threat to the Curia, having the potential to stir up the people of Rome at any moment. Worse still, he could have persuaded Frederick that he had a useful role to play in containing the pope's authority in Rome. According to John Julius Norwich, a Church tribunal condemned Arnold of heresy and rebellion, but since everything happened so quickly, that must have been held in absentia before he was arrested. Arnold's summary execution was harsh, but his challenge to both Church and social order were sufficient justification in the custom of the age. Arnold had received many warnings, all of which he had obstinately ignored, to his ultimate peril. St Francis of Assisi (1181–1226) challenged the Church in a similar way although, unlike Arnold, he never disobeyed it.

We do not know who was responsible for authorising Arnold's death and there is no evidence to indicate that Adrian was directly involved in his execution. Certainly, he was not in Rome when it took place. Peter may have exceeded his authority and taken matters into his own hands, but he was close to Adrian, who usually took him into his confidence. It is unlikely that Peter would have executed Arnold without first consulting the pope. Boso had remained in Rome throughout this time, in effect operating as the pope's deputy, and he might have been responsible, but again there is nothing to confirm this.

Killing Arnold, however, failed to eliminate the threat to the Curia. Immediately afterwards, Boso tried without success to prevent the Republicans of Rome from sending their own deputation to seek out Frederick. Even without their leader, the rebels still thought they could persuade Frederick to take their side.

In the meantime, back on the chessboard, Frederick had moved his camp to Viterbo, only a few miles from the pope at Civita Castellana. Adrian was desperate to learn how the rebels would be received by Frederick, but he need not have worried. The deputation of Romans met Frederick a little south of Sutri and without the experienced Arnold to guide them they struggled. They were not used to the niceties of diplomatic exchanges and they played their hand badly, making haughty demands that almost seemed to be calculated to annoy the emperor. They asked Frederick to help them win concessions from the pope over the governing of Rome. In return, the senate and people of Rome offered to welcome Frederick as their liberator, claiming that the people of Rome were the inheritors of the ancient Roman Republic. This was hardly an approach to win over the German successor to the Roman Empire. Adding insult to injury, they also demanded an indemnity of 5,000lb of silver from Frederick. They had wasted their time. Frederick delighted his entourage of German nobles with a tirade that Edward Gibbon described as being worthy of Cicero himself:

> Famous indeed have been the fortitude and wisdom of the ancient Romans; but ... your strength and freedom have long since been exhausted by the

Greeks and Franks. Are you desirous of beholding the ancient glory of Rome, the gravity of the senate, the spirit of the knights, the discipline of the camp, the valour of your legions? You will find them in the German republic ... They will be employed in your defence, but they claim your obedience. From its foreign and domestic tyrants the city [Rome] was rescued by Charlemagne and Otho, whose ashes repose in our country: and their dominion was the price of your deliverance.[12]

Credit for this oratory probably belongs more to his biographer, Otto of Freising, writing after the event around 1157, than to Frederick himself.

It is hard to see how the deputation could have been more comprehensively dismissed, and it scurried back to Rome. Adrian was delighted. This cleared the stage for his cardinals to go back to Frederick in the company of the two returning archbishops and this time no one went astray. There was an uninvited addition to the pope's team: Cardinal Octavian, eager to give his personal welcome to Frederick, had wheedled his way into the deputation. Octavian belonged to a family long supportive of the imperial throne and he would remain Frederick's man in the College of Cardinals throughout Adrian's reign. Loyal Boso was scathing about Octavian's involvement:

Octavian, cardinal priest of the title of St Cecilia, already dreaming of sedition and schism, had come to him, not sent but sent away by the pontiff. But after the said cardinals had entered the king's presence and taken counsel concerning their legation to fulfil the instructions of the Roman pontiff, the said Octavian began to vomit forth the venom which he had swallowed and to disturb the peace: but quickly and for good reason, he was silenced by his brethren, the cardinals.[13]

Boso was writing with the benefit of hindsight: in the schism after Adrian's death it was Octavian who became the antipope. At this point, however, he had the pope's trust. Adrian would use Octavian for several future missions, taking advantage of his close German links. Nonetheless, John of Salisbury had also been critical of Octavian when he had been sent by Eugenius as a legate to King Conrad of Germany with a view to arranging his imperial coronation (which never happened), calling him proud and pompous and a sycophant of the Germans.[14]

This second meeting of the cardinals with Frederick went better and they were able to return to the waiting pope with the emperor's promise that he had no hostile intentions against the Church. In return, Frederick formally asked the pope to crown him with due solemnity in St Peter's. Despite this good report, the still cautious and strong-willed Adrian wanted more. He needed absolute reassurance and told Frederick that, if he were to swear on the gospels and on the cross before the papal ambassadors that he would protect the pope and protect the dignity of the papal office, and would not usurp any papal functions, he would ride out to meet him and then crown him as he wished.

Frederick was always going to agree. He wanted his coronation too much and he accepted Adrian's terms. On 8 June Frederick, in front of the cardinals and his own nobles, and in front of the sacred emblems of the gospels and the cross, delegated one of his princes to make the oath on his behalf. His solemn promise was not to harm in any way either Adrian or his cardinals.[15] In this way, Frederick vowed to serve Adrian and to take vengeance on all who tried to harm him. That Adrian had found it necessary to protect his cardinals from harm or imprisonment shows just how worried the Curia had been about Frederick. Emperors had a habit of using force to achieve their aims. Those fears now allayed, all the pieces were in place and everything was ready for their first meeting.

✠ ✠ ✠

Still the game between the two leaders continued. Adrian made his way to Nepi, 8 miles east of Sutri, while the emperor brought his camp forward to Campo Grasso, closer to Sutri. At last the time had come for the set-piece meeting of the two most important leaders in Europe. On 9 June Adrian, mounted on a white palfrey, a docile riding horse, and surrounded by his cardinals robed in scarlet, rode towards the emperor's camp with the full panoply of papal banners and trumpeters. On their approach they were met by an equally colourful deputation of German princes and bishops who led the pope towards the royal tent. A throne to befit a pope was ready and waiting for Adrian. They knew how to put on a staged event in the twelfth century.

Immediately there was friction. Following protocol, the emperor approached the pope to help him dismount but he did not, as tradition demanded, hold the pope's stirrup for him, the homage of *strator*. This role recalled a soldier chosen to act as a groom for a senior officer. Just as now, protocol was all-important when leaders met. The pope was dealing with an uninvited and armed German king whose true objectives were less than clear. Adrian was arguably entitled to be wary, but perhaps he was less than tactful. There was a stand-off. Neither pope nor emperor would budge. All those watching, even the Germans, knew Frederick had slighted the pope. It certainly shocked the attending cardinals, who took it as an omen of bad will. The disrespect to the pope confirmed their worst fears and they turned and fled to Civita Castellana, leaving Adrian to his own devices. Clearly the cardinals did not feel that they could rely on the oath to protect their safety given on behalf of Frederick only the day before.

Adrian himself was not panicked. He held his temper, dismounted and proceeded into the royal tent, taking his allocated throne. Frederick advanced and kissed the pope's feet. Ordinarily Adrian would have then offered a kiss of peace, but instead he drew back. He would not be intimidated and told the emperor that until he showed him the traditional sign of respect, to act as his *strator*, he would not give the customary kiss of peace. Frederick was equally stubborn and would have none of it, insisting that it was not part of his duty to act as the pope's groom. Two stubborn men were at an impasse. Adrian maintained his dignity and returned to Nepi.

Adrian was correct in that there had been a breach of protocol. Emperor Constantine had set the precedent of an emperor acting as groom for the pope back in the fourth century when he performed this service for Pope Sylvester I. Without doubt, the German princes surrounding Frederick were aware of the precedents. Some would even have been present in 1131 in Liège when Emperor Lothair III had paid this same homage to Pope Innocent II. They counselled the emperor to concede, putting Frederick under pressure. Adrian was brave, if not a little reckless, in forcing this issue over protocol when the Sicilian army was only four days' march south of Rome, not to mention the continuing hostility of the Roman Republicans. Frederick kept Adrian waiting a further two days before capitulating. Through gritted teeth he agreed to perform the office of groom to the pope 'out of reverence for the blessed apostles'.[16]

Yet again the emperor's camp moved forward, this time to Lake Janula near the town of Monterosi, 10 miles south-east of Sutri. On 11 June the meeting was restaged. Adrian rode to greet Frederick as if for the first time. The emperor held the stirrup as the pope dismounted and the pope then gave Frederick the kiss of peace. Two equally strong-willed leaders were reconciled.

Adrian's dogged insistence may smack of arrogance but in the twelfth century, as the representative of Christ on earth, the absence of this homage would have been inauspicious for the Church that Frederick had vowed to protect. It has been suggested that Frederick had not been deliberately awkward but just performed the ceremony incorrectly, perhaps holding the left stirrup rather than the right stirrup, and that Adrian was petulant to make a fuss about it. Boso wrote about the event some ten years after it had taken place and so, knowing of the later conflicts between pope and emperor, he may have exaggerated a simple mistake. However, the incident is not mentioned at all in Otto of Freising's biography of Frederick, suggesting that it was an embarrassment for Frederick and a victory for the pope. Perhaps, but it came with the cost of a missed opportunity for friendship.

Even if unwise, Adrian had been courageous. Frederick had learnt that the pope was not someone he could coerce. After only seven months on the Throne of St Peter, the raw English pope had bearded the mighty German Emperor. This was not a harmonious start to the relationship but for the time being at least they had avoided conflict.

THE LEONINE CITY
Coronation of the Emperor

The king approached the pontiff to be crowned, and having presented the imperial insignia, he received sword and sceptre and the crown of the empire from the hands of the pope. So loud and strong was the Germans' acclamation of praise and joy, that it was believed that a terrible thunderbolt had just fallen from the heavens.

Cardinal Boso
Vita Adriani IV[1]

Adrian and Frederick had patched up their quarrel and both were eager to get to Rome and hold the coronation. The sooner it was held, the sooner they could face up to William, although at this point Adrian still did not know if he could rely on Frederick's help to join the fighting in the south and defend the threat to the papal territories. He would soon find out. In the meantime, they took advantage of their mutual respect and spent a week together on the relatively short journey to Rome. Over several days of pleasant conversation, pope and king covered ecclesiastical and secular matters of mutual concern.[2] Sadly, the harmony would not last. Pope and emperor would never be as close again as they were in the early summer days of 1155.

For now, though, some progress was made. Adrian confirmed to Frederick that he would stand by the Treaty of Constance, made two years earlier with Pope Eugenius. They agreed on the menace posed by the followers of Arnold, who had been the first victim of their alliance. Adrian was relieved that Frederick had not succumbed to the entreaties of the Republicans of Rome, yet even without any support from Frederick they were still holding sway in the city. Frederick may not have been over-concerned about control of Rome, but he was aware that its Republicans still had the capacity to disrupt his coronation. Adrian counselled the emperor as to how to deal with them:

> My son, you will learn more about the guile of the Roman rabble as time goes on. For you will discover that in treachery they came and in treachery they departed. But aided by the clemency of God, who says, 'I shall take the wise in their own craftiness',* we shall be able to circumvent their shrewd schemes. Accordingly, let brave and knowing young men of the army be quickly sent ahead to seize the church of St Peter and the Leonine stronghold. Our knights are there within the fortifications; upon learning our wishes they will straightaway admit them.[3]

Frederick could not trust the Republicans any more than Adrian could, and did exactly as the pope recommended. Early on Saturday, 18 June 1,000 knights, the pick of Frederick's army, rode to the Leonine City guided by Octavian, the cardinal with good imperial links. By dawn they had quietly secured St Peter's Basilica on the right bank of the Tiber, making it safe for Adrian to follow. Messages were sent back to him and the emperor that all was ready for the next step. Adrian went first with the rest of his cardinals to await the emperor on the steps of St Peter's. Still early on a beautiful summer's day, the soldiers protecting Frederick looked splendid, their armour gleaming in the bright sun.[4]

Frederick had been camped about 2 miles north of Rome and entered the Leonine City by its golden gate, early in the morning. In order to prevent any disruption of his coronation by the rebels, he stationed some of his knights just outside the walls. Here they would secure the bridge over the Tiber which led directly to the heart of Rome. Neither Frederick nor Adrian was welcome in Rome and setting this guard proved to be a wise precaution.

At last the emperor's moment had arrived. He had been the German king for three years and was about to receive the imperial crown, something his uncle Conrad had never managed. Just as for Adrian's papal coronation there was a well-established procedure. Frederick changed out of his armour and donned the state robes befitting an emperor. The ceremony started at the Chapel of St Maria in Turri. This ancient church, demolished in the Renaissance, was one of several small churches that adjoined the atrium outside St Peter's Basilica. The altar contained relics of St Maurice, who had been designated as a patron saint of German Roman emperors in 926.

---

*   1 Corinthians 3:19.

The moment was recorded by the same anonymous twelfth-century poet who recounted the time that Frederick made an example of Tortona:

> There sat the reverend Adrian as Pope,
> A man known for character and learning.
> According to the custom, he received
> The Monarch in the portal of the church
> And led him into the building with great praise.[5]

The first part of the ceremony was conducted by the cardinals rather than by the pope. At the altar of the chapel, with his hands held in those of the pope, Frederick swore to be the defender of the Holy Roman Church.[6] Adrian then led Frederick in procession into St Peter's itself. Adrian's successor as Cardinal Bishop of St Albano pronounced the first of many prayers over the emperor at the Silver Gate:

> Oh God in whose hands are the hearts of kings ... grant to thy servant Frederick, our Emperor, the shield of Thy wisdom, and that, drawing his counsels from Thee, he may please Thee, and may preside over all the kings of the earth.[7]

This prayer cautioned Frederick that, despite his earthly power, he was still answerable to God. We know that Frederick was God-fearing and even when he fell out with the pope he never lost his faith.

Inside the church Frederick reached a great red disc of porphyry set into the floor. Porphyry is a hard purple and white igneous rock associated with Roman emperors and found only in one mountain in Egypt. Here the Cardinal Bishop of Porto recited a second prayer addressing God as 'the ruler of empires':

> Firmly establish this sovereign ... in the throne of empire. Visit him as Thou did Moses in the burning bush ... and pour on him the dew of Thy wisdom ... Be Thou to him a shield in all difficulties, and grant that the nations may be true to him, that his nobles may keep the peace, and that his people may ever enjoy the blessings of happiness and peace.[8]

This second prayer recognised the power of the emperor and reminded him of the difficulties he would be up against. Not all would be true to his authority and God would be his protection.

Frederick next moved to the space directly in front of St Peter's tomb, known as the confession in reference to the confession of faith which led to his martyrdom. Here the Cardinal Bishop of Ostia anointed the prostrate Frederick on his right arm and between the shoulders with holy oil while beseeching:

> God, in whom all power resides, to grant him a happy period of imperial rule, that nothing may hinder his care for the Church, and that he may rule his people with justice.[9]

The pope now took the lead for the second part of the ceremony. Adrian began the Mass. Immediately after the reading of the Epistle, Adrian approached Frederick and presented him with the sword and sceptre and placed the crown on his head. The deed done, Frederick was now the Roman Emperor, the heir to Charlemagne. The German soldiers were ecstatic. The crown Frederick received had not been used before, having been made in the tenth century but then remodelled in the early 1150s for his uncle Conrad, who in the event never came to Rome for a coronation.[10]

There had never been a medieval emperor without the active participation of the papacy.[11] Only after their supplication to the pope had previous kings of Germany become Roman emperors. For successive popes, the prime objective of the ceremony was to secure physical protection for the papacy from the Byzantine Emperor in Constantinople, who was always intent on extending his empire into papal territory in Italy, something the Church could not accept, of course.

The imperial coronation had largely followed tradition, but Adrian had introduced some subtle changes. They may seem insignificant now, but they mattered then in emphasising that the secular power of the emperor was subservient to the ecclesiastical power of the Church.[12] That the anointing had been done before the start of the Mass, with an inferior oil, and not at the high altar, all showed that he was not being given a liturgical office. Furthermore, that Frederick was anointed on the shoulder rather than on the head marked that it was his physical strength to support the papacy that was being recognised. Adrian conferred the insignia himself, and at the high altar, to emphasise the dominance of the ecclesiastical power over the secular. The sword conferred on the emperor by the pope was part of a medieval allegory referring to the 'two swords' in Luke's gospel.* One sword, the spiritual sword, was wielded

---

*   Luke 22:38.

directly by the pope, and the second was handed by the pope to the secular king for him to wield to suppress evil as directed by the pope. At no time had the papacy regarded the Roman Emperor as autonomous and the prayers of the ritual set out exactly how the emperor was expected to use his sword.

For the same reason, the coronation ritual did not provide a throne for the emperor. As a minister of the pope, the emperor was not entitled to sit on a throne. Only the pope sat on a throne. All this subtlety was probably lost on Frederick; the emperor had no Latin and he had followed the rituals meekly. In the formal scrutiny by the pope, the *scrutinium*, he answered the pope's Latin questions unknowingly, giving the Latin responses fed to him by the attending clerics.

Regardless of what he did or did not understand, Frederick saw things differently. He had always insisted that his authority came directly from God alone, quoting St Peter's doctrine, 'Fear God, respect the Emperor'.* It is not difficult to see how the emperor's rather different understanding of his own authority would cause problems for all popes in due course, especially for Adrian. Having had to accept his imperial authority from the pope would rankle with Frederick and return to the surface in later events.

For the moment, at least, Frederick was happy. His imperial coronation, and main purpose for the German mission to Italy, had been completed and he was in high spirits. The brand-new emperor, wearing his crown and riding a caparisoned steed, returned in a victory procession to the camp his army had established just outside the wall.

Back in the Leonine City, Adrian was wary. He still had nagging doubts as to whether Frederick would now fulfil his part of the deal and help him stand up to William or take his prize and hightail it back to Germany.

The coronation had been held deliberately early, and on the Saturday rather than the more usual Sunday, to wrongfoot the rebels of Rome who might well have interrupted the ceremony with their protests. This proved wise: when the news of the secret coronation reached the Roman senators they were infuriated at having been tricked. In a rage, they and the rebels advanced on St Peter's with some considerable force and killed some of the guards that Frederick had posted at the gate. When this alarming news reached Frederick, at about 4 p.m., he immediately ordered his tired knights to turn back to protect the pope.

June in Rome is hot, and the knights had set out early that Saturday morning. They were already exhausted but nonetheless, with the new emperor

---

* 1 Peter 2:17.

at their head, they joined what was a bloody battle by the Tiber, near the
Castel Sant'Angelo. The fighting lasted until nightfall, by which time 1,000
Romans had perished and a further 600 had been captured.[13] During this
combat, prompt action by Henry the Lion saved Frederick from mortal injury.
Previously these two German leaders had not been close, coming from rival
branches of the family that both desired the German throne, but on this day
Henry's life-saving action reconciled him to Frederick. This was not the only
time Henry would show such courage. He would step in heroically again in
1159 to rescue two of Adrian's cardinals from robber-barons.

Frederick's biographer, Otto of Freising, exaggerating the success of the
Germans in this foray, strained credulity by claiming that only one German
was killed and one captured:

> You should have seen our men ruthlessly and ferociously killing and wound-
> ing, wounding and killing the Romans, as if to say, 'Take now, O Rome,
> Teutonic iron instead of Arabian gold. This is the price your prince offers
> you for your crown. Thus do the Franks purchase empire.'[14]

It was an unequal fight, with unskilled civilians battling against trained troops.
Otto points out with good reason that the bigger threat to the Germans was
not the Romans but the weather. The unhealthy climate and the extreme heat
of that season in the city was a greater danger than the enemy.

Many Romans were captured, and Adrian took pity on them, as a churchman should. Although some were executed before he could intercede with
Frederick on their behalf, he managed to save the rest who were handed over
to Peter, the Prefect of Rome.[15] We do not know how they were then treated.

✠   ✠   ✠

Despite this victory, pope and emperor dared not drop their guard. The
Commune had been beaten but had not surrendered, and the entrances to
Rome were still barricaded by the rebels. Frederick's victory had not been as
overwhelming as his chroniclers would have us believe, and his knights could
not be expected to guard the Leonine City for long. Nor could they expect
to be supplied with food by the Romans across the Tiber. A siege was always
a time-consuming operation and besieging Rome was out of the question.

Frederick's army was now camped near Tusculum, south-east of Rome,
where the climate for his soldiers was no better. The nearby swamps made the
air heavy and unpleasant to breathe.[16]

Discretion prevailed. Adrian and Frederick left the Leonine City together the next day, heading north along the west bank of the Tiber. This effective retreat emphasised the relative weakness of Frederick's forces, as had the siege at Tortona a few months earlier. Up to this point Adrian and Frederick's differences had been relatively minor, but growing friction between their competing claims of imperial and papal sovereignty broke the surface. First, Frederick had taken the monastery at Farfa under imperial protection, as it had been before 1120. This Benedictine abbey still exists, about 40 miles from Rome. Ever since 1120 popes had considered the monastery to be part of the Apostolic See, but Adrian chose not to make an issue over Farfa and let Frederick keep it.

He was less accommodating over the second tussle. When Frederick moved to Tivoli, 20 miles north-east of Rome, he made its citizens submit to him as their lord, and Adrian took exception. Tivoli had been a popular resort for the great and the good of the Roman Empire. The most impressive villa there was Villa Adriana, the home of Emperor Hadrian. Adrian insisted that Tivoli was papal territory and must be restored to his authority. Frederick backed down, writing to the people of Tivoli on 29 June 1155:

Frederick, by God's grace, emperor of the Romans and forever Augustus, to all the citizens of Tivoli, his grace and goodwill.

We wish all of you to know that we have restored the city of Tivoli to our very dear and reverend father in Christ, Pope Adrian, out of respect for blessed Peter, Prince of the Apostles, saving only in all things imperial right. For this reason, we have absolved each and every citizen of Tivoli from the fidelity which they have recently sworn to us, ordering and commanding you very firmly that you should stand faithfully by our venerable father, Pope Adrian, serve him with devotion, and strive to obey him as lord; knowing, as has just been said, that you are absolved from the oath of fidelity which you have recently taken, saving imperial rights in all things.[17]

Frederick's letter to the citizens of Tivoli was written on the feast of the martyrdom of Saints Peter and Paul, which is one of the most important feast days in the Church's calendar. Adrian celebrated High Mass in Tivoli in the presence of Frederick, and both leaders wore their crowns. Adrian took the opportunity during his sermon to absolve all those who had spilt blood in the recent fighting with the Romans.

Adrian and Frederick had managed to reach the end of June without a serious falling-out, but this did not last. Adrian was getting increasingly impatient with Frederick's delay in tackling William. Frederick had hardly even been south of Rome and was not shaping up to providing any help in challenging the Normans. It is possible that Frederick was still contemplating a further attack on Rome, which could explain his slow meandering up and down both banks of the Tiber.

Frederick's decision was made for him by the climate. When he reached Albano, he allowed his soldiers, still uncomfortable in the summer heat, to rest and recover. Having had enough of the Italian weather, the German barons were ready to go home. They pressurised Frederick to leave and an outbreak of fever, probably malaria, at Albano settled the matter. The emperor reluctantly agreed that it was time to return to Germany. He was perfectly well aware of his obligation to help Adrian further, but he also knew that he would struggle to persuade his under-strength army to stay in Italy any longer. Adrian was naturally furious about the decision and both literally and metaphorically parted company with the emperor; they never met again. Adrian had been abandoned to confront the threat of William on his own.

✠   ✠   ✠

German armies were never keen to stay in Italy for long and the year 1155 was no different. Their king had been crowned emperor and as far as the German barons were concerned their mission had been accomplished. All that they wanted now was to get back to cooler climes. Frederick had agreed to return but he was in less of a hurry than they were. He took his time, wandering slowly along the course of the Tiber. He reached Spoleto, 80 miles north of Rome, where the citizens, not having heeded the lesson of Tortona, had foolishly paid the tribute due to him in counterfeit money. They had also imprisoned Frederick's loyal ally, Count Guido of Tuscany, whom Frederick had earlier sent south with other barons to Campania and Apulia to regain cities and *castra*, fortresses or small castles, lost to William. Spoleto reaped the whirlwind. Frederick laid waste to it on 27 July. In a further blunder, rather than staying within the safety of its strong city walls, the men of Spoleto had decided to face Frederick in the open. After six hours' hard fighting, they were overcome. The surviving citizens fled, half-naked, to the surrounding hills, saving only their lives.

Moving further north to Ancona on the east coast, Frederick received ambassadors from Manuel, the Byzantine Emperor, ready now to pursue his own ambitions in Italy. Manuel never stopped believing that he was the true Roman Emperor, the direct successor to Constantine. He was hoping to rekindle with Frederick the good relationship that he had had with Conrad III, and he could afford to pay Frederick handsomely for his support in a joint attack against William. Manuel's ambassador, Michael Palaeologus, the Governor of Thessalonica, begged Frederick to stay longer in Italy and join with the Byzantine army in dealing with William.

Palaeologus was no more successful than Adrian had been. Such a Byzantine alliance would have been a blatant breach of the Treaty of Constance, and yet that was not what constrained Frederick. He wanted the Sicilians defeated, but he wanted others to do it for him. Even if he were tempted by the offer of enormous sums of money, he knew that his German princes and their men would not accept a change of mind. They had had enough. What is more, his army's foot soldiers had fulfilled their feudal obligation to support Frederick in arms and were entitled to return. Frederick was content to let the Greeks confront the Sicilians; he was more anxious to reinforce his position back in Germany.

At the same time, disaffected Apulian barons were appealing for Frederick's help in the restoration of their estates. Frederick was generous with words and sympathy but, as with Palaeologus, he was not willing to offer them any military support. He had left Adrian adrift and now he left the Apulian barons and the Greeks to their own devices. His *Romzug*, his march to Rome, was done. Some of the German contingent returned to Germany via the Adriatic and Venice, some over the Alps via the Great St Bernhard Pass, and Frederick led the rest back the way he had come, over the Brenner Pass.

Frederick's one-year *Romzug* had achieved its main objective, the imperial coronation. He had helped remove Arnold, but had he brought a stronger army he might have supressed the Commune and fully liberated Rome. He had not done so because, as a still-new king, he did not have solid support throughout Germany. Had he kept a more disciplined timetable, he could have dealt more firmly with the rebellious Milanese; instead, he would have to come back in three years to do that properly. Had he helped the pope face up to King William, he could have established a good relationship with Adrian, joining with the pope in controlling Emperor Manuel's Italian ambitions. He did none of these things and, focused only on his coronation, all these opportunities slipped away. Frederick knew himself that he had achieved little. In a letter to Otto of Freising he admitted that the campaign had been 'a toilsome journey'.[18]

Adrian had mixed emotions. He was pleased that the coronation had happened on his terms, emphasising for him at least that the emperor's authority came from the pope. Frederick had delivered a significant blow against the

Commune. However, Adrian was not pleased that the new emperor had not faced up to William as the Treaty of Constance required. Nonetheless, Adrian, the new foreign pope, had held his own. The firmness we had first seen at St Ruf had transferred to the larger stage.

With Frederick on his way back to Germany, Adrian now had to deal with events in southern Italy without the protection of the Roman Emperor's sword.

BENEVENTO
A Victory of Sorts from Defeat

Desiring with the grace of God to protect the recognized possessions of the
Holy Roman Church, we forbid under pain of anathema any military person to
invade or forcibly hold Benevento, the city of St. Peter. If anyone act contrary to
this, let him be anathematized.

Canon 8
The First Lateran Council, 1123

Adrian now dismissed Frederick from his thoughts. He had other things to
worry about: if anything, the problems for his papacy were deteriorating. He
was still denied safe access to Rome and, more worryingly, papal territory
in the south was falling to King William of Sicily. Consequently, Adrian and
his cardinals decided to move south to be a little nearer to the action. In
September they based themselves at Ferentino, a hill town about 40 miles
south-east of Rome. Here they discussed what to do about William.

The tension could potentially have been avoided if Adrian had responded
differently to William when he was first elected pope. William's first thought
when news reached him of Adrian's election had been to seek a rapprochement. This had been the purpose of William's deputation that Adrian had
rejected at the end of 1154. Unfortunately, Adrian believed at the time that
Frederick would provide the papacy with all the support that it needed.
Frederick was seen as a stronger and more reliable partner, whereas William
had been *persona non grata* with the Curia ever since his unauthorised coronation. Adrian's impetuousness had come back to haunt him.

Events had moved on, and Adrian was now in some difficulty. He could hardly ignore William's incursions, but he did not have sufficient armed forces to oppose him on his own. He and his cardinals now knew that they could not rely on any German help under the Treaty of Constance. What was even more concerning was the information they received about Frederick's discussions in Ancona with General Michael Palaeologus, the ambassador of the Byzantine Emperor. For all they knew, Frederick had made a secret deal to cede Italian territory to the Greeks and thus breach the treaty. If that were true, the papacy could only be a loser. Adrian needed to strengthen his position should there be another threat in the north, and it looked like he was going to have to broker his own deal with William. Adrian was hesitant to do this, even though the treaty did not explicitly prevent the pope from making a pact with William. Nevertheless, Adrian knew that Frederick would regard a Sicilian pact as implicitly forbidden and would be infuriated.

Having previously opposed negotiations with William but now without Frederick to protect them, the cardinals started to come round to Adrian's way of thinking. They could now see that they might have a better chance of recovering Church lands in the south by reaching an agreement with the Sicilian king. Alliances in Italy were always fragile and again they were shifting. However, engagement with the freshly excommunicated William would not be comfortable or come easily. Much bad blood between the kingdom of Sicily and the papacy would have to be overcome. William's current challenge to Adrian was like a rerun of the battle between his father Roger and Pope Innocent II. Could Adrian and William find the accommodation that had eluded their predecessors?

While Adrian pondered his next move with his cardinals, William's authority was being threatened by his own subjects. His father Roger owed his kingship to his brutal repression of the Norman barons, and his firm hand had ensured peace throughout the final ten years of his reign. Nevertheless, the enmity of the Norman barons in Apulia had never gone away. The changing of the guard in Palermo on Roger's death presented a new opportunity and they were not slow to challenge William. They perceived him to be less forceful than his father and therefore vulnerable. William and his chief officer knew that a challenge was inevitable. Maio, known as the 'emir of emirs', was an Italian from the largely Greek town of Bari and was close to William, a relationship that was another source of friction with the mainland Norman barons, who resented Maio's power. William had more trouble even closer to home, in Sicily itself. While Frederick had been busy in Lombardy and Rome, Manuel, the Byzantine Emperor, had incited the Greek population of the polyglot island into rebellion. This was part of a Byzantine plan to soften up Sicily before the Byzantines mounted their own challenge to William in the south of mainland Italy.

Meanwhile, in Ancona up in the north of Italy, the Byzantine ambassadors were indeed working up their plans to win back a foothold on the mainland. They had not been surprised that Frederick would not stay to help them, and nor were they too concerned. They found the support they were looking for from these same Norman barons who were unhappy with rule from Sicily and were ready to rebel. The barons had previously taken the view that tying themselves to the German Empire was better than being subject to Sicily, but Frederick had deserted them. They now reckoned that an association with distant Constantinople would suit their purpose just as well and might even be better. They had seen that Venice had benefitted for many years from a hands-off Byzantine association and the profitable trade that it brought.

As they pondered, the ambassadors presented the unsettled barons with documents claiming that before he left Italy Frederick had agreed to grant the Adriatic coast to Byzantium. These letters could well have been clever forgeries, but if they were genuine, and had become known to Adrian, he would have seen the surrender to Byzantium of cities along the Adriatic coast as the most blatant of all Frederick's breaches of the crumbling Treaty of Constance.

If the documents did not sufficiently persuade the barons to join the Greek cause, copious payments of gold did the trick. United by a common enemy, the Norman barons decided to join the Greeks in a challenge to William under the joint leadership of General Palaeologus and their own figurehead, Robert III, Count of Loritello. Robert, a nephew of Roger II, had always felt excluded from William's court and particularly resented the pre-eminence given to Maio. Robert believed that the significant role as William's right-hand man should always have been his and had already plotted to seize the Sicilian throne from his cousin. Robert had never hidden his ambition and William had ordered his viceroy, Asclettin, to arrest him but, getting wind of this plan, Robert escaped to safe refuge in the Marches of Abruzzi. The alliance with Palaeologus gave Robert the opportunity to make a comeback and he jumped at it.

Robert of Loritello and Palaeologus were well matched as leaders. They had similar personalities and complementary military resources. Robert had the important local support and credibility, whereas Palaeologus had the money. They met in Viesti, a little south of Rome but on the opposite coast. Once the alliance was sealed, they combined their fighting men into a single formidable army. The Greek knights, distinguished by their effective scaled armour, were well equipped with the latest weapons. They also had a navy, renowned for its use of a flame-throwing weapon known as Greek fire, the chemical composition of which is still uncertain. Palaeologus contributed ten ships to the joint endeavour and had additional funds to buy further help as and when needed.

Robert soon had almost complete support from the barons along the Apulian coast. Morale was already high and was boosted further when rumours of William's death reached mainland Italy. The king was indeed seriously ill in Palermo, but he recovered. Nonetheless, this fake news quickly sapped the morale of the remaining Sicilian loyalists on the mainland. William was not powerless, however, and the allies still had their work cut out. Asclettin, William's viceroy on the mainland, led a Sicilian army which was made up of some 2,000 knights and a good number of men on foot. This was a more than decent force, but it was too slow in moving from Salerno on the western coast. When Robert and Palaeologus made their first armed strike towards Bari the Sicilian army was still over 100 miles distant, on the wrong side of the Apennines and too far away to intervene.

Bari was the main Italian port on the southern Adriatic and was where the allies had their first major success. Until 1071 it had been the Byzantine capital in Italy and its citizens were still largely Greek. Success came easily to the allies when some Greeks freely opened Bari's city gates to Palaeologus and Robert. With Asclettin too far away to help, the defenceless city soon surrendered. Other coastal towns then fell like dominoes. Trani fell first, and then Andria, a small coastal town 15 miles north-west of Bari. Count Richard of Andria, the loyal royalist defender of Giovinazzo, managed to escape and join Asclettin's forces.

By September 1155 Asclettin and his army caught up at last with the fighting but immediately walked into a trap. They entered the fray only to be ambushed by Robert just outside Barletta, 40 miles up the coast from Bari. Richard of Andria broke out of this encirclement and fled for the second time. Robert gave chase and caught up with him just outside Andria's city walls. Richard knew that Andria was not secure enough to withstand a siege and bravely turned on the spot to face battle. At first Robert and the chasing Greeks were in disarray but then Richard's luck finally ran out. He was struck by a stone, unhorsed, and then disembowelled by a sword-wielding priest.[1] At this the town surrendered.

With every humiliating defeat William was becoming less of a threat to Adrian and the need for a deal less obvious. Meanwhile, and to William's dismay, his agents had become aware that the Greeks were now courting the pope. Adrian was unexpectedly drawn into the fray when Palaeologus, having given up on Frederick, made an offer to him. On behalf of Manuel, his emperor, Palaeologus offered the pope 5,000lb of gold and more troops to help drive William out of Italy. In return, Adrian was asked to grant three Apulian coastal cities to the Byzantine Empire. Adrian listened, even though he knew well that a deal with the Byzantine Emperor would put him too in open breach of the Treaty of Constance. That treaty was already dead, but the obedient man in Adrian was still willing to honour it from his side and hold the moral high ground.

Although tempted, Adrian was also conscious that he could not easily sign a formal alliance with Byzantium and so with the eastern Church. Even after 100 years, the wounds of the Great Schism of 1054 were still raw and the theological differences between east and west remained unresolved. Adrian did harbour dreams of healing the rift and thought that an alliance with Byzantium might somehow lead to a reconciliation of the two churches. As a non-Italian, Adrian was perhaps ideally placed to achieve that reconciliation, although he had no doubts about the superiority of the western Church. Nonetheless, an alliance now could unite the two churches by pivoting the papacy away from the German Emperor and towards the Byzantine one. The snag was that only one emperor could be recognised by the pope, and he had only just crowned Frederick. The Curia habitually referred to Manuel as 'King of the Greeks' rather than as emperor, even though it was Manuel and not Frederick who in reality could claim a direct succession from Constantine.

It was too great a risk. Adrian decided not to conclude an explicit deal with the Greeks, but he was ready to take advantage of the opportunity they presented to chase William out of Italy, and even out of Sicily itself. He could see that the Greeks, together with the restive Norman barons, had the power to achieve this and he was happy to be seen to support the rebel Norman part of the alliance. Adrian's earlier act of excommunication had not bothered William himself, but it had prompted some of the barons rebelling against William to send envoys to Adrian pleading for him to support their struggles and restore their lands which, after all, were held under papal fiefs. The pope was ready to oblige.

In September 1155, just as Asclettin was walking into the ambush at Bari, Adrian met Robert of Capua, Andrew of Rupecanina and other rebel barons at San Germano, the town lying in the valley below the great abbey of Monte Cassino. The barons acknowledged the pope as their lord and in return Adrian was happy to re-establish papal suzerainty over Apulia. The latest news of the fighting was good and the mounting difficulties for William had encouraged Adrian. He agreed to support the rebel barons, while turning a blind eye to their alliance with the Greeks. On 29 September 1155, having collected such troops as he could, Adrian set off south for Benevento. After only nine months on the throne, the English pope was going to war.

✠   ✠   ✠

That churchmen should bear arms for their beliefs was hardly new. Jesus always preached a message of peace, refusing even to let his disciples defend him in the Garden of Gethsemane when he was arrested.* However, Christians had endured violence ever since the time of Jesus and were always prepared to fight in defence of their faith when necessary. By the end of the eleventh century, and at the time of the First Crusade, militant Christian knights had no qualms about extending the influence of the Church by force. By the early twelfth century, and born of dire need in the Holy Land, it became accepted that even clerics could bear arms.[2] As we have seen, Pope Lucius II had himself been killed in 1145 leading a papal force against rebels in Rome.

There were no standing armies as such. Adrian could draw on papal garrisons, led by papal castellans or governors, appointed by him. These troops were better organised than those of recent popes and Adrian had no qualms about employing extra mercenary forces. He explained that 'no one can make war without pay'.[3] Battles were fought by mounted knights accompanied by motley foot soldiers fulfilling their obligation to their feudal lord. The knights did not have plate armour but instead wore quilted, hooded tunics covered with small iron rings, known as mail. Over the hood they wore an iron helmet with a protruding bar to protect the nose. Their weapons were swords and spears. The foot soldiers did less well and only some had helmets. Their weapons included bows, slings, spears and axes, but they were of limited use as defences against mounted knights. There was little military discipline and no subtlety to their tactics: a twelfth-century battle was a head-on contest of brute force. Bishops and clerics would fight too but wielding clubs and so respecting in a literal sense the Church's ruling that men of God should not spill blood. Adrian rode to battles at the head of his knights, but he would not himself enter the fray, instead watching from a safe distance.

Pope and barons reached Sora, halfway between Rome and Naples, by 9 October and their forces easily took Capua, just north of Naples, which was burnt down on 2 November. They reached Benevento by 21 November, by which time, after heavy fighting, most of Apulia had fallen to the allies. Adrian

---

*   Matthew 26:52.

was warmly received by the citizens of Benevento and he welcomed their city back into the papal fold.

Benevento, meaning 'fair wind', is a former Roman colony on the Via Appia about 30 miles north-east of Naples. The triumphal Arch of Trajan, erected in 114, still forms the eastern gate in the city walls. The nearby church of Santa Sofia, a Unesco World Heritage Site, dates back to 760 and is a stunning example of Lombard religious architecture. Its adjoining cloister dates from Adrian's time.

Adrian's arrival at Benevento spelt trouble for William. By now the Sicilian king had lost control of all of Campania and most of northern Apulia. Emperor Manuel was so delighted by the news of the progress that he dispatched reinforcements for Palaeologus. William was in a desperate situation as the threesome of pope, barons and Byzantine troops closed in against him in a pincer movement. In the south, Palaeologus and Robert had already bottled up William's viceroy, Asclettin, and Adrian and his allies were now threatening from the north. William panicked. He decided that he had no option but to sue for peace with the pope as soon as possible. He sent Bernard, the bishop-elect of Catania, in Sicily, to Salerno to make overtures to the pope on his behalf. In return for papal absolution William offered to swear homage and fealty to the pope and cede to the Holy See three towns: Montefercolo and Morcone, in the territory of Naples, and Padule, which was 5 miles south of Benevento. He also promised to defend by arms the authority of the Church and to match the 5,000lb of gold that Palaeologus had offered Adrian. This was quite a package and achieved without any help at all from Emperor Frederick.

William had offered enough to tempt the pope, but first Adrian wanted to make sure that William was not just playing for time. To do this, he sent one of his cardinals, Hubald, to Salerno to form a view on the sincerity of William's offer. Hubald reported back positively, convinced that the deal was genuine, and Adrian was inclined to accept it. As ever, the collegiate pope wanted his cardinals' support and he sounded out their views. On this occasion he might have wished he had not done so, as the cardinals were of a different mind. They counselled Adrian to delay any treaty with William as the fighting was still going in favour of the allies. Some cardinals, known as the German group, were particularly nervous about making any compact with William.

Things did seem to be getting worse for William. Emperor Manuel's reinforcements included a fleet which was besieging Brindisi, on the heel of Italy, and there were real hopes of a complete allied victory. The Greeks were skilled fighters and in April 1156 Brindisi fell to them, apart from some of William's staunch loyalists who were bottled up in its citadel. All the signs suggested that

William's days in Italy were numbered and the cardinals saw no need to parley while they had the upper hand.

Adrian was pleased with the shape that events were taking, but not so his future nemesis back in Germany. In autumn 1155, Frederick had been content to let the Greeks and the Apulian barons take on William, but he quickly changed his tune when he saw how successful they had become. He refused to see the Greek envoys who came to him at Würzburg, complaining bitterly that Michael Palaeologus had betrayed him and had deceived the Apulian barons with forged letters.[4] A permanent Byzantine presence in southern Italy was a threat to his own interests.

Frederick did not have to worry for too long. The tide was about to turn.

✠　✠　✠

Back in Benevento, the cardinals could not see the change coming. Even if Adrian did, he did not want to gainsay them, knowing the importance of consulting the cardinals before making decisions. Pope Eugenius had only appointed him as Cardinal of Albano 'with the common consent of his brethren'[5] and as recently as 9 February 1156 at Benevento Adrian himself overturned a decision by his predecessor, Pope Anastasius IV, because the latter had not first sought the consent of the cardinals.[6] So, against his better judgement, Adrian accepted the advice of his cardinals and rejected William's terms outright. He would soon rue his decision. Boso marked the hubris with a quotation from Luke:

> Everyone that exalteth himself shall be humbled, and he that humbleth himself shall be exalted.[*]

And so it proved. William, under enormous pressure, pulled himself together. The allies had at first achieved success in southern Italy, but overconfidence was their undoing. Perhaps not yet fully recovered from his illness, William had hastily marshalled his army and navy in Messina in north-east Sicily, the closest port to the Italian mainland. Asclettin was summoned to William to explain his dire performance and, getting no support from the court, was held responsible and cast into prison where he died several years later.

William's army crossed over to the mainland and his fleet set out for Brindisi just as the allies were starting to wobble. Their long siege of Brindisi had tried

---

[*]　Luke 18:14.

their patience and tensions had arisen between the Greeks and the Normans. Together they occupied the town but could not break the citadel, where William's loyal troops were hanging on. Despite their run of successes over the past six months, Robert of Loritello and Palaeologus fell out badly. Palaeologus then died of a sudden illness in Bari and was replaced by his deputy John Ducas, an equally able military leader. He and Robert patched up their differences, but some of Ducas's mercenaries chose the moment to demand impossible increases in their pay and when these were refused they deserted.

William's forces now outnumbered the allied troops, were too powerful for them. William's navy reached Brindisi before his land forces and it barricaded the narrow entrance to the harbour, shutting off any escape by sea for the Greeks. Julius Caesar had blocked the same harbour to Pompey's fleet in 48 BC. For a time, the Greeks in Brindisi held firm against the Sicilian navy, but when William's army joined the battle from the land side a couple of days later, the Greeks were completely overwhelmed. William raised the siege of his citadel in Brindisi on 28 May and rescued his loyalists who had been trapped there. John Ducas was taken prisoner. William's navy even captured the reinforcing Byzantine fleet that Manuel had sent. Their catapults of Greek fire could not save them, and the fleet had missed its chance to retreat to the safety of Bari. This was a crushing defeat; the Greeks, so close to re-establishing their control over southern Italy, had lost everything in an instant.

Robert of Loritello, William's rival for the Sicilian throne, knew that he was now in serious trouble. He deserted the Greeks for the second time and managed to flee ahead of William's army. Other Apulian barons were not so lucky. They were captured and dealt with harshly. Nor was there any magnanimity for the defeated Greek citizens of Brindisi, whom William regarded as nothing but traitors. Many were hanged, blinded or drowned in the sea. To the victor the spoils, and unfortunately for Adrian, William's spoils included the 5,000lb of gold that the Byzantine Emperor had intended for him. Adrian had been following news of the fighting from Benevento and his delight over the earlier victories of the Greeks had completely evaporated. He had thought William was getting the comeuppance that Frederick had failed to deliver. Now he was aghast.

Situations in war can change quickly, and William's enemies began to fade away. As so often in defeat, allies fell out and it became every man for himself. Count Richard II of Aquila restored himself to William's favour by betraying his own leader, Robert of Capua.[7] Like the Apulian barons, Robert was blinded and taken in chains to a prison in Sicily, where he died soon afterwards. William moved on swiftly to Bari, whose citizens had surrendered without a fight, hoping for generous terms. Since they had destroyed William's 'house', his citadel in Bari, at the start of the fighting, he did not spare their houses, but he did at least give them two days to remove their possessions to safety outside the town. Apart from St Nicholas's cathedral, the whole town was then razed.

The savagery of William's victories quelled dissent in the other towns of Apulia. William regained the remaining territory that he had lost without the need for further fighting. He then turned to attack Benevento, to where the surviving barons had already fled, joining a now disheartened Adrian and his meagre forces.

William chased them and was more confident than he had been when his army had failed in its siege of Benevento the year before. He had the stronger forces, and it was now Adrian who was vulnerable. To all intents and purposes, the pope had become William's prisoner. Remarkably, the father, Roger, and now the son, William, had each captured a pope. There could be no rescue for Adrian by Frederick, who was long since gone. The Greeks had been annihilated so they could be of no help either. Nor could Adrian flee to Rome, which was still blocked by the rebels. Surrounded, Adrian had no choice but to negotiate with the victor, and worse still, from a weak position. He could only hope to minimise the damage.

He first dispatched most of his cardinals to the relative safety of Campania then sent three of them, led by his chancellor, Cardinal Roland, to face the king and his army on the crest of a hill 2 miles outside Benevento. They bade the king, in the name of St Peter, to cease further hostilities. The cardinals had no means to back up this demand; however, to their surprise, William gave them a warm welcome. He knew that he had already won. The cardinals were hardly in a position to bargain, but they did ask for clemency for the remaining barons. William magnanimously agreed. He did not seek to press his advantage against the pope's supporters, preferring to make a settlement. Just as Frederick had sought papal recognition from Adrian in 1155 to enhance his credentials in Germany, William too wanted papal approval of his own throne and was happy to pay a fair price for it.

Naturally, terms of settlement were drawn up by William's team rather than by the cardinals. William's own advisers were his chief minister Maio, the English Bishop Hugh of Palermo, and Count Romuald of Salerno. The treaty was finalised on 18 June 1156. Whether by coincidence or design, this was one year to the day after Frederick's coronation in Rome. So much had changed in a mere twelve months.

William was more generous than a victor need have been, although not as generous as he would have been in winter 1155, when Adrian had rejected his entreaties. Robert of Loritello, William's cousin and leader of the uprising, Andrew of Rupecanina and the remaining barons were expelled from his kingdom but were permitted to take with them their possessions. They fared much better than their fellow barons who had been captured at Brindisi. Such is the caprice of war.

The Treaty of Benevento started with a glowing account of William's victory and self-importantly emphasised that William had always been humble at the moment of his successes. The original manuscript is still held in the Vatican Archive, and, rather less humbly, inscribed around William's royal seal are the words:

> The right hand of God gave me courage;
> The right hand of God raised me up.[8]

William borrowed these words from his grandfather, Roger, the Great Count of Sicily, who had inscribed them on his sword after the decisive victory of the Normans over the Sicilian Muslims at Cerami in 1063.

William was anxious to mend the quarrel with the papacy and his treaty made this clear. He conceded papal authority over ecclesiastical matters in Apulia and Calabria, namely 'mainland Sicily', but not for Sicily itself. The pope was free to send legates and would have the right to consecrate and visit all the churches and monasteries throughout the Sicilian realm except on the island of Sicily. He was even entitled to receive tributes from them. Meanwhile, William reserved the right to reject clerical nominees if they were found to be traitorous or unsuitable in any way. Once again, a state was usurping the Church's privilege.

Adrian had previously worked hard to separate sovereign power from ecclesiastical issues, and this concession stuck in his craw. He owed his papacy to his success in establishing Church authority in Scandinavia and had he not been surrounded by William's victorious army he would never have let him get away with a kingly veto over Church appointments in Sicily. At Benevento he had no choice but to give way. With great disappointment and humility, he accepted for William and his heirs the right to the kingdom of Sicily, the duchy of Apulia, the principality of Capua, and the cities of Naples, Salerno, Amalfi and Marcia. Worse still, Adrian had to agree to support the king in maintaining these territories. In return, William agreed to pay annual tributes to the pope for these mainland territories.

Considering the awful position in which he had found himself, Adrian accepted the outcome at Benevento philosophically, while bitterly regretting that he had turned down William's earlier offer. The next day he processed with the remaining cardinals across the milky-brown River Calore to the nearby church of Saint Marciano,* where he marked the new peace with the celebration of a Mass. William humbly prostrated himself at the pope's feet and swore fealty to him. Adrian presented William with three lances each flying a pennant – a narrow tapering flag – so investing him formally with his three dominions: the kingdom of Sicily, the duchy of Apulia and the principality of Capua.[9] William, satisfied with results, returned to Palermo a happy man. He also reached a settlement with the Byzantine Emperor Manuel, who had other troubles in the east that needed his attention. Manuel also agreed to recognise William's kingship in Sicily in exchange for the release of the Greek prisoners taken at Brindisi.

Almost overnight William had switched from being the enemy of the papacy to its defender. When all was said and done there proved to be a surprisingly good meeting of minds between pope and king. William's terms were generous enough, and to mark his satisfaction he gave Adrian and the cardinals gifts of gold, silver and silk, an increasingly fashionable material in Italy. It was William's father, King Roger, who had first brought silk weavers to Europe.

William's victory was either a lucky chance or cleverly planned from the start. The wily William may always have intended to make a last-minute intervention to relieve Brindisi. His earlier offer to the pope at Salerno might well have been a deliberate delaying tactic while he marshalled his resources, even though Cardinal Hubald had been convinced it was genuine. Whether fortuitous or not, William had snatched victory from the jaws of defeat.

After the agreement had been completed William asked the pope a further favour. He asked Adrian to remove the dioceses of Agrigentum and Mazarium, both in Sicily, from being sees of Rome to being suffragan sees of Palermo. That Adrian agreed to this demonstrates mutual goodwill that was never evident in the dealings between Adrian and Frederick. While it had looked like a defeat for the pope at first, the peace of Benevento now looked like a genuine alliance. Events have always dictated policies: the astute Adrian had come to realise that, while a close alliance with mighty Emperor Frederick sounded good at a practical level, he would likely get more support from a Sicilian

---

* This church disappeared in the sixteenth century. The site is now bare and unexcavated.

king nearer to the papal territories, from someone who actually needed the reciprocal support of the pope. Ever a diplomat, Adrian had worked a victory of sorts at Benevento. It marked the watershed of his papacy, but it was the end of any relationship with Frederick.

Some historians have suggested that an alliance with William had always been Adrian's strategy and that he deliberately sent away from Benevento those cardinals known to favour close ties with Frederick. This is surely disingenuous. There were indeed empire-favouring cardinals, but only a few. Adrian did what he did at Benevento because he was in a hole. To have fled Benevento with the cardinals would have drawn William's army into the heart of the Patrimony, and not to have made a treaty would have left Rome itself vulnerable to William's army. The events at Benevento were not of Adrian's choosing and his stance in facing William was courageous.

The new peace between papacy and Sicily lasted forty years, well beyond Adrian's pontificate. In the schism that followed Adrian's death, William's support for his elected successor, Pope Alexander, was invaluable and Adrian deserves credit for that.

✠ ✠ ✠

All was now peace and harmony between Adrian and William, but trouble was brewing in the north. Frederick saw events at Benevento very differently. He had been on a rollercoaster of emotions: first happy to let the Greeks and the barons have a tilt at William; then dismayed by the extent of the Greek alliance's early successes; and pleasure when their success came to an end when William recaptured Brindisi. Now he was livid about the treaty at Benevento that brought Adrian and William together. Frederick was furious that the pope had gratuitously granted away what he regarded to be imperial lands. He saw this rapprochement between Adrian and William as a direct breach of the Treaty of Constance endorsed by Adrian at Sutri only the year before, and he was not alone: some contemporary writers agreed with him.[10]

However, it is far from clear cut. The words that Pope Eugenius had signed up to obliged the papacy to help Frederick to maintain and increase his realm, but it was never clear whether this extended to southern Italy. Eugenius had agreed not to concede any land in Italy to the Byzantine Emperor but had made no similar commitment regarding the King of Sicily. Cardinal Roland had been a member of Pope Eugenius's negotiating team at Constance and would have known all of this when he met with William. It is easier to argue that Frederick had already broken the treaty by leaving

Italy as soon as he had been crowned and without facing up to any of the pope's enemies in southern Italy. Adrian had completed his part of the deal by crowning Frederick. That Frederick had then chosen not to support the pope made it reasonable for Adrian to consider himself free to make whatever arrangements he could to secure his position. Whatever the arguments, the reality of the situation was that Adrian's agreement with William looked to Frederick like nothing less than blatant treachery.

Frederick also saw Adrian's implicit alliance with the Byzantine troops under Palaeologus as a further breach of the treaty, even though Frederick had made his own accommodation with the Greeks when his emissaries met Palaeologus in Ancona. At one point Frederick had even contemplated a marriage with the daughter of Emperor Manuel. In all probability Frederick had offered some territory in Italy as a reward to Manuel for his support. Whatever reasons Adrian and Frederick each had for collaborating with the Greeks, the latter had their own agenda. Somewhat duplicitously, Manuel had sent emissaries to both Frederick and Adrian, and he did not mind which of them came to the party. He grasped the opportunity provided by the unrest in Apulia to try to recover the old Byzantine possessions on the Italian mainland. There was no reason for the Greeks to have supported the opposition to William with their money and navy if there was nothing in it for them. The Greeks were aware that Frederick had chosen to do nothing to thwart William's advance but instead had left it to others to do the dirty work.

While Frederick seethed in Germany, Adrian remained in Benevento. He did not leave until July 1156, and it was while he was there that he received a welcome deputation from England. Henry II had assembled an embassy to travel to Rome to congratulate his compatriot. Henry's embassy had taken some time to get organised and the party would then have taken at least two months to travel to Italy, arriving at Benevento in late 1155 or early 1156. The embassy included the bishops of Lisieux, Le Mans and Evreux, and Robert of Gorham, Abbot of St Albans. The town of his childhood now basked in the reflected glory of Adrian's achievements and, whatever the true circumstances of his leaving St Albans, there were never any hard feelings. Abbot Robert would have been of similar age to Adrian, but it is unlikely that they had met before. Adrian's friend, John of Salisbury, also arrived at Benevento around the same time as the embassy but he may not have been an official member of it. Archbishop Theobald of Canterbury may have so arranged things that John would be his ear to the ground at Benevento.

News of Adrian's election had caused enormous excitement at St Albans. Abbot Robert eagerly prepared for his journey across the Alps and the chance to regain papal privileges for his abbey. He set off for Rome on 9 October, the feast day of St Denis, accompanied by the three bishops. Matthew Paris describes a difficult journey that Abbot Robert was lucky to survive:

> Leaving England they boarded ship. But as the sea swelled up they were soon at risk of submersion. The abbot, however, particularly invoking the aid of blessed Margaret, virgin and martyr, contrary to the expectation of all, experienced her protection in the shipwreck. He vowed therefore that her name should be inserted in the church's litanies to be honoured more readily. Landing safely, therefore, and afterwards travelling and avoiding many robbers' ambushes, they came finally to Benevento where they found the lord pope.[11]

All chroniclers of the age liked to include a miracle as an accompaniment to a venture as a sign of divine approval.

King Henry asked his delegation to conduct 'certain difficult royal business'.[12] Henry wanted a release from an oath that he had given to renounce the county of Anjou in favour of his brother Geoffrey, and which he now regretted. Before he died Henry's father had instructed the bishops and nobles of Anjou not to allow his body to be buried until Henry had agreed to do this as soon as he ascended the throne of England and Normandy. Henry claimed that this oath had been forced on him by the shame he would have suffered if his father's body had remained unburied. The pope agreed.[13]

Among their luggage the embassy carried copious gifts from Henry. There were also sealed letters, including one purportedly advising Adrian as to how he should choose his cardinals:

> And since the control and management of all the churches belong to the pope, let him, without delay, create cardinals of such a character that they will be able and willing to carry his burden.
>
> Since an unworthy clergy is a hindrance to the churches, let him watch with great care that no unworthy person may receive from him an ecclesiastical dignity or living.
>
> The pope is urged to gird himself up for the reconquest of the Holy Land, that is, to make a crusade.
>
> There is a general desire that the pope should give aid to the Greek empire, once so illustrious, but now woefully devastated.[14]

Advice on choosing cardinals is ironic coming from a king who insisted on choosing his own clergy for the English Church, something which ultimately led to Becket's murder in Canterbury Cathedral. It seems suspicious. The Greek Empire was actually in decent shape in Henry's time. The letter was likely written by an ill-informed student as a teaching exercise, perhaps as late as the fourteenth or fifteenth century, when the Greek Empire was indeed in trouble.

From his luggage Abbot Robert drew out his own gifts for Adrian, including substantial amounts of gold and silver, three mitres and an elaborate pair of sandals made by Christina, prioress of Markyate.[15] Christina was a lady born of a comfortable Anglo-Scandinavian family who resisted attempts to marry her off by seeking refuge at St Albans, where she was professed as a nun. However, there was no convent at St Albans. Monasteries combining monks and nuns had been usual in western Europe until they were forbidden by the Second Council of Nicaea in 787, a restriction that took many years to take effect. It was only in the eleventh century that the Benedictines outlawed mixed monasteries. Instead, Christina founded a small community in Markyate, about 8 miles north-west of St Albans. The needlework of English nuns was prized throughout Europe and the sandals were magnificent.

Adrian was embarrassed by gifts and often followed the practice of Pope Eugenius by refusing them. On this occasion, after considering everything laid out before him 'with a smiling countenance', he 'accepted only the mitres and the sandals, because of their admirable workmanship', and declined the rest:

> He greatly commended the devotion and urbanity of the abbot and said jokingly, 'I refuse to receive your gifts because you refused to receive me once when I once sought refuge under the wings of your church and asked in charity for the monastic habit.' To which the abbot replied, 'My lord we were never able to receive you; for the will of God, whose providence directed your life to higher things, opposed it.' And the lord pope replied 'You have replied elegantly and courteously,' and he was pleased by the form of the response and added 'Dear abbot, courageously you can ask whatever you wish; his Albano cannot fail St Alban.'[16]

Adrian's play on the word *albano*, meaning 'white' in Latin, his seat when cardinal as well as being from St Albans, was indicative of his sense of humour and underlined his affection for St Albans.

Those gifts that Adrian declined were distributed by Robert to the cardinals and staff of the Curia. Paris wrote that Abbot Robert did this 'knowing that those Romans are insatiable sons of bloodsuckers, thirsting for money'.[17] This harsh verdict from Paris reflects his own partiality. In his writing he misses no opportunity to extol St Albans but like many in the English Church he had always resented appeals from Rome for funds.

Adrian proved that the abbot could ask for whatever he wished. The abbey's link to England's first martyr had always worked wonders in keeping it visible in Rome, but during the civil war of King Stephen's reign St Albans had lost its independent status and had come under the control of the Bishop of Lincoln. At the request of Abbot Robert, Adrian freed it once more from Lincoln's control. St Albans would be answerable only to the pope, a privilege shared by no other English abbey.[18]

Robert asked another favour of Adrian: he wanted the relics of St Alban to be returned to his abbey. He complained that the monks of Ely Abbey were claiming possession of them. Relics do not now matter much to Christians, but they were significant then, miraculous even. They were a magnet that attracted pilgrims to the shrines of important saints and brought an important source of income for abbeys; until the thirteenth century, St Albans was the main pilgrim attraction in England.

There may have been some truth in Ely's claims. There is a curious tale about St Alban's bones recorded by Matthew Paris in the thirteenth century.[19] At some point in the ninth century, Danish raiders attacked the abbey and carried off the bones to Odense, where there is indeed a priory dedicated to St Alban and where the sainted King Cnut IV was murdered in 1086. The monks of St Albans were distraught and one of them, Egwin the Sacristan, was determined to retrieve the bones. He saw an apparition of St Alban who told him where they could be recovered. The story goes that he travelled to Denmark, in mufti, and inveigled himself into the Danish priory, in time becoming one of their monks and eventually their sacristan. He discovered the hiding place of the bones and secreted them in a chest he had made, which he then gave to an English merchant to take back to St Albans, where there was much rejoicing on their return. Egwin too returned to the English abbey. Sometime later, fearful of further raids, the monks of St Albans gave the bones to Ely for safekeeping and it seems the Ely monks then refused to return them. Adrian had always believed that the bones of St Alban were at St Albans and gave this as one reason for the favours he bestowed on its abbey. The relics have long since disappeared, although the church of St Pantaleon in Cologne claims to have them. In 2002, when the shrine to St Alban was being restored, the German church donated one of the bones back to St Albans.

✠ ✠ ✠

Abbot Robert was not the only friendly face in the English delegation to Benevento. John of Salisbury had visited Adrian at Ferentino in 1150 when he was still a cardinal and both were pleased to see each other again. Adrian enjoyed the company of a fellow Englishman and after the rest of the English delegation left Benevento he allowed John to stay with him for three months, during which time their friendship grew. Adrian shared intimate confidences with John, who recorded the conversations, giving us a rare insight into Adrian's private feelings.[20] Adrian had asked his friend's candid opinion of both himself and the wider Church, and John was bold enough to accuse the Church of greed:

> I related openly to him the evil uses of spiritual liberty, about which I have heard in various provinces. For it was said by many that the Roman Church, which is the mother of all the churches, presents itself not so much like a mother as like a stepmother than a mother of the others.

Even then stepmothers had an unfair reputation. John continued:

> Scribes and Pharisees sit within Rome, placing upon the shoulders of men insupportable burdens with which they themselves do not dirty their own fingers ... They accumulate valuable furnishings, they pile up gold and silver at the bank, even economising too much in their own expenses out of avarice.[21]

It was brave of John to be so outspoken to the leader of the Church, and shows just how close he was to Adrian. The pope then asked him for his own view, putting John in a quandary. He replied with courage that he agreed with the complaints, pointing out that Cardinal Guido had also shared these criticisms openly in a recent meeting of the cardinals. John added that he had met many honest clerics who did despise avarice in the Church.[22] Adrian did not take offence and replied in good humour with an analogy, just as he had with King Sweyne in Denmark in 1154. He pictured the eyes, hands and feet of a man conspiring to deprive the belly of its food, with the result that those limbs then found their vitality and powers diminishing. This was not a new comparison. It had first been seen in Plutarch's biography of Coriolanus and was later used by Shakespeare in his play about the same man.[23]

By now Adrian had been pope for only eighteen months and they had been stressful months. Adrian needed a sympathetic ear, and he opened his soul to John, who recorded the tribulations of a pope. He complained that the distress of his papal responsibilities far exceeded all his previous unhappiness. Adrian told John:

> The chair of Peter is full of thorns, his mantle is seeded throughout with the sharpest needles, and so heavy as to press and scarify and break the strongest shoulders, and his crown and tassels dazzling indeed because they are on fire.[24]

In a short space of time, Adrian had indeed been scarred by many thorns, facing up to challenges from Arnold of Brescia, Emperor Frederick and William of Sicily. Adrian had never sought the papacy and his first reaction had been to turn it down. He had been ambitious for learning but never for high office for its own sake. He knew where his duty lay, accepting the will of God, but he told John that he would rather have stayed in England or remained hidden from the world in the cloister of St Ruf except that he dared not disobey God. He admitted that as he had climbed from cloistered clerk to supreme pontiff his happiness had never increased. Only with the help of the Lord could he carry the burden imposed upon him.[25]

These honest words on human frailty would have rung true with John. He was familiar with the burdens imposed on a pope, having been in the service of Pope Eugenius at the Council of Reims in 1148 and probably having worked in the papal office for much of the time after then until 1153.[26] John would have been impressed by his friend's candour and delighted to find during his stay that Adrian was of the same reformist mould as Eugenius. Both popes wanted to free the Church from the influence of secular rulers and powerful families. John knew well that both the popes had come to the papal throne from outside the Curia and so were more alert to the wider concerns in the Church at large.

John was the good friend that Adrian needed in these tough times. John returned to England full of enthusiasm for the papacy and re-joined Archbishop Theobald of Canterbury's staff as his secretary from the middle of 1156.[27] He kept in touch with Adrian through correspondence, on his own behalf and for the archbishop.

IRELAND

Henry II's Intended Invasion

He sent moreover by me to the king a golden ring, adorned by a fine emerald, in token of his investiture with the government of Ireland.

John of Salisbury
Metalogicon[1]

While Adrian strived to restore peace where he could, there is a shadow that hangs over his pontificate. Although he never went to Ireland, for many he was defined by it, for there was a second item of 'certain difficult royal business'[2] that Henry II had asked his deputation to raise at Benevento. Henry was looking for papal approval for a conquest and conversion of Ireland.

Henry controlled more land in England and France than his predecessors had, yet he harboured ambitions to provide his younger brother William with a territory of his own, and Ireland fitted the bill nicely. Henry had held a council at Winchester on 29 September 1155 to discuss a plan. In attendance was his mother, Matilda, who vetoed the idea. Her opposition might have seemed to dissuade him, but it is more likely that Henry just kept his territorial intentions hidden.[3]

England and Ireland have long had a tense relationship and it has been argued that the problems between the two countries started with Adrian and Henry. It made sense for Henry to seek the approval of the newly installed English pope for his ambition for Ireland and to use the cover of expanding the Church's spiritual authority for a land grab. Adrian is said to have given the English king permission to subjugate Ireland, which he eventually invaded in 1171.

Adrian and Henry II acceded to their thrones in the same year, but they were quite different in age. Adrian was in his early fifties and already an experienced man of the world whereas Henry was only 21 and fresh to the scene. Henry was committed to implementing real changes and to improving the lands under his control, which stretched from the Cheviot Hills to the Pyrenees. This gifted young man saw that, to ensure success, he needed a structured system of royal government and he wasted no time in establishing it. While Frederick was busy reinforcing Roman law in his empire, Henry was laying a firm foundation for what would become English Common Law. His excellent work in this field has stood the test of time and the local assizes Henry established from 1163 still exist today.

Like all European sovereigns, Henry was conscious of Adrian's influence as the supreme arbiter of all disputes. Henry would have his own fierce quarrels with the Church, never willing to concede his own secular powers over the English Church, which led eventually to the brutal murder of Thomas Becket in 1170. Relations between English kings and Roman popes were always uneasy, with one surprising exception. In 1207, King John refused to accept Pope Innocent III's nomination of Stephen Langton as Archbishop of Canterbury. During a quarrel lasting six years John was excommunicated but in 1213 he and the pope made up, and as part of the deal John surrendered England to the pope as a fief. For the rest of his reign, and throughout his quarrels with the barons, John enjoyed Innocent's support. Nearly 400 years passed before the influence of the Roman pope in England was removed.

John of Salisbury wrote about a 'privilege' that Adrian had granted to Henry for the submission of Ireland. John is usually reliable and, soon after he learnt of Adrian's death, he wrote that Adrian had 'granted and given Ireland to the illustrious Henry II king of the English to be held by hereditary right'.[4]

John does not explain when this grant was given, and opinions remain divided to this day about what precise permission was given and the form it took. Many writers claim that the source of this privilege was a papal bull, called *Laudabiliter*, but John does not himself mention this. Bulls, or privileges, are named after their opening word: *Laudabiliter* means 'in a praiseworthy manner'.

The earliest text of *Laudabiliter* comes from Gerald of Wales, Archdeacon of Brecon, who was writing in the late 1180s. There is no mention of a 'hereditary right', and it appears that only John made this claim. Gerald nevertheless confirms that, during his visit to Benevento, Adrian had handed to John a gold and emerald ring as a present for Henry to be used as a sign of investiture of the right to rule Ireland. This ring was kept in Henry's royal treasury at Winchester.

Gerald's starting point was that the sovereignty of all Europe's islands was in the pope's gift, as provided in the 'Donation of Constantine'. This was the fourth-century document that endowed Pope Sylvester and his successors with temporal power in the western empire, and in particular over all of its islands, including Ireland. At this time in history, Gerald would not have known that the 'Donation' was a fake. Indeed, it had been relied on by many popes, most recently by Pope Urban II to justify granting Corsica to the Bishop of Pisa in 1090. Adrian too would have sincerely believed that Ireland was a freehold of the Church transferred from the Roman Emperor, even though Ireland was one of the few parts of Europe that had never been conquered by Rome.

Gerald's writing is the only record of *Laudabiliter* and no copy of it has been found in the papal archives, hence the mystery as to whether it ever really existed. Gerald later claimed that Adrian had written to King Henry in response to his request to enter Ireland with his support and so that the king could enlarge the boundaries of the Church.[5] However, the well-connected Gerald may have been partial and writing with hindsight. He was highborn, of Anglo-Norman and Welsh stock, and had close connections to the English royal family. He would have been keen to defend Henry's triumphs in Ireland. For this reason, his account, which omits any dates, is not regarded as reliable on its own.

Adrian is most unlikely to have given Henry carte blanche over Ireland. In 1159, when Louis of France and Henry of England together sought Adrian's blessing for a proposed invasion of Castile, Adrian had declined, requiring the prior consultation of the Church and people of Spain. This approach is more typical of Adrian's caution. If Adrian did in any way endorse Henry's submission of Ireland, it was likely to have been conditional on winning the support of the Irish. Had Ireland not already been Christianised then Adrian might well have given the neighbouring Christian ruler encouragement to subjugate and convert the country, but this was not the case. Christianity had come to Ireland sometime before the fifth century from interactions with Roman Britain and the missionary work of St Patrick. Only recently Pope Eugenius had drawn Ireland closer to Rome by establishing an archdiocese in Ireland, free of Canterbury's control.

The authenticity of *Laudabiliter*, as given to us by Gerald, has been a painful bone of contention and, even if it was genuine, opinions as to its true content have long raged. That it could have been a forgery is plausible. In an age when papal support was valuable to any enterprise there would have been an industry of forged papal privileges. In the early twentieth century, historian Oliver Thatcher reached a plausible conclusion about Gerald's report of

Adrian's letter to Henry. Thatcher regarded the letter as not a forgery in the sense that it was written to deceive, but rather that it was an exercise in Latin by a twelfth-century student practising letter writing. This was a well-known part of student training in the Middle Ages. Analysis of the text of the letter shows no sign of having been written with the care expected of experienced papal secretaries.[6]

Even if *Laudabiliter* is discredited, it does not mean that Adrian had not given some grant to Henry's embassy at Benevento in late 1155. It is likely that Abbot Robert of St Albans, who, as we have seen, was at Benevento as part of the embassy, did ask Adrian to confirm England's absolute possession of Ireland. This might have been based on a historical 'right' of England over Ireland, dating back to the legend of Arthur. The pope would have had no reason to endorse that stance and the Irish would also have a different view of this claim. Nor would Adrian have given away the freehold of an already Christian Ireland which was therefore entitled to papal protection.

Abbot Robert must not have succeeded in this request for confirmation, something Matthew Paris never mentioned in his writings, hiding a failure by a fellow monk of St Albans. John of Salisbury, who had been at Benevento at the same time and had stayed on with Adrian, would have been aware of Robert's failure on this point. It was perhaps John who stepped in with a compromise. He could have persuaded Adrian to make a lesser grant, offering Ireland to Henry as a feudal possession. This would explain the gift of the gold and emerald ring to Henry as a sign that, in Ireland, Henry would be the pope's man. This is exactly what happened a little later when the King of the Isle of Man gave his kingdom to Pope Honorius III in 1219, receiving it back as a fief from the pope, sealed by the gift from the pope of a gold ring.[7]

If that had been the case, Adrian's grant of a feudal right was never going to be acceptable to Henry, who knew all about the difficulties that came with fiefs. Most of his French possessions were held as a fief from the King of France and they had given him no end of trouble. Worse still, accepting Ireland as a fief would have meant to accept that England too, as an island, was a papal possession held by him only as fief. Henry could not possibly have tolerated that. In any event a fief did not come into effect unless and until there had been a formal investiture. Henry kept the pope's token ring, but he never formally sought to be invested, and certainly never swore homage to Adrian for Ireland as practice then would have required. Henry wanted to hold Ireland absolutely and not as a papal vassal.

Not only was the authenticity of *Laudabiliter* called into question, but there were also claims of a conspiracy. According to some rumours, the See of Canterbury, not pleased that it had lost authority over the Irish Church at the Synod of Kells in March 1152, might, unbeknown to him, have used John of Salisbury on its own behalf, intent as it was on reclaiming its authority over the Irish Church. Such a plot is not impossible, but there are no reliable records to confirm it and this is a conspiracy too far.

Ironically, John's attempt to help Henry's claim to Ireland at Benevento annoyed Henry, who resented John's closeness to the pope and perceived their friendship as a threat to his own authority. The villain of this enmity was Bishop Arnulf of Lisieux, who had also been part of the delegation visiting the pope at Benevento. Arnulf did have the ear of the king and had indeed warned Henry against John's close friendship with the pope. Henry was not willing to accept the implication that the papacy had the freehold of Ireland, and his position would have been that he had only been seeking papal approval to enforce his pre-existing right to Irish sovereignty. For John to imply that Adrian, an Englishman of low birth, should treat King Henry as his vassal was completely unacceptable. John paid the price as the messenger who upset his king and was excluded from Henry's circle in the summer of 1156. John appealed to Adrian for help, complaining that Arnulf had falsely denounced him to the king and to the Archbishop of Canterbury.[8] Reconciliation with the king only came in summer 1157 after a direct intervention on his behalf by Adrian.[9]

Henry's wish to subjugate Ireland was real enough. Both William the Conqueror and Henry I would have done so had they not had their hands full in dealing with internal unrest. In the event, Henry's aim was thwarted for a similar reason. The troops that he had earmarked for an Irish invasion had to respond to another emergency: in 1156 he needed them in France to put down his brother Geoffrey's rebellion in Poitou and Anjou. The intention to install Henry's younger brother William in Ireland, first discussed at the council at Winchester in September 1155, had been deferred but not dropped. Ireland remained on Henry's agenda. Writing in the late 1180s, after Henry's invasion of Ireland in 1171, Gerald of Wales says that Henry sent messengers to Adrian's successor, Pope Alexander III, this time getting ratification of his right to rule over the Irish.[10] Gerald was again being partial in seeking to justify Henry's invasion.

Papal privilege was never a claim that Henry himself made. When he invaded in 1171 he never justified it by reference to a grant by Adrian and would never have wanted to accept that he was in Ireland as the vassal of the pope. Adrian certainly made some kind of grant to Henry around 1155–56 but it is too big a leap to suggest that Henry's 1171 invasion was a direct consequence of whatever Adrian had done.

Henry's invasion was a direct consequence of later events. Richard, Earl of Striguil, 'Strongbow', had crossed to Ireland in 1170 in defiance of Henry and with 12,000 men, intent on forging an independent kingdom for himself in Leinster. By 1171 Ireland was in turmoil and the opportunistic Strongbow had become a threat. Henry needed to enforce his own authority before Strongbow took root. It also suited Henry to be away from England at that time to avoid the papal legation on its way to excommunicate him for Becket's murder in December 1170.

Henry was recognised as the legitimate ruler of Ireland by much of the Irish Church, including the bishops of Waterford, Dublin and Cashel. They did this at the request of Diarmait Mac Murchada, the King of Leinster, who owed Henry a favour. In 1167 Diarmait had been deposed by the High King of Ireland, Rory O'Connor, but Henry intervened on his behalf and reinstated him on his throne. Now was the time to return the favour and Diarmait honoured his obligation.

This public recognition of Henry was made without any reference by either king or bishops to *Laudabiliter* or any other papal authority. Henry became the Lord of Ireland and claimed the whole island but, in reality, his rule only extended to the 'Pale' around Dublin and some provincial towns, including Cork, Limerick, Waterford and Wexford. The rest of the island, 'beyond the Pale', remained under the control of various Gaelic chiefs.

Diarmait died in 1171 and Henry then allowed Strongbow to hold Leinster as his fief. Henry's successors used the title 'Lord of Ireland' until 1541, when Henry VIII first styled himself 'King of Ireland'.

One year after Henry's invasion, in 1172, Adrian's successor Pope Alexander confirmed Henry as Lord of Ireland, which is doubly surprising since it was only two years after Becket's murder, and it was in spite of the fact that Henry had initially given his support to Alexander's rival, Antipope Octavian, in the papal election of 1159. Unlike Adrian, Alexander knew Henry well and he must have forgiven Henry for Becket's murder and for supporting the anti-pope by then.

Rebellion resurfaced in Ireland in 1175 and Henry felt the need to bolster his authority by papal support from Pope Alexander. That Henry sought support on this occasion, rather than permission, also suggests that papal support was all Henry had ever sought for his ventures in Ireland.

Any grant from Adrian played no significant part in Henry's invasion of Ireland. Nonetheless, the Irish would continue to regard Adrian's supposed *Laudabiliter* as the starting point for English claims over Ireland and the contentious issue would run for hundreds of years. Some 140 years after

Henry's invasion in 1171, Robert the Bruce, fresh from his victory at the Battle of Bannockburn, sent an army under his younger brother Edward to invade Ireland and drive out the Anglo-Norman settlers. During the 1315–18 campaign, Edward had the support of Tyrone Domnall Ó Néill, who had been troubled by Norman incursions to the south and east of his lands. In 1317 Ó Néill asked the recently installed Pope John XXII to revoke *Laudabiliter*, writing that Adrian deserved to be called Anti-Christ rather than true pope.[11] The Irish Church backed up Ó Néill, claiming that King Henry II had misled Pope Adrian and that, rather than giving away Ireland, Adrian should have taken away from Henry the kingdom that he already had.[12] Despite this indignant and impassioned plea, Pope John ignored the request and Edward Bruce's campaign eventually failed.

Feelings have run high ever since, and the arguments have been nuanced. Some Catholics in Ireland could not accept that according to Gerald their pope could have described Ireland as barbarous and needing freeing from vice.[13] Nor could they believe that the pope could have described Henry's ambition a 'pious and laudable desire'.[14] It follows that they could not believe *Laudabiliter* to be genuine. It must be a forgery. Other Catholic authors did believe Adrian was responsible for the following 700 years of unhappy history of Anglo-Irish relationships. Some Protestant writers took pleasure in seeing the pope blamed for the humiliation of Ireland.[15]

In the end, the authenticity of the bull is immaterial. Even if it was a forgery, it is likely that in some way Adrian did grant conditional authority over Ireland to Henry, probably the feudal use of Ireland, a compromise that Henry never took up. What Adrian had or had not done would never have mattered were it not for the eventual conquest in 1171. Any grant Adrian made did not cause the subjugation of Ireland and the consequences were still invisible when Adrian died. While Henry never accepted a fiefdom of Ireland by making the necessary oath of homage to the pope, Adrian had acted unwisely in offering it to Henry. Nonetheless, it is unreasonable to hold Adrian responsible for Ireland's future troubles.

Whatever the reality of the situation, Adrian played his part in the grant of Ireland to Henry not as an Englishman helping an English king, but as a pope. He never provided any favours for the king of his native country. All popes of the era believed that they had responsibility for all the realms of Europe and any one of them would have given Henry the same guidance.

FERENTINO
Dealings with the East

It must be the work of the Pope to remove the slight obstacles which hinder the perfect union of the Greeks and the Latins.

Archbishop Basil of Achrida[1]

Adrian left Benevento soon after John of Salisbury had returned to England. By the summer of 1156 he reached Ferentino, about 50 miles south-east of Rome, staying at one of the several summer papal houses. In no sense was this a break for him. Even amid his campaigns, the hectic business of a pope was unceasing. This included dealing with matters relating to the extensive papal estates and no end of petitions brought to him on ecclesiastical disputes. Two of the many issues that followed Adrian wherever he went give a sense of the papal workload.

The first concerned Jerusalem. Sometime in August 1156, a deputation of Greek bishops arrived at Ferentino after an arduous journey from the Holy Land, bringing accusations against the Knights Hospitaller. Archbishop Peter of Tyre and no fewer than six suffragan bishops were led by Fulcher, the Latin Patriarch of Jerusalem, who was supposedly almost 100 years old.[2] The deputation waited until the good winds of spring 1156 and sailed to Brindisi, arriving there in May at the height of the chaos as King William of Sicily was trying to raise the siege of its citadel. They appealed to Asclettin to allow them safe passage to the pope using the shortest and most direct road to Adrian, then still at Benevento, but Asclettin refused to let them travel into this dangerous area. Instead they had to sail north to Ancona, on the east coast, and then travel overland to Ferentino.

Once they had found Adrian they laid out their grievance against the Hospitallers. Also known as the Order of St John of Jerusalem, the Hospitallers had started as a group of individuals from Amalfi and Salerno who were associated with a hospital in Jerusalem. Founded in about 1023 by Gerard Thom, the hospital was dedicated to John the Baptist and was established to provide care for sick, poor or injured pilgrims coming to the Holy Land. Christian pilgrims travelled in some numbers to Jerusalem, just as today Muslims endeavour to visit the Kaaba shrine at Mecca at least once in their lives. A pilgrimage to the holy sites earned a Christian complete atonement from all their sins. After the conquest of Jerusalem in 1099 during the First Crusade, the Hospitallers became a formal military religious order under a papal charter charged with the care and defence of the Holy Land. They were forced to move their base to Rhodes in the fourteenth century and next expelled from there by Suleiman the Magnificent in 1522, when they took refuge in Malta. The order survives in Rome to this day as a charity now known as the Knights of Malta, and enjoys observer status at the United Nations.

A cleric named William recorded the accusations in his chronicle written around 1180.[3] William, who later became Archbishop of Tyre, had been born in Jerusalem around 1130 and was of French or Italian stock. Jealousy had arisen between the Hospitaller Knights and the Latin clergy in Jerusalem, and in particular between Raymond, the Master Hospitaller, and Archbishop Peter. This was exacerbated in 1154 when Pope Anastasius IV exempted the Hospitallers from paying tithes to the local bishops. Their specific complaint now was that the Hospitallers were allowing excommunicated people to receive the sacraments. In addition, the Greek bishops were furious that the Hospitallers had built for themselves a large and elaborate headquarters which completely overshadowed the neighbouring Church of the Holy Sepulchre, the holiest site in Jerusalem.[4] Their complaint about excessive magnificence was quite unreasonable. The Hospitallers' main building needed to be large to serve its many purposes. In addition to taking care of sick pilgrims in Jerusalem they provided hospitality to other pilgrims, especially women, and it was also home to a complement of as many as 400 knights. The Greek bishops' grievances went further, complaining that whenever the lord patriarch gave a sermon at the site of the crucifixion the Hospitallers set their great bells pealing so loudly as to drown out his words. As if that was not enough, the Hospitallers were accused of loosing arrows on the church.[5]

Adrian listened to their complaints for three or four days and then found against the Greek bishops. Their long journey had come to naught. William of Tyre complained bitterly of Adrian's partiality:

The pope and his entire court had received the Hospitallers with great cordiality, but had on the contrary, repelled the patriarch and his people with contemptuous wrath, like illegitimate and undeserving sons.[6]

William, who was close to the patriarch, doubtless exaggerated the treatment of the visitors. He went further, suggesting that Adrian had been bribed by the Hospitallers to give them a favourable ruling. There is no evidence for this, though it was true that Latin patriarchs were not close to the Curia, whereas the Hospitallers were held in great esteem by the papacy. Adrian was naturally well disposed towards both the military orders in the Holy Land, the Templars and the Hospitallers, together in effect the regular Christian army guarding the holy places. However, in the wider Church the military orders were a favourite subject for attack. John of Salisbury was no fan of the Hospitallers and criticised their greed in England, accusing them of soliciting the wealth of generous supporters under the pretext of charity, abusing the generosity of pontiffs and arbitrarily withdrawing their churches from the control of diocesan bishops.[7]

As usual Adrian had not given his ruling without consulting his cardinals. He was never indecisive, but he was always a team player, taking every opportunity he could to ensure that he had their loyalty. While he gained their support, it may not have been unanimous and Cardinal Octavian may have dissented.[8] This dispute now appears comical, but it would not have been seen as such by Adrian, and the episode must have reminded him of the complaining monks of St Ruf ten years earlier.

A second major issue, and one that Adrian himself chose to address, was the Great Schism of 1054 between the Roman and Orthodox churches. He had probably been musing about a reconciliation ever since his unofficial alliance with the Greeks the previous year. The immediate cause of that schism 100 years earlier had been the pope's excommunication of the Patriarch of Constantinople, but the tensions had been there for some years.

One of many religious disagreements between east and west was whether or not it was acceptable to use unleavened bread for the sacrament of the Eucharist. While the west supported the practice, the Church in the east did not. Other disagreements occurred over the exact wording of the Nicene Creed and priestly celibacy, something that the western Church held in esteem. Politics was involved too. The Curia had always been adamant that the pope had authority over the patriarch and of course Constantinople disagreed.

Naturally, Adrian was always firmly of the view that it was pope not patriarch who was the true successor to Peter's throne, which would have made any rapprochement extremely difficult. Adrian would also have realised that, no less than Frederick, the Byzantine Emperor would ever accept that his imperial power was dependent on the pope. Nevertheless, there was a flicker of hope when in 1157 William of Sicily concluded a treaty with Emperor Manuel, whereby William conceded the eastern Mediterranean to Manuel and in return Manuel recognised William's rule in Apulia. This treaty may well have been brokered by Adrian himself.[9]

Whether it was or not, prompted by this outbreak of peace, Adrian lost no time in sending legates, Baldwin and Baldizo, to Emperor Manuel himself urging the reunion of the two churches. He followed this up with a letter to the leader of the Orthodox Church, the Patriarch of Constantinople Luke Chrysoberges, and a letter also to Bishop Basil of Thessalonica requesting the help of both to work towards an end to the schism. Adrian regarded the pope as responsible for all the Christian churches and he made this clear in his appeal to the Patriarch of Constantinople:

> To work to bring those who recognise themselves to be the Lord's sheep back to the flock of St Peter, who had undertaken their care at the Lord's command.[10]

Adrian's words might have been better chosen, and came over as insensitive to the readers. His pleas certainly fell on the deaf ears of the patriarch, but Bishop Basil did respond. He told Adrian positively that 'he will find a powerful auxiliary in the emperor whose will all the Greeks obey', yet added a mild rebuke:

> The Pope must not regard the Greeks as sheep that have gone astray. There is the same faith in the East and in the West, there is the same sacrifice.[11]

Adrian may not have won any favours with the patriarch when he had made an extraordinary appointment in Venice. Enrico Dandolo was a member of a noble Venetian family. Since 1134, he had been the Patriarch of Grado, an island between Venice and Trieste, although he was based in Venice itself. Venice had strong trading ties with the Byzantine Empire but because it was in schism with the Roman Church, Dandolo would not support Venice coming to the aid of Greeks defending Corfu against a Norman invasion. Bitterly, the Doge of Venice had expelled Dandolo to Rome in 1147, where he was provided with a safe haven by Pope Eugenius. After the death of the doge in 1151, Dandolo was able to return to Venice and soon after his election Adrian had consecrated him Primate of Dalmatia. Two years later, Adrian went further, authorising

Dandolo to ordain bishops for the Roman Church in any Byzantine cities where Venice had churches, including Constantinople itself. This remarkable precedent effectively created an eastern patriarch in the west.[12]

Had Adrian's papal reign lasted longer, he would have continued his efforts towards reunification. Had he managed to make headway with the Great Schism it would have been the defining point of his papacy and Church history would have been different. He never got the chance.

From Ferentino, Adrian continued north, first to Narni, the geographic centre of Italy, and by September and after a long and mountainous trek he reached Orvieto. This town occupied a spectacular rocky site and held an important defensive position. Adrian's arrival coincided with Orvieto's torrential autumn rains and its River Paglia flooded.[13] Orvieto had been outside papal jurisdiction for some time but Adrian brought it back into the Church's fold. He showed his gratitude to the citizens of Orvieto by establishing the Curia there and staying put for some time, which no previous pope had done. Boso writes for the first time about the pope's 'temporal power':

> For until his time, as everyone said, no Roman pontiff had entered that city
> [Orvieto] or exercised any temporal power within it.[14]

In October, he then moved a little further south, arriving at the pleasant town of Viterbo, only 50 miles north of Rome, a mere two-day journey away. In a period when Rome was often barred to them, Viterbo had become another residence favoured by popes, especially Eugenius.

Pleasant though Viterbo was, Adrian did not linger: he was eager to get back to Rome. Once in Rome, he concluded the formal agreement with Prior Rocco of St Costanzo, representing the citizens of Orvieto, whereby the town swore a lasting oath to perform homage and fealty to the pope, and to provide the pope with much-needed military aid. Adrian also had the chance to catch up with his friend from Scandinavian days, Archbishop Eskil, who was visiting Rome. As we will see, Eskil's return home would prove more difficult.

Rome was safer for Adrian now that Arnold of Brescia had been removed, but difficulties remained. The leaders of the Roman Commune were as awkward as ever, but Adrian was intent on finding an agreement with them and the dialogue must have gone sufficiently well because by 12 November he was able to re-establish his Curia in its official base in the Lateran Palace.

How Adrian managed to win over the Romans, we do not know. He had proved himself to be an effective negotiator, and he may also have been generous with financial support. The passage of time had also helped heal the furious reaction to the overthrow of Arnold, and the rebels would have realised that their prosperity depended on good relations with the pope. It would not have helped the commercially minded Romans to prevent his return to his city: they needed the pope to be in Rome. Whatever, there would be no more quarrelling with the Romans until the very end of his pontificate. This improved situation made Adrian much more comfortable, and it also helped consolidate his control further afield. He was kept as busy as ever, including with various issues concerning his homeland.

Pope Adrian IV: Pope Adrian wearing his papal crown, a modest Phrygian-style, white linen conical cap with a circle of bejewelled gold. (Hertfordshire County Council)

**Mediaeval
St Albans Abbey:**
When the abbey
church was
completed in 1116
its walls were covered
in gleaming white
plaster to protect
against the weather.
(Friends of St Albans)

The Merton plaque showing Breakspear and Becket with King Henry III: In 2012 the London Borough of Merton commissioned a bronze plaque for Queen Elizabeth II which shows King Henry III (1216–72) standing between Becket and Breakspear, 'both pupils at Merton Priory'. (Antony Dufort)

Abbaye de Saint-Ruf at Avignon: The barred-off chancel and bell tower are all that remain to be seen of the Abbaye de St-Ruf in Avignon. (Marianne Casamance)

The west front of Nidaros Cathedral: Breakspear chose Nidaros Cathedral in Trondheim as the seat of the new Norwegian archbishopric, an obvious choice as the resting place of the sainted King Olaf II. (Erik A. Drabløs)

Frederick Barbarossa greets Pope Adrian at Sutri in 1155: Barbarossa approached the pope to help him dismount but he did not do as tradition demanded and hold the pope's stirrup for him, the homage of 'strator'. (Peter1936F/Wikimedia Commons)

Coronation of Frederick Barbarossa: Barbarossa supported by two robed German dukes is crowned Holy Roman Emperor by Pope Adrian who is assisted by two clerics dressed in white. (Peter1936F/Wikimedia Commons)

Crown of the Holy Roman Emperor: The Lombard crown is octagonal, made of eight hinged plates of high-carat gold, each arched at the top, and studded with pearls and precious stones. (Gryffindor/Wikimedia Commons)

Frederick Barbarossa: A copperplate engraving of Holy Roman Emperor Frederick I by Abraham Bogaerts 1697. (Florilegius/ Alamy Stock Photo)

Castel Sant' Angelo: Castel St Angelo was built by Emperor Hadrian between 134 and 139 as his mausoleum and later came to be used by the popes as a fortress. Today it is a museum. (Adrian104/ Wikimedia Commons)

Tomb of Pope Adrian IV: Adrian's tomb is in the crypt of St Peter's. On the wall above his third-century red marble sarcophagus is the inscription HADRIANVS PAPA IIII. (Alan Howard)

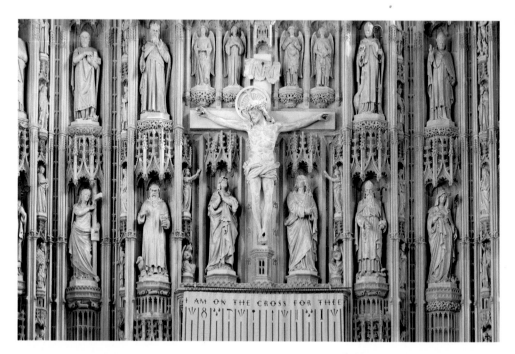

High altar screen at St Albans Cathedral: The Victorian patron of St Albans, Lord Aldenham, restored the high altar screen it to its present glorious state. Pope Adrian is on the extreme right on the top row. (Robert Stainforth/Alamy Stock Photo)

15

ENGLAND
Appeals to the Pope

We approve your just requests and receive that monastery in which you devote yourself to divine service, together with the adjacent churches and everything pertaining to that monastery under the protection of blessed Peter and ourselves and confirm by the privilege of this present document. Moreover ... the church of St Alban and everything pertaining to it shall be free from all tribute to king, bishop, earl, viscount, duke, judge or tax collector.

Pope Adrian IV
Incomprehensibilis[1]

Judging by the fact that Adrian told John of Salisbury at Benevento in 1156 that he wished he had never left England, you might think that he might have liked to retire to England. But popes, like monarchs, never retired voluntarily, although Benedict XVI broke this long-held tradition in 2013 and paved the way for future pontiffs to do the same. Nor did a single pope set foot in England until 1982, when John Paul II finally walked upon England's 'mountains green'.[*]

Adrian never returned to the land of his birth after he became pope. Nonetheless, he was responsible for matters there and played his role in England from afar. King Henry had naturally taken pride in Adrian's election and would have seen the pope as a valuable ally, but the transactions between the English pope and the English king were not always smooth.

---

[*] William Blake, *Jerusalem*.

Adrian and Henry never met, although Adrian had regular communication with English abbots on matters that concerned the king.

The most senior churchman in England was the Archbishop of Canterbury, and until the Reformation in the sixteenth century he was under the direct authority of the pope. From 1139 to 1161, which included all of Adrian's reign, the See of Canterbury was occupied by Theobald, the Norman former Abbot of Bec in Normandy who had been chosen by King Stephen in 1138. Adrian's friend John of Salisbury was secretary to Theobald from early 1154 and remained in that post under his successor Thomas Becket. John was present in Canterbury when Becket was murdered in 1170.

We know from John's correspondence that Adrian had a rocky relationship with Theobald. There had also been a running conflict between the archdioceses of Canterbury and York ever since the Norman Conquest. Adrian supported freedom for the Archdiocese of York from Canterbury's control and also gave York authority over the Scottish bishops, and neither of these decisions helped his relationship with Theobald. Nor did it help that the archbishop was closer to King Henry than to Adrian both geographically and politically. So much so that in January 1156, almost as soon as he had been elected, Adrian complained in strong terms to Theobald about his obstructing justice for the monks of St Augustine's Abbey in Canterbury and accused him of being in the king's pocket. Adrian's letter, probably drafted by John while he was in Benevento, complained to Theobald that English clerics' 'right of appeal is so smothered by you and the king of England that no-one dares to appeal to the apostolic see in your presence or his'. Adrian did not stop there: 'In addition, you are in every way lukewarm and remiss in dispensing justice to those who suffer injustice.'[2]

He then went on to accuse Theobald of being too focused on currying favour with the king to perform his duties objectively. Theobald protested his innocence in replies also written by John from France in the spring of 1156. John was playing each end from the middle and this spat may have been exaggerated deliberately since both John and Theobald were trying to demonstrate to a sceptical King Henry that they were not slavish to the pope's views. Henry had been greatly annoyed by Adrian's letter to Theobald and saw it as an unwarranted interference in English affairs. Theobald later came to learn, probably from John, that the Curia in Rome thought he, Theobald, was obstructing some of the cardinals as well as some junior clerics. Theobald was alarmed by this and sought to defend himself against the accusations. Indignant, he felt the need to complain that Adrian had unfairly favoured the monks of St Augustine's. He wrote three separate letters to

Cardinal Roland, Cardinal John of SS John and Paul and Cardinal Boso, declaring his devotion to the Church and asking all of them to reassure all the cardinals of this.[3]

Henry had been cross about Adrian's censure of Archbishop Theobald, but the relationship between English pope and English king remained civil. In the twelfth century it was customary for privileged boys at around the age of 7 to be removed from their mother's household and sent for the next stage of their education to an aristocratic court. King Henry himself had been sent away from his mother Matilda's household when he was 7, first to his father, Count Geoffrey of Anjou, and then three years later to the household of his uncle, Earl Robert, in Bristol. Henry's son, known as Young Henry, had been partly brought up in the Becket family home. According to Bishop Arnulf of Lisieux, Adrian too adopted this practice on behalf of his protégés, sending some to Henry's court for their education, which included training in hawking, hunting and arms.[4] We do not know who they were.

✠　✠　✠

We might think that opposition to the slave trade started at the end of the eighteenth century, but it has always troubled people, including Archbishop Theobald, who asked John to write a letter to Adrian about slavery.[5] He complained that the Welsh were carrying on a regular slave trade, selling Christians into foreign parts, where they became the captives of infidels. This was true but it was hardly only the Welsh doing it. The slave trade was flourishing then in Bristol and Chester although, unlike the south of Europe, slaves themselves were still relatively rare in England.

Adrian shared Theobald's concerns for slaves and other unfree men. While he could not abolish the practice, he did use his authority to implement changes to at least improve the lives of those in bondage. He was personally responsible for a change in Church law which eased the marriage rules for serfs. In the twelfth century serfs, while not exactly slaves, were not free either. They had inherited from slaves the requirement to obtain their master's consent before contracting a marriage. Gradually this became more relaxed and it was only when a serf married someone bound to another master that consent was needed. Adrian legitimised marriages of serfs in all conditions, albeit subject to a fine.[6] In answering a challenge to his ruling from Archbishop Eberhard of Salzburg, he pointed out that St Paul had decreed:

> There is neither slave nor free ... for you are all one in Jesus Christ.[*]

All, slave or free, were entitled to the Church's sacraments, so marriages between serfs should not be forbidden on any account. Marriages contracted against the wishes of a feudal lord should not be dissolved for that reason.[7] Adrian, the compassionate reformer, had taken a firm step for human rights, such as they were in the twelfth century.

✠   ✠   ✠

Adrian took a similar step towards fair play by addressing an issue that had been bubbling up about exemptions for privileged monastic orders from paying tithes otherwise due to local parish churches or dioceses. These favours had originally been granted to help Cistercians and regular canons with few resources to establish new foundations. However, once the monasteries had become established they became wealthy through their agriculture, and the exemptions from tithes jarred with the local churches. Adding insult to injury, as these wealthy institutions then acquired more land they claimed the same tax exemptions on their new holdings. Even the poorest of peasants paid tithes to their baptismal churches and Adrian, alive to the injustice, responded favourably to those seeking to reclaim their previous tithes. This had become an issue not just in England but also in Italy, Germany and France. Ever the diplomat, Adrian skilfully took the gentlest approach that he could and drew a line between virgin land newly cultivated by monks, for which the tithe exemption should continue to apply, and previously cultivated land, where it should not. The policy as applied to England was set out clearly in his undated ruling:

> Out of regard for discretion and justice we have decreed that the said Cistercians may keep tithes from the new lands which they cultivate by their own labour; but they must without delay restore the rest to the churches in whose parish the lands and properties are known to belong. We define as new lands those of whose cultivation no memory survives.[8]

Adrian had grasped the nettle, not being afraid to change the policy of his predecessor Eugenius when he thought he had been wrong. Naturally, Adrian's ruling caused a stir in the monastic orders. John of Salisbury, who was always concerned about greed in the Church, was pleased with Adrian's

---

[*]   Galatians 3:28.

clever solution to limit the scope of the privilege yet keep intact the original intention to help new foundations.[9] A pragmatic Adrian was applying his talents for compromise which had been burnished during his mission to Scandinavia. This reform was interrupted by his successor, Alexander III, who reversed the change for the Cistercians before Adrian's ruling was reinstated in full by the Fourth Lateran Council in 1215. Adrian's decision had been the correct one.

✠ ✠ ✠

Adrian was not pope for long, but he was kept busy writing many bulls, then known less formally as 'decretals', meaning decisions. These decretals were not the theological encyclicals of today and were usually rulings of a pope in direct response to questions and disputes raised by bishops and abbots on ecclesiastical business, often regarding property rights. Several of these concerned England, where appeals to the pope over the head of the English king were common. These appeals to Rome were forbidden 400 years later by the Ecclesiastical Appeals Act 1532, drafted by Thomas Cromwell and passed by parliament in 1533. This act proved to be the cornerstone of the English Reformation and by forcing it through Henry VIII was taking a cue from Frederick in claiming that England was an empire and so the English crown was an imperial crown.

Adrian exercised his judgements without fear or favour to England's King Henry, as clearly shown in a dispute between them concerning Battle Abbey. William the Conqueror had built this abbey close to the site of the Battle of Hastings in atonement for the slaughter caused by his invasion. He endowed it with the valuable privilege of independence from the Bishop of Chichester, in whose diocese it lay. After William's death the English bishops refused to accept Battle Abbey's continued independence and took their complaint to Pope Eugenius, who found in their favour. After becoming pope, Adrian concurred with his predecessor's verdict. At a council held in Colchester in May 1157 by the new Chancellor Thomas Becket, the Bishop of Chichester won the argument. Abbot Walter of Battle Abbey was incensed at the loss of his independence and turned to Henry for help; not surprisingly, Henry supported Walter and designated Battle Abbey a 'Royal Peculiar'*and by doing so earned a censure from Adrian.[10] These were still

---

*   A Royal Peculiar is a church exempt from the jurisdiction of the diocese in which it lies. Westminster Abbey is one such.

early days for both rulers and fortunately this disagreement did not provoke an open breach between them.

This was just one of many rulings made by Adrian concerning abbeys throughout England. Disagreements between abbots and diocesan bishops were frequent and invariably fractious. Just as at Battle Abbey, the bishops resented the independence of abbeys and in particular their exemption from paying tithes to their local diocese. On the other hand, all the leading Benedictine monasteries aspired to win papal exemption from diocesan control and, in return for annual tributes to Rome, they would receive protection for their rights and privileges. St Albans Abbey, where Adrian's life's journey had started, had regained its independence from the Diocese of Lincoln when Abbot Robert visited the pope at Benevento. Adrian always retained a soft spot for his first church and St Albans was not slow to take advantage of this. Adrian's decretal *Incomprehensibilis* had been granted at Benevento on 5 February 1156.[11]

A second decretal written shortly afterwards, *Religione ac pietate*, was sent to all English bishops instructing them to mark St Alban's feast day, 2 August, for special celebration.[12] All parishes were required to publicise the feast and offer indulgences for the remission of sins for pilgrims who visited St Albans. Two days later, on 26 February 1156, Adrian wrote to Archbishop Theobald of Canterbury, requesting him to support St Albans Abbey proactively. Together these grants gave an enormous commercial advantage to the abbey and Adrian went further still and granted to St Albans the patronage of the churches of Luton, Hartwell, Biddlesden and Potsgrave, which meant that their tithes now accrued to the abbey. These payments were set at one halfpenny from each plough in the province of Hertfordshire, due on the Friday after Ascension Day, and a further penny for each plough and a penny from each household on abbey lands every 2 August.

All this attention and support confirmed St Albans as the leading abbey in England and caused a significant increase in its community. There had been about fifty monks around 1150; by 1166 their numbers had almost doubled. During this period Abbot Robert found it necessary to rebuild the chapter-house to twice its previous size. He took the opportunity to inter several abbots in the central space between the rows of chapterhouse benches and, in a signal honour, Adrian's father, Richard Breakspear, was also buried there.[13]

Soon after Abbot Robert had returned from Benevento, Archbishop Theobald called a synod of archbishops, bishops, abbots, earls and barons in London to discuss general affairs of the English Church. Bishop Robert of Lincoln, already made aware of the new privileges of St Albans, pleaded ill health – doubtless a diplomatic illness – and took no part in the synod. Had he attended he would have been obliged either to accept the pope's ruling, and so incur the wrath of his own clergy, or to speak against the ruling and so suffer the pope's displeasure. In his absence the synod accepted the pope's decision. Predictably, the clergy of Lincoln were incensed, and unholy dissent raged between St Albans and Lincoln. Bishop Hugh of Durham was close to both sides and stepped in as honest broker to temper the arguing prelates.

Abbot Robert was highly pleased with the outcome of his trip to Italy and wanted to give further thanks to Adrian. The pope had apparently requested candlesticks, and Robert had a pair made of gold and silver and sent two of his monks to present them to Adrian. In return they secured yet another letter from Adrian reconfirming the independence of St Albans from Lincoln. Matthew Paris writes that these monks also returned with some relics of the 'Theban Legion', given to St Albans so that the monks would forever keep Adrian in their memory. The Theban Legion, commanded by an Egyptian Christian, Maurice, was an entire Roman legion of 6,666 men and, according to legend, every single one of them had converted to Christianity and been martyred in 286 for refusing to attack fellow Christians. This grisly event took place in what is now St Moritz in Switzerland. The coronation ceremony for Frederick had commenced at the altar dedicated to St Maurice in the Leonine City.

Adrian also gave to St Albans a pallium, precious sandals, an expensive ring, and other things which Matthew Paris called 'tedious to describe'.[14] One of these things too 'tedious to describe' was a chasuble, the outer vestment worn by a priest at Mass, which was so finely made that it continued to be worn at St Albans for a further 300 years. The chasuble was affectionately called 'Adrian'.[15]

Not everyone was as delighted as Abbot Robert about the abbey's independence. Gerald of Wales made clear his thoughts on whose side he was. He was extremely critical of the wealth and avarice not just of St Albans, but also the two other leading English abbeys, St Edmund's at Bury and St Peter's at Westminster. These three, wrote Gerald, by pride and love of excessive wealth had freed themselves from the churches of Lincoln, Norwich and London.[16] Adrian's latest generosity to St Albans was too much for the clergy of Lincoln, and once more Bishop Hugh of Durham had to step in to reconcile the clerics. The Bishop of Lincoln wisely realised that he would have to bide his time while Adrian remained pope before making any further complaints.

Adrian reconfirmed the privilege of St Albans in 1157 but took the opportunity to impose his own tax on the abbey. Perhaps on reflection he thought he had been over-generous to St Albans:

> As a mark of the reception of this freedom from the Apostolic See, you are to pay one ounce of gold to us and to our successors every year.[17]

This tax would hardly have distressed Abbot Robert: the privileges that St Albans had won were well worth the ounce of gold that it had to pay annually in tribute to Rome.

The clergy of Lincoln waited for the right time to challenge the decision of St Albans' independence. On Adrian's death they appealed to his successor Pope Alexander III, but to no avail. Undaunted, they then forced a trial at Westminster before King Henry in 1162. The king was not pleased that St Albans had agreed to make the annual payment to Rome of 1oz of gold but he too found in favour of St Albans, which in return agreed an annual payment of £10 to Lincoln as compensation.[18]

Even that was not the end of the squabble. Again, in 1186, the independence of St Albans was challenged by Hugh, the then new Bishop of Lincoln. Perhaps as a gesture of goodwill, he tried to visit the abbey on his way back from his consecration in London to his installation at Lincoln. Fearful that allowing Bishop Hugh to say Mass in the abbey would imply that they were conceding authority to him, and in a blatant breach of Benedictine hospitality, the monks of St Albans turned him away.[19] Hugh did not stand for this and swiftly excommunicated St Albans and its churches. Chastened, the monks of St Albans quickly repented. They had the last word, however, when Pope Clement III restated in 1188 that St Albans fell under the sole jurisdiction of the pope.

Adrian not only granted independence to the abbey at St Albans, but he also ensured that Abbot Robert was treated well. When he had been with the pope in Benevento, the abbot had boasted of the hospitality given to travellers at St Albans; being so close to London, there were many of them. Abbot Robert contrasted this to the poor hospitality given to him and his bishop companions by the monastery of St Benoît-sur-Loire while on their way through France. This prompted Adrian to write to the Abbot of St Benoît instructing him to mend his ways and to recompense Robert for the expenses he had incurred. This showed both affection for Robert and the importance Adrian placed on monastic hospitality.

✠ ✠ ✠

St Albans was not the only English abbey to gain privileges from Adrian. Byland Abbey, now ruined, is in Ryedale, North Yorkshire. It was founded in 1137 by the Savigniac order of monks and was taken over by the Cistercians ten years later. Other abbeys in the north such as Furness, Calder, Rievaulx and Newburgh Priory resented this parvenu and Byland's early years were spent in disputes with these more established abbeys. Like Rievaulx, Byland's wealth would come from sheep farming. On 23 November 1156 Adrian conferred a similar privilege to Byland, giving it the papal protection it sought and permanent title to all its present and future possessions. A well-briefed pope set out the detailed boundaries of its land and freed the abbey of tithes to the local bishop and state. It seems remarkable now that a pope in Rome had authority to exempt landowners in faraway England from local taxes, but sovereigns accepted this power in those deeply ecclesiastical times.

Rufford Abbey in Nottinghamshire also gained by Adrian's benevolence. It had been founded by Gilbert de Gant in 1147 as a daughter house of Rievaulx Abbey in Yorkshire. Adrian gave his blessing to the abbey in 1156 following which the abbey's lands increased. This expansion was done brutally, with the villagers of nearby Cratley, Grimston, Rufford and Inkersall all being displaced to a new village of Wellow. Adrian's bull protecting the rights of Rufford Abbey still exists today and is in the British Museum with its leaden seal still attached.

Adrian also bestowed benefits on St Mary's Benedictine convent at Neasham on the River Tees near Sockburn, County Durham. This was an established convent but nonetheless its ownership of the church there was challenged. Adrian intervened and confirmed the convent's title and furthermore exempted the nuns from payment of tithes and granted them free right of sepulture or burial. This bull, dated 3 February 1157, is also held in the British Museum. It is an impressive document on vellum measuring 2ft 6in by 1ft 7in. The seal on the bull, inscribed *Adrianvs PP IIII*, is slightly bigger than a modern £2 coin and is affixed by twisted strands of green and crimson silk.

Merton Priory also got in on the act of looking for papal favours. Its canons complained that the Bishop of Winchester was usurping their authority in their churches at Effingham and Upton, and Adrian intervened on Merton's behalf.[20] Merton has a link to the emergence of Oxford University by its establishment of Merton College, and Adrian can also claim such a link. Oxford town grew up in the shadow of what was first a nunnery, St Frideswyde, which had been founded in the eighth century. In the eleventh century it had become a priory of Augustinian canons and Adrian's letter to Prior Robert confirmed its rights, giving Oxford an early confirmed status.[21]

✠ ✠ ✠

Adrian dealt with more than diocesan disputes and was called upon regularly to judge bad conduct by clerics, and even murders. Three cases concerning England are described in the correspondence of John of Salisbury, the first of which shines a light on Adrian's sense of justice and the importance he attached throughout his life to living by the rules.

There had been a serious falling-out between the Bishop of Norwich and the Archdeacon of Suffolk, a man called Walkelin. The archdeacon was a worldly man and well connected in Norwich, but following some unspecified crimes levelled against him he had travelled to Benevento to appeal directly to the pope, probably while John of Salisbury was there. Adrian took Walkelin to task for bad conduct and ordered the Bishop of Worcester to hold proceedings against him. John tells us that Walkelin returned from Italy unreformed and committed more offences. While travelling, his mistress gave birth to a son and Walkelin had the effrontery to christen him Adrian. As if that were not cheek enough, his mistress was soon pregnant again and he instructed that if this child were a boy he would be named Benevento, or if a girl to be called Adriana. This was too much for John:

> O what a true friend of the Roman pontiff! Even in his sins he remembers him and labels the fruits of his wickedness with your name.[22]

Adrian set much store by clerical celibacy and was appalled that a celibate cleric should father children. Walkelin faced his charges at a council held by the Bishop of London in June 1156 but no conclusion was reached because the Bishop of Worcester was absent for some reason.[23] This episode shows Adrian's concern for justice, but despite his misdemeanours Walkelin survived the censure and remained Archdeacon of Suffolk until 1186.

John's second example case involved a judgement on theft that drew out Adrian's sense of mercy. Bishop Nigel of Ely was another English bishop who had to answer to Adrian. He had acquired some valuable items from a church in Ely; in an order issued by Adrian from Benevento in February 1156 he was told to return them within three months or face suspension as a bishop. Nigel did not comply and a year later, in March 1157, Adrian, now in the Lateran, generously gave him more time. Later still, in January 1159, and after an intervention on the bishop's behalf by Archbishop Theobald suggesting that the items in question were in truth recoveries of property lost during the storms of the civil war, the threat of suspension was relaxed provided he swore an oath in front of the Archbishop of Canterbury to restore the property.[24] Adrian's patience in this case was exemplary and showed how just and compassionate he was too.

In John's third case, Adrian was called to judge on a possible murder. Archdeacon Osbert of York was charged with murdering Archbishop William in 1154 by poisoning him through wine in the Communion chalice. An ecclesiastical trial was held in 1156, and even though Osbert's accuser did not produce any witnesses, Osbert was unable to establish his innocence. Not for Osbert was the concept of innocent until proved guilty applied. In a move that was either foolhardy or brave, he offered to prove his innocence by the ordeal of white-hot iron, or boiling water, or even by single combat,[25] gruesome tests that were increasingly frowned upon and which Pope Innocent III would ban early in the next century. The case was transferred to the papal court in France and Osbert apparently appeared there at some time. Adrian had been intending to visit France during 1158 but never did, the chaos of Frederick's second Italian campaign having commenced in early 1158.[26] No record of the judgement on Osbert exists, but we do know that he was stripped of his clerical status.

All three cases show Adrian to be a fair man. He was willing to dispense justice to clerics whatever their seniority and without fear of any repercussions for the reputation of the Church. This was more easily achieved at this time when there was total respect for the Church's teaching than in the twentieth century when unquestioning acceptance had dramatically diminished and too many clerical scandals were hidden for fear of damaging the Church.

These papal rulings were so important and valuable during Adrian's pontificate that they were often forged. The twelfth century was the golden age of medieval forgery and Archbishop Theobald was alert to the threat, seeing it as a peril to the Church, leaving guilt unpunished and innocence condemned.[27] A series of forgeries came to light during a serious dispute between Bishop Nicholas of Llandaff and one Robert, the son of his predecessor bishop. Robert had been accused of all manner of crimes including carnal vice, arson and robbery and was excommunicated by the bishop. Robert later appeared at Llandaff defending himself with letters purporting to come from Adrian. Theobald had the letters sent back to Adrian for verification and as a result forgery was added to Robert's alleged crimes.[28]

❊ ❊ ❊

Ever since the tenth century a pope had the more pleasant responsibility for canonisations. Before then sainthood had been less formalised, with local bishops governing the veneration of holy men and women in their dioceses. In 993 Pope John XV formally canonised the first official saint, St Ulrich of

Augsburg. In 1158 Adrian took pleasure in canonising an Englishman and a fellow missionary in Norway. We know little about Sigfried, the so-called Apostle of Sweden, but it is likely that he first went to Norway around 1000. He was probably an early missionary-bishop in Nidaros and then worked in Sweden from the mid-1020s where he became the first bishop of the new Diocese of Skara.

While in office Adrian took advantage of his Englishness to provide England with common prayers in the vernacular. Although there is no firm evidence, he is credited as the author of a twelfth-century English translation of both the Apostle's Creed and the Lord's Prayer written for the benefit of King Henry. The Lord's Prayer in Old English is easily recognisable:

> Vre Fadir in heuene riche,
> Thi name be haliid euerliche
> Thou bring vs to thi michilblisce
> This will to wirche thee vs wise
> Als hit is in heuene ido
> Euer in earth ben hit also,
> That holi bred that lasteth ay,
> Thou send hit ous this ilke day,
> Forgiue ous all that we hauith don,
> Als we forgiuet vch other mon,
> He let vs falle in no founding,
> Ak scilde vs fro the foule thing. Amen.[29]

In addressing matters related to his home country Adrian proved himself to be methodical and fair. His favouritism to St Albans is understandable and, that apart, his rulings were given without any English chauvinism. It is unfortunate that he never developed a rapport with his chief lieutenant in England, the Archbishop of Canterbury, and this is especially puzzling since both shared the support of John of Salisbury, and Theobald had had a good relationship with Adrian's mentor, Pope Eugenius. The archbishop led the English Church through stressful times, and after the difficult dealings he had endured with King Stephen it is not surprising that Theobald worked hard to keep close to King Henry. Perhaps it was his closeness to Henry that had made Adrian wary of him.

THE PATRIMONY
Strengthening the Papal State

Italy recognizes the full ownership, exclusive dominion, and sovereign authority and jurisdiction of the Holy See over the Vatican as at present constituted,
together with all its appurtenances and endowments, thus creating the Vatican
City, for the special purposes and under the conditions hereinafter referred to.

Article 3, The Lateran Pacts of 1929

Adrian had been busy with English matters but had so much more to do closer
to Rome. His wide travels had revealed to him the poor state of the fabric of
the Patrimony and the two years of relative peace between the agreement
with William at Benevento in June 1156 and Frederick's second foray into
Italy in June 1158 proved to be his only opportunity to give papal lands the
attention they needed. The pope, as ruler of the Patrimony, had become the
most important person in Italy. The Church's lands were the largest landhold-
ing on the Italian mainland, but there had been no shortage of challengers for
control of individual cities and their wealth. By the time Adrian inherited the
Patrimony it had been considerably reduced by a combination of the German
and Byzantine emperors, the noble families of Rome, and the Norman barons
who had established themselves in southern Italy and Sicily. The Patrimony
Adrian inherited consisted only of the modern regions of Lazio, Umbria,
Le Marche and part of Emilia-Romagna.

By the end of the eleventh century the papacy's accumulated wealth had
largely been dissipated in endless struggles, and the important relationship with
its main protector, the Roman Empire, had soured. In 1076 Pope Gregory VII

excommunicated Emperor Henry IV in a furious quarrel over the appointment of bishops and abbots. In turn, Henry tried to have the pope deposed.
Most German and northern Italian bishops remained loyal to Henry and
elected an antipope, Clement III. From 1081 Henry followed up with a series
of military campaigns, leaving Italy in a complete mess.

Henry entered Rome, and on 1 April 1084 was crowned emperor by
Antipope Clement. In desperation Gregory, hiding away across the Tiber in
the Castel Sant'Angelo, accepted the support of Robert Guiscard, a powerful Norman in southern Italy, who came to his rescue. However, some of
Guiscard's Sicilian troops joined in the sack of the city, and the alliance between
the pope and the Normans so incensed the people of Rome that they forced
Gregory to leave Rome altogether.

Rome had all but been destroyed in this fighting. Two important Roman
churches, San Clemente and Santi Quattro Incoronati, were so severely damaged that they had to be rebuilt.[1] The Capitol and the Palatine were gutted
and there was hardly a building still standing between the Lateran and the
Colosseum.[2]

As the twelfth century, began the papacy was still short of secular alliances
to secure papal control over the Patrimony but the obvious supporters, the
German Roman Emperor in the north and the Normans in the south, had
not always obliged. With papal coffers nearly bare, popes had to rely on their
own limited resources to hire mercenaries to hold and recover papal lands.
Papal authority in the south ebbed away after Duke Roger of Apulia had
become the single ruler of the Normans after overcoming Pope Honorius II
in 1128. More precious papal money was frittered away in attempts to buy
off various barons who, at any sign of weakness, seized control of unde-
fended territory. On the death of Honorius in 1130 the cardinals split and a
schism took another toll on Church finances. With the support of Bernard
of Clairvaux, Pope Innocent II won the power struggle against Antipope
Anacletus, but Innocent was only able to gain possession of the Leonine
City after Anacletus died in 1138. When Innocent at last entered Rome, he
found its properties in a terrible state of repair. He set about renovating the
churches as best as he could and restoring to them the lands that had been
stolen by the various barons.

This constant fighting, the limited funds and the papal schism had all slowed
down the recovery of the Patrimony and the rise of the anarchic Roman
Commune in 1143 had hardly helped. Ironically, at the same time as the fabric
of the Patrimony became threadbare the papacy itself had grown in international stature, becoming recognised as a power by rulers throughout western

Europe.[3] The pope's temporal responsibilities had grown too but St Bernard of Clairvaux was not the only one aggravated by this intermingling by the papacy of the worldly with the divine. He was mindful of Jesus's response to Pontius Pilate after his arrest:

> My kingdom is not of this world. If my kingdom were of this world, my servants would have been fighting, that I might not be delivered over to the Jews. But now my kingdom is not from the world.[*]

The political role of the Church would always leave it exposed to criticism and there is no doubt that it distracted the attention of popes in general, and Adrian in particular, away from matters of the divine. Papal wealth and power had been the major complaint of Arnold of Brescia and this difficult divide would persist throughout history. In the fourteenth century William Langland, writing an alliterative Middle English verse, *Piers Plowman*, blamed the Church's confusion of temporal and spiritual on the Donation of Constantine:

> Whenne Constantyn of hus cortesye holy kirke dowede
> With londes and leedes (teniments), lordshepes and rentes,
> An angel men hurde, an hih at Rome crye –
> Dos ecclesie this day, hath ydronke venym
> And tho that han Petres power. aren pysoned alle.[4]

Notwithstanding Bernard's misgivings, Pope Eugenius had made a start on restoring the Patrimony to its former glory. In the Concordat of Worms, Emperor Henry V agreed to restore to the Church its possessions including the powerful monastery of Farfa and its twenty-seven *castra*, or forts. Not all its previous holdings had been recovered so Eugenius resumed the post-Worms papal policy of purchasing *castra* to defend the Patrimony. Thanks to him, the papacy's hold on its lands and its financial affairs had improved a little by the start of Adrian's reign. Adrian was not himself a worldly man, but he never doubted his obligation to manage the temporal side of the Church and not just the spiritual. Continuing where Eugenius left off, he set out to recover control of more of the lost territories.

Adrian concentrated on further fortification of the Patrimony. He took direct control of the individual *castra* he acquired, naming them 'special fortresses of the Church'.[5] Some had long been deserted and were in a bad state

---

[*] John 18:36.

of neglect. Following the practice of previous popes, once the abandoned buildings had been purchased Adrian sought out new tenants. He instructed them to restore the *castra* and where necessary he provided a papal subsidy to help them to afford this.[6] After the restoration was complete he charged the tenants an annual rent calculated on a graduated scale according to their means. In addition, he charged them *fodrum*, a hospitality tax, and asserted himself as their suzerain. In return for the *fodrum* the papacy agreed to protect the fort and defend it against challengers. The papacy would also have the right of first refusal in the event of a sale. This clever purchase and lease out arrangement helped to fortify the Patrimony at minimum cost for the papacy and provided the Church with an ongoing income.

There seemed less advantage for the tenants in these deals, but it must have proved attractive enough as even some sitting owners were happy to sell their strongholds to the papacy in return for the same package of protection. Like Eugenius before him, Adrian wanted papal ownership of the freehold of the forts to be acknowledged, but was then happy to hand them back to their recent occupiers, even allowing some tenant barons to take control of further surrounding land. He did not mind his vassal tenants being strong provided they were obedient. If they failed him he was quite prepared to take the forts back by force. Adrian had a passion for his faith but recognised the necessity of power and using it justly.

In this way Eugenius and Adrian had established a series of fortified strongholds throughout the Patrimony and Adrian now made good use of them. He spent half of his short papacy on the move around the Patrimony, partly due to his need for safety but also partly to address its refortification. Also, as today, the climate in Rome during midsummer was hot, and in the twelfth century when there was little sanitation it was positively unhealthy. As temperatures rose in summer Adrian would withdraw to the cooler hills, especially to Anagni, which is a little to the east of the current papal retreat of Castel Gondolfo.

On his journeys Adrian would not have travelled lightly. When he could not stay at the papal houses, tents or pavilions would have to be carried. His entourage could be considerable. On a visit in 1159 to the *castrum* of Sgurgola near Segni, 40 miles south-east of Rome, his team included Cardinal Boso, his chamberlain; Peter Gaitanus, his papal official; Roger, a sub-deacon; Rodolfo, Adrian's chaplain; Peter and Alexius, Adrian's butlers; Donellus and John Ritius, his papal doorkeepers; Bovacannus and Gisilbertus, the marshals; Malavolta, the constable, and many other servants from the pope's domestic household.[7]

✠   ✠   ✠

Adrian was an efficient administrator, and he set up a first-class team around him. It is a real skill to choose the right people and his appointments showed just how competent he was. A key player in his team was the experienced Boso, whom he had known since the Scandinavian mission. He became Adrian's *camerarius*, or chamberlain, in December 1154 and so right from the start Adrian had a reliable manager of papal finances. Boso was also head of the papal household. He kept good records of all the tax receipts, property purchases and was the paymaster of the papal troops. He knew his way around the papal archives and was able to help Adrian determine the titles to papal lands and so recover any lost papal dues. Boso's efficient records became the nucleus of the *Liber Censuum*, the papacy's financial record of property revenues. This book, running to eighteen volumes, became the most helpful source of the history of papal finances in the Middle Ages. Boso was more than a competent servant; he was also a loyal friend to Adrian and he was rewarded for all his hard work when Adrian elevated him to cardinal in January 1157.

The second key member of Adrian's team was the learned and reliable Cardinal Roland, who had first been singled out for senior office in the Curia by Pope Eugenius at the same time as he had selected Adrian. The intellectual Roland brought legal training to his office, having been both student and teacher at the blossoming law school in Bologna. Roland, originally from Siena, also became a close friend to Adrian. Eugenius had appointed Roland as his papal chancellor in 1153 and he filled the same role during the short papacy of Anastasius IV. Roland must have had some expectation of being elected pope in 1154, having been the chancellor to the two previous popes.

Another strong candidate in that election must have been Cardinal Octavian, who was well connected in Rome and a staunch supporter of the German king; he was the same Octavian who had been over-eager to greet Frederick in 1155. Neither can have felt any resentment towards Adrian and both must have voted for him since he was elected unanimously. For his part, the first thing Adrian did as pope was to re-appoint Roland as his chancellor. Roland, like Boso, supported Adrian in his work to regain the lost territories, as did two other cardinals, Cardinal Julius of Palestrina and Cardinal Hubald of St Prassede, the future Pope Lucius III (1181–85). Roland was well regarded in the Church and was elected pope after Adrian died.

Another key team member was Cardinal John of SS Giovanni e Paolo. He had been employed as the Rector of Campania by Eugenius, who had created the post especially for him. Adrian kept John in that office and his duties included the arrangement of all Adrian's journeys around the Patrimony.

His appointment was significant and ensured stability of policy at a time when the papal territory was being strengthened.

Adrian's appointments demonstrate his effectiveness. It was necessary for a pope to keep the number of cardinals up to strength. Since the closest advisers to rulers were often senior clerics, bringing some of them into the College of Cardinals created good international contacts, although Germans were rarely made cardinals because of the papacy's continuing conflicts with the Roman emperors. During Adrian's reign there would be about thirty-five cardinals at any one time, most titled after the twenty-five to thirty parishes within Rome plus the seven suburbicarian sees immediately surrounding the city.

Adrian created cardinals on three occasions, as ever first seeking the agreement of his existing cardinals. In January 1157 he promoted eight new cardinals including Boso. In March 1158 he appointed ten more, including one Cardinal Walter, whom he assigned to his own former See of Albano. Little is known about Walter, but he is likely to have been a fellow canon from St Ruf. If so, Adrian could have known Walter – who appears to have been an Englishman – and he was certainly known to Thomas Becket. Nonetheless, before appointing Walter a cardinal, Adrian first asked Archbishop Theobald to provide a reference for him:

> The facts which you demand need but little enquiry; for they shine so brightly in themselves that they cannot be hid; so great is the brilliance of his noble birth and the glory of all his kin. For Walter, as we know for a fact, was the son of a distinguished knight and born of a noble mother in lawful wedlock ... Moreover for a long period he lived most honourably in the diocese of Chichester and adorned the fair fame which he inherited from his ancestors by the distinction of his own virtue, while he has always and in all things walked among us blamelessly.[8]

This was the kind of reference that Adrian could never have received for himself. Adrian now had a least one friend from his own days at St Ruf and Walter became a distinguished member of the papal Curia.[9]

Finally, in 1159, Adrian created twelve more cardinals.[10] The sixteen popes who served from 1099 to 1198 appointed about 300 cardinals so Adrian's thirty new appointments in five years was a higher rate than the average for that century. Two of the thirty cardinals he created became popes themselves: Ubaldo Allucingoli, Cardinal of S. Prassede, became Pope Lucius III in 1181 and Alberto di Morra, Cardinal of S. Lorenzo, became Pope Gregory VIII in 1187. Just as he had been chosen on merit, so too did he make his own appointments on merit. Adrian the manager was never criticised for appointing anyone incompetent.

Adrian worked closely with his senior team, always determined to keep all the cardinals onside in all his decisions. He did this as any good manager would, by always keeping them fully informed. Having been a regular canon, he had experienced first hand St Benedict's rules for monasteries which stipulated that if some important action concerning an entire monastic community must be taken, the abbot should convene his monks. He did just that throughout his pontificate, always taking the view that as pope he was first among equals, ever-conscious that most of his cardinals were senior to him in both age and experience.

He was wise to seek their support. A pope who lost the backing of peers could only be a weak pope. Gregory VII (1073–85), so like Adrian in many ways, lost the support of his cardinals. So driven was Gregory to enforce the laws of the Church that he would invariably take immediate action without consultation. Nothing unsettles a management team more than being out of the loop, and his cardinals' unhappiness turned to open rebellion in 1084 when Emperor Henry IV installed Antipope Clement III.[11]

That flaw apart, Adrian probably regarded Gregory VII as his role model. When Pope Alexander II died in 1073 his successor, Archdeacon Hildebrand, had already been wielding effective power in the Curia for twenty years, supreme in all but name. His election immediately after Alexander's funeral was a formality. Curiously Hildebrand had spent all those years in high office without ever having been ordained a priest, and this was done in haste and he was then enthroned as Pope Gregory VII.[12]

Unlike most popes of this era, although just like Adrian, Gregory was not of noble birth; he was the unprepossessing son of a Tuscan peasant. He gained the throne of St Peter after his long apprenticeship in the Curia and by his sheer ability. He was a man of conviction, eschewing compromise and, just as Adrian would show at Sutri, was never intimidated by the Holy Roman Emperor. Unlike Adrian, his lack of flexibility eventually failed him in his struggle with Emperor Henry IV. Gregory had however laid down a marker that emperors defy the Church at their peril.

Gregory was a reforming pope, standing firm against simony, the purchase of clerical offices which was then a common abuse in the Church, and enforcing celibacy for priests. He was an enthusiastic supporter of regular canons and their communal lives. Unquestioning obedience to the Church was his own constant guide and he expected the same from others. Gregory strengthened the hierarchy of the Church and it was because of his reforms that the cardinals who would later desert him became increasingly involved in the administration of the Church. Adrian had a lot to admire in Gregory but he could also see Gregory's mistakes and was not going to repeat them.

✠　✠　✠

Adrian had the skills needed for his role, and the team to help him achieve his objectives. He had no qualms about using the wealth that accrued to the papacy and, barring distributing some of the papal funds to curry favour with the Roman Commune when he was elected, he spent it wisely. However, Adrian had to find additional funds to meet his ambitions.

Unlike many of his predecessors he had no wealthy family supporting him. There was no explicit Church taxation; the main source of income was rent from papal land holdings. Earlier in the century feudal landholdings had become commonplace in the Patrimony, and feudal obligations included not just the provision of knights when needed but also payment of fief to the overlord, often the papacy. There was also regular income from the monasteries in the Patrimony, which had to pay dues in return for papal protection. The hospitality tax, *fodrum*, which was due to the pope and the cardinals when they visited the vassal territories in the Patrimony also helped.

Adrian and Boso were intent on taking full advantage of these sources of income to cover the costs of rebuilding. They applied their administrative skills to good effect, keeping meticulous records of what was being paid and what was not and chasing up overdue rents. Some further money was raised by property sales, but Adrian needed more to complete his purchases of *castra*, and he turned to Boso to sort that out. It is most likely that his *camerarius* raised the considerable sums needed through the payments of Peter's Pence and donations made by the steady flow of visitors to the Holy City.

Not all money from the pilgrims reached the papal treasury as the citizens of Rome expected their cut from these gifts. The city's economy depended on this and Romans developed a reputation for being aggressive in taking money from pilgrims:

> A people drunk with insane fury ...[who] would shed the blood of citizens even over the bodies of the saints, whenever they could not satisfy their lust for money.[13]

Another source of income for the papal treasury came through the courts. Archbishops and bishops had started to bring controversial questions to the

pope for settlement, and supplicants for such rulings or judgements on ownership disputes and spiritual matters had to pay a fee to the Curia. Finally,
when necessary, the papacy would raise loans from the major noble families
of Rome. One mortgage for 1,000 marks* was raised from Pietro Frangipane
in 1158 and secured against a number of papal *castra*, a loan not paid off until
1190.[14] All these sources added up to a considerable sum and it did not go
unnoticed. John of Salisbury's frank criticism of his friend Adrian was not the
first time that papal thirst for gold was deplored.[15]

Regardless of what people thought, this expansive income gave Adrian the
wherewithal to consolidate the Patrimony, build new churches and carry out
the obligations of a state, such as hiring soldiers when he needed them. Adrian
spent the money available to him in a relatively short time. Despite being
young for a pope, he was always in a hurry to get things done. It was just as
well that he did: although he could not know it, he would not have long on
the papal throne to achieve his ambitions.

Adrian caught up with overdue repairs to the Church's estate following
the fighting of the 1130s and the later neglect in the time of the Republicans.
He restored the Lateran Palace and other churches of Rome. He reorganised
the papal doorkeepers and guardians of the important churches in Rome, the
Lateran and the basilicas of St Lawrence and St Silvester. The new guardians
made a solemn oath:

> To be true to the pope, to guard the places committed to their charge during
> his life or at his death, and not to steal any of his property or that of the places
> entrusted to them.[16]

These guardians were placed under the direct control of the chamberlain,
Cardinal Boso. Adrian had built a new portico for the church of SS Giovanni
e Paolo and there is a memorial of him in that beautiful church. He raised the
wall along three sides of the oratory of St Giovanni in Fonte, making it the
same height as the nave. The Lateran Palace was given a long overdue restoration and the church of SS Cosma e Damiano was furnished with a new stone
altar. The roof of the baptismal fonts at St Processo, a chapel at the south end of
St Peter's Basilica had collapsed some years before and was rebuilt.[17]

Adrian did more than maintain churches in Rome. His projects included
building a new church at Ponte Lucano. He purchased 'two excellent mills
at Santa Cristina'.[18] These mills were on the north shore of Lago di Bolsena

---

*   A mark was a weight measure equal to 8 troy ounces of silver, today worth about £150.

and, for 190 pounds of Lucca money,* they came with ironwork, paddles and a water channel. He bought land at Policastra near Naples. He sent sculptors to Pisa to help in the building of a monastery.

The intent behind much of this work was to make travel around the Patrimony safer. Ever since Arnold had run loose in the north, Adrian had been eager to tighten control there and throughout all papal lands. As a frequent traveller himself he wanted pilgrims, clerics and merchants journeying to Rome to enjoy access to well-guarded roads. His network of *castra* belonged to the Church and the privileges the occupants had been granted were conditional on an obligation to defend the roads. The tenants had control of the surrounding land, but they were ordered not to block roads.

The counts of Calmaniare were feudal tenants of the pope for the land they held around the Lago di Bolsena near Viterbo, and their agreement was typical. The Calmaniare brothers swore an oath to Adrian on 11 October 1157 that they would:

> Watch over the routes to Rome, at all times and on behalf of all persons, particularly for pilgrims identified by their badges (*formae*), and excepting only publicly acknowledged robbers, enemies of the Roman church, and their own enemies.

Adrian also obliged them to 'observe a truce with local lords' and threatened that if roads did not remain safe 'the Rocca San Stefano would then be returned wholly to the right and dominion of St Peter'. [19]

Pilgrims could be recognised by the badges they wore, which were usually made of a lead alloy and represented the saint they favoured. In protecting travellers, Adrian completed a noble act, but he had also strengthened his Patrimony and so too his authority. It made good financial sense to facilitate access to Rome where travellers would leave gifts and swell papal coffers.

Tenants ignored at their peril these obligations to keep roads safe. In 1158 Baron Adenulf of Aquapuzza, near Sezza, south of Rome, thought he was strong enough to defy the pope. He had started to threaten travellers along the nearby Via Appia. Without hesitation, Adrian excommunicated him and sent Cardinal Boso with knights and foot soldiers to lay siege to Aquapuzza. Eventually the baron capitulated and Boso raised the papal banner from its

---

* A strong currency in Italy, and the equivalent value today of 190 Lucca pounds would be about £500,000.

tower. Adenulf was brought to the pope and the cardinals at nearby Albano barefoot and with a halter around his neck. This humiliation was the price he had to pay to be absolved from his excommunication. Adenulf presented Adrian with a myrtle bough, a military signal of defeat, and swore homage and fidelity to the pope. Having made it clear who was boss, the benevolent Adrian then returned Aquapuzza to him as a fief.[20]

Adrian particularly wanted to make the roads at the borders of the Patrimony more secure. He agreed to pay 300 pounds of Lucca to his new friends in Orvieto to help them secure the road from Sutri to the northern border. Adrian had tried to reach refuge in Orvieto in 1155 before Frederick's advancing army. Orvieto was a strong strategic position on the road to Sutri and Adrian was wisely anticipating future threats from the north. Orvieto became the most important city in the Patrimony north of Rome. The castle of Radicofani, also on the northern border of the Patrimony, had been made over to Pope Eugenius in 1153 and Adrian strengthened it by building a strong new tower within the castle. He purchased the fortress of Montichello and rebuilt the ruined *castrum* of Orcia on the junction of the Nar and Tiber rivers 'which was a den of thieves, and fortified it with a wall and towers, not without great expense'.[21]

In only a brief time, Adrian achieved much in the recovery of the Patrimony. He secured more *castra* than either Pope Eugenius before him or Pope Alexander immediately after him. Adrian did this while tackling serious threats both north and south, even though he himself was not settled in the Lateran during most of his papacy. This reflects well on Adrian and demonstrates the efficiency of his team in the Curia.

All these new fortifications came not a moment too soon. Emperor Frederick was stirring again, and Adrian was keen to support the opposition to the empire growing within Lombardy. The empire was just as eager to support opposition to the pope's temporal powers in the Patrimony. Frederick had no doubt about who was in charge. He was adamant that the Holy Roman Emperor ruled Christendom on behalf of the pope while the pope only had direct control of Rome and all spiritual matters. This was not how Adrian viewed it, so more trouble was inevitable.

BESANÇON

A Bitter War of Words

In the middle of the month of October 1157 the emperor set out for Burgundy to hold a diet at Besançon. Now Besançon is the metropolis of one of the three parts into which the renowned Charlemagne divided his empire for distribution among his three sons.

Rahewin
The Deeds of Frederick Barbarossa[1]

While Adrian was spending time and money strengthening the fortifications around Orvieto, the strategic heart of the northern Patrimony, Frederick was planning a second foray across the Alps, and with greater military support than before. As early as March 1157 he had commanded Otto of Wittelsbach to start gathering troops for a second Italian campaign.[2]

This time there was not even a pretence of friendship between pope and emperor. Adrian's accommodation with King William of Sicily at Benevento had put paid to that, even though it must have been obvious to Frederick that Adrian was effectively William's prisoner and had no option but to agree terms with William. Adrian now had to put aside his rebuilding work to prepare a difficult re-engagement with Frederick. He was not sure exactly what Frederick had in mind, but he knew that the emperor had punitive business to finish with Milan and was seeking to establish his control over northern Italy to compensate the loss of Swabian lands surrendered to his cousin. But might Frederick be intending to go further, targeting Rome and the papacy itself?

Although trust between the two had evaporated, Adrian did keep trying to reach out to Frederick. He had to: if it came to fighting Adrian could not match Frederick's power. In January 1157 Adrian wrote to a senior member of Frederick's entourage, Abbot Wibald of Stablo, a town in the Ardennes region of Belgium. Adrian asked for the abbot's help to mend the post-Benevento fences with Frederick, 'There are about the emperor ... certain men who strive by all means to extinguish devotion for the holy Roman church in his mind'.[3]

Adrian sought to improve the chance of reconciliation with Frederick by pinning the blame for their quarrels on the imperial advisers. The 'certain men' that Adrian had in mind were led by Rainald, Frederick's chancellor, but his tactic to make Rainald responsible did not work and his appeal to Wibald came to nothing.

Taking aim at Rainald was a reasonable ploy, but Rainald was far too close to the emperor for it to succeed. Frederick had appointed him as the Chancellor of Germany on 10 May 1156, some eight months after the first *Romzug*.

Rainald, born around 1120 and the clerical younger son of a Saxon noble, was clever and well educated, and later in 1159 he became Archbishop of Cologne. He was the typical career churchman that Adrian was not. As a staunch German patriot, Rainald, unlike the calmer Wibald, never sought to restrain Frederick in exercising his imperial authority, becoming Frederick's enforcer par excellence. Word of Adrian's criticism of Rainald reached Frederick and that only made matters worse.

Another bar to any meeting of minds between pope and emperor was the resurfacing of a longstanding issue, namely Frederick's recent second marriage, or rather the divorce that enabled it. Frederick had first married Adela of Vohburgh in around 1147, just before his departure on the Second Crusade. No contemporary source mentioned where or why they had married, and the union was short: they lived together for at most three years.[4] There were no children, which would not have helped matters since all rulers needed heirs, and in 1153 Frederick divorced her. This first marriage was never mentioned by Frederick's biographer, Otto, and it was clearly a touchy subject that Frederick wished to write out of history.

The Church never recognised divorce per se, but it did in some instances grant an annulment if it could be shown that the marriage had never been 'valid' in the first place. In royal marriages the reason often put forward for invalidity was consanguinity, which was convenient for Frederick as Adela's grandmother and his own great-grandfather were siblings, children of Emperor Henry III and Agnes of Poitou. Consanguinity may have been no more than an excuse, though, as some chroniclers accused Adela of adultery.[5]

For whatever reason, Frederick's marriage had failed, and he was glad to have the excuse to dissolve it in 1153.

Three years later, in June 1156 and still only 33, Frederick married again, this time to the 12-year-old Princess Beatrice of Burgundy. Marriage at such an early age is shocking now, but at the time it wasn't unusual for adult men to marry young girls. The special attraction for Frederick was that this match brought Burgundy under his control, giving him another power base. It also opened an alternative route to Italy from Alsace. Instead of using the high and cold Brenner Pass, he would now be able to reach Italy by the easier Soane and Rhône valleys.

Pope Eugenius had reluctantly permitted the annulment of Frederick's marriage to Adela in 1153. Adrian knew this and was unwilling to overrule his predecessor. Instead, he and his chancellor, Cardinal Roland, aimed their criticism at the German bishops for supporting the second marriage. Rome's stern disapproval had not gone unnoticed by Frederick and later proved a contributory factor to the papal schism that followed Adrian's death.

Just over a year after his second marriage, in October 1157, Frederick called a diet* at Besançon, close to the Jura Mountains and the modern border with Switzerland. Frederick's intention was to win public formal recognition of his new title as King of Burgundy. All the nobles of Germany were there along with representatives from Rome, Apulia, Tuscany, Venice, France and even England and Spain. Frederick wanted to put on a show and no expense was spared in arranging splendid festivities worthy of the occasion.

At this time Adrian was at the papal retreat in Anagni. He wanted a better relationship with Frederick but, unlike in 1155, he had nothing to offer the emperor in return. Frederick had won his imperial crown and their common enemy, Arnold, was no more. In any event, Frederick was still fuming about Adrian's treaty with William, and his criticism of his second marriage. At such a fragile moment, Adrian tried hard not to let himself be provoked by Frederick. He said nothing when he heard that Frederick had banned German bishops from travelling to Rome. When the emperor appointed his own man, Albertus, as Bishop of Verdun without consulting the pope, Adrian again bit his tongue. He did not want to give Frederick another excuse to return to Italy by force, yet he could only take so much, and another dispute soon erupted.

Adrian's friend from his Scandinavian days, Archbishop Eskil of Lund, had been exiled in France during Denmark's civil wars of the 1150s. These wars ended in 1157 and Eskil decided it was safe to return to Denmark, travelling

---

* A formal assembly of the Holy Roman Empire.

from Rome where he had been visiting Adrian. On his way home, sometime before the Diet of Besançon took place and while passing through Burgundy, he was seized by bandits at St Blasien, in the southern part of the Black Forest. His goods were stolen, and he was held in captivity for ransom.

It is not clear who or what lay behind this kidnapping. It is doubtful but not impossible that Frederick was directly involved, though he certainly did nothing to help Eskil. He may have long been nursing a grudge against both Adrian and Eskil for the earlier freeing of the Scandinavian Church from the control of the German Archbishop of Hamburg-Bremen in 1153.

While he had held back on other issues, Adrian could hardly ignore the plight of a senior churchman, especially one whom he had just appointed as the permanent papal legate to Scandinavia. He wrote to Frederick requesting the immediate release of his friend. Frederick ignored the letter. He felt he owed Adrian nothing and thought he could intimidate him.

In that, Frederick was wrong. He had misread Adrian's passivity on those other issues for weakness. Adrian had no personal fear of Frederick or indeed anyone except his God. He felt even stronger since the Treaty of Benevento in having the protection of William, and so better able to face up to Frederick. Still, he had not yet given up on the emperor. Although he stopped short of attending the Diet of Besançon himself, he sent the two most senior cardinals, Cardinal Roland and Cardinal Bernard of St Clement, ordering them to press hard for Eskil's release.

At first the two cardinals were well received by Frederick, but things soon turned sour. Frederick's biographer, Otto of Freising, was seriously ill and his chronology was being continued by Rahewin, who shares for us the dramatic events. In front of all the gathered dignitaries the cardinals opened their address to Frederick with the words:

> Our most blessed father, Pope Adrian and all the cardinals of the Holy Roman Church salute you, he as father they as brethren.[6]

This greeting seems innocuous, even friendly, but that is not how it was received. The familiar term of 'brethren' is harmless in a spiritual sense, but it was taken in a political sense to be impertinent. Not only that, but the term also implied that the emperor, like the cardinals, owed his position to the pope.

Things got worse. Frederick could not read Latin himself and Adrian's letter was translated and read out by Chancellor Rainald. The contents went down even more badly. Adrian naturally complained about the seizure of Archbishop Eskil in Burgundy and asked Frederick to punish those responsible, suggesting that he 'ought with great determination to arise and bring down heavily upon the necks of the wicked the sword which was entrusted by divine providence to you' with the authority invested in him through Adrian at his coronation, 'which was entrusted by divine providence to you for the punishment of evildoers'. So far so good. Adrian went on to remind Frederick of the favour he had done for him by his coronation:

> For, most glorious son you, should recall before the eyes of your mind how willingly and how gladly your mother, the Holy Roman Church, received you the other year ... and with how much pleasure she conferred the emblem of the imperial crown.

And to further hammer home the point:

> Nor do we regret that we fulfilled in all respects the ardent desires of your heart; but if your excellency had received still greater benefits at our hand.[7]

Adrian's use of the word 'benefits' was explosive. Today, words in communiqués after international conferences can be controversial, but seldom with such consequences. Using the word 'benefits' implied, not for the first time, that the German kings only possessed their imperial power by a 'benefit', namely a gift, from a pope.[8] According to Rahewin, the assembled German nobles were incensed:

> What had particularly aroused them all was the fact that in the aforesaid letter it had been stated, among other things, that the fullness of dignity and honour had been bestowed upon the emperor by the Roman pontiff, that the emperor had received from his hand the imperial crown.[9]

Adrian knew that this was a sensitive point. In 1155 Frederick had objected when he heard that a painting of Emperor Lothair prostrated at the feet of Pope Innocent II was hanging in the Chapel of St Nicholas at the Lateran Palace above the inscription 'Coming before our gates, the king vows to safeguard the City, then, liegeman to the Pope, by him he is granted the crown'.[10] Rahewin tells us that Adrian had agreed at that time that the offensive picture and its inscription would be removed. Yet, once again, the Germans saw in Adrian's letter the same suggestion that Frederick's crown was a gift of the pope.

The actual Latin word that Adrian had used, which so upset Frederick and his advisers, was *beneficium*. English is not the only language where words can have more than one meaning, and Adrian's intended sense appeared to have been lost in translation. In German, *beneficium* could mean 'fief', being land held in return for service to one's feudal lord, or suzerain. That the German Empire was an enormous fief from the pope was completely anathema to them. Some writers have suggested that Adrian slipped the word in deliberately. This is possible but unlikely. Adrian knew Frederick to be impetuous and that he was already gathering troops for his second foray into Italy, and the last thing he would have wanted to do was to goad the emperor unnecessarily. The cardinals, whether in ignorance or deliberately, did that for him. They poured fuel on the Besançon fire, asking, 'From whom then does he have the empire, if not from the lord pope?'[11]

This was too much. One of Frederick's senior nobles, Count Otto of Bavaria, unsheathed his sword and aimed a blow at the cardinals. Fortunately for them, Frederick stepped in to prevent bloodshed, giving the cardinals safe conduct to their lodgings. In a diplomatic breach, Frederick forcefully searched their baggage and confiscated the pre-sealed blank papal documents that he found, claiming they were intended for nefarious purposes. He ordered the cardinals to return directly to Rome first thing the next day. They returned empty-handed to Adrian, who was by now back in the Lateran Palace.

✠ ✠ ✠

Adrian's biographer Cardinal Boso says nothing about this incident at Besançon, possibly because he thought it reflected badly on Adrian's judgement in the same way that Otto of Freising had omitted all reference to the dispute at Sutri in 1155 from his biography of Frederick. We cannot be certain that Adrian deliberately set out to upset Frederick with provocative language, but the outcome at Besançon still represented a rare diplomatic failure for Adrian, and it all happened in the public gaze.

Adrian suspected that the situation had been deliberately aggravated by someone close to Frederick, and with good reason thought that it might well have been Rainald's handiwork again, in deliberately mistranslating *beneficium*. Rainald had respect for the Church, but he opposed the pope on political grounds and it would have suited him to embarrass Adrian and so reduce the influence of Rome on ecclesiastical measures in Germany.[12] Frederick's constant need for adulation was fertile soil for any such mischief. Ever since 1155, any suggestion that he was emperor only because it had been conferred on him by the pope had rankled Frederick and this pent-up anger had broken the surface.

Inevitably, there were consequences. After his summary dismissal of the two cardinals, Frederick felt the need to get the German Church on his side. He guessed that the pope might excommunicate him as he had William, and if he were to lose the support of the German bishops, his own position in Germany could be challenged. Just in case he was excommunicated, Frederick even went as far as secretly laying the groundwork for a new papacy based at Trier on the German side of the Alps, a first hint of the schism that followed in 1159.[13] Frederick wrote immediately to inform the German bishops of the dispute, reckoning correctly that Adrian too would soon be writing to them. Frederick was eager to get his side of the story out first.

The letters on the Besançon fiasco capture the power struggle between the two most important people in Europe, and Rahewin gives us both texts in full. Frederick's hard-hitting letter to the German bishops opened with his emphasis that his authority as emperor came directly from God not the pope:

> The Divine Sovereignty, from which is derived all power in heaven and on earth, has entrusted to us, His anointed.

Frederick acknowledged his obligations to defend the Church, writing, 'the peace of the churches is to be maintained by the imperial arms'. However, at the heart of the letter was a bitter complaint about the pope's behaviour:

> After we had honourably received them on the first day of their arrival, and on the second, as is customary, had seated ourselves with our princes to hear their message, they, as though inspired by the Mammon of unrighteousness,* by lofty pride, by arrogant disdain, by execrable haughtiness, presented the message to us that we ought always to remember how the lord pope had bestowed upon us the imperial crown and that he would not regret it if Our Excellency had received greater benefits from him.

Frederick closed his argument succinctly:

> Whosoever says that we received the imperial crown as a benefice from the lord pope contradicts the divine ordinance and the doctrine of Peter** and is guilty of a lie.[14]

---

* Luke 16:9.
** 'Fear God, honour the king', 1 Peter 2:17.

There is a contradiction here. If Frederick did receive the imperial crown direct from God then that could only happen through the action of the pope, God's representative on earth.[15] Frederick would not have seen it like that. He also remembered that his predecessor, Conrad, used the title emperor even though he had never been crowned by the pope.[16] Frederick's letter continued with a justification for his diplomatic breach in searching the baggage of the two cardinals, saying the sealed blank parchments would have been used to steal from German churches, 'as has been their practice hitherto':

> They were endeavouring to scatter the venom of their iniquity throughout the churches of the German realm, to denude the altars, to carry off the vessels of the House of God. [17]

It is difficult to understand why possession of these blank parchments was an indication of malicious intent, but it does show that Frederick had lost all trust in the motives of the cardinals. He wanted the German bishops to see Rome as a threat.

Back in Rome, Cardinals Roland and Bernard described to Adrian and the other cardinals their treatment at Besançon. The listening cardinals fell into two distinct camps. In the majority were the 'Sicilian' cardinals who had strongly supported the rapport Adrian reached with King William. On the other side, the smaller group of 'German' cardinals, who had always been uneasy about the alliance made at Benevento in 1156, were inclined towards humouring the emperor, believing that the Church's interests would be best served by remaining close to Frederick. These included Cardinal Octavian about whom Adrian's biographer Boso had complained of 'vomiting forth venom' at the first meeting of the cardinals with Frederick at Sutri back in June 1155.[18] The 'German' cardinals thought that Roland and Bernard had been clumsy at best, but in a heated discussion Adrian defended them robustly.

Adrian always worked hard to keep the cardinals united and this emerging split between the two groups would have concerned him greatly. Their division was an ominous sign. The diplomat in him did not want to make the imperial relationship any worse so he too wrote to the German bishops, keen to learn where they stood on the dispute and wanting their support just as much as Frederick did. His considered letter, unlike Frederick's, sought to calm things down, telling the bishops that the Besançon incident was 'a matter of which we cannot speak without the deepest sorrow'. Nonetheless, Adrian insisted that Frederick's treatment of the two cardinals was unprecedented. Although they had been received politely at first, the atmosphere quickly changed:

On the following day, when they returned to him and our letter was read in his hearing, taking advantage of a certain expression therein employed, namely 'we have bestowed upon you the favour of the imperial crown,' he blazed forth with such agitation of spirit that it would be disgraceful to hear and painful to repeat the insults that he is said to have hurled at us and our legates, and how dishonourably he compelled them to retire from his presence and with all speed from his land.

Frederick, writes Adrian, then took the extraordinary step of banning German clerics from visiting Rome, setting guards to 'forcibly call back those who desired to come to the Apostolic See'. Adrian tried to win the bishops over by suggesting that Frederick would not have acted as he did if only he had first consulted his bishops. He closed his letter with a direct appeal:

Although we are somewhat disturbed by this act, yet at heart we draw very great consolation from the fact that he did not do this on your advice and that of the princes. Hence we are confident that by your counsel and persuasion his wrath may easily be calmed.[19]

Adrian made no attempt to explain or defend his use of the word *beneficium*, which had caused the uproar. This might have been because he thought it would prove a fruitless debate, or perhaps, if using the word *beneficium* had been a deliberate calculation, he was hoping the German bishops would accept its use. Adrian's line, calculated to appeal to the bishops, was that Frederick had shown disrespect to the German bishops by not taking their counsel on a serious quarrel with the Church of God. His great worry, with good cause, would have been that if this quarrel got out of hand Frederick might seek to sever the Church in Germany from Rome. He might have been made aware of Frederick's musing of a new, alternative German papacy. It was only 100 years since the schism with the eastern Church and he would have been terrified of another schism happening during his reign. He had to forge a path which would maintain his dignity and at the same time keep the German bishops on side.

Such direct approaches of both emperor and pope put the German bishops in a difficult position. They had two masters and they could not please them both. Their starting point would be to support the pope in spiritual matters and the emperor in political matters, but that was precisely the difficulty: the distinction was not clear cut. The bishops were 'gravely disturbed and alarmed at these developments' and knew that this quarrel helped nobody. Their wish was to temper the row between 'your holiness and your most devoted son, our lord, the emperor'. Their carefully written response recognised the standing of Adrian's emissaries:

> Your messengers, those most prudent and honourable men, the lord Bernard and the lord Roland, the chancellor, venerable cardinal priests.

Nonetheless, claiming that 'our empire has been thrown into confusion', the bishops included a rebuke to the pope for the words that he had used:

> We dare not and cannot uphold or approve in any way those words, by reason of their unfortunate ambiguity of meaning, because they were hitherto unknown and unheard of.[20]

At least the German bishops accepted that the word *beneficium* had more than one meaning, but they felt obliged to remind Adrian of the German dismay at his recent pact with William at Benevento, which was still an open sore. The bishops closed their letter by asking Adrian to write again to Frederick, this time in more conciliatory terms:

> As for the rest, we humbly ask and beseech Your Holiness to pardon our weakness and, like a good shepherd, calm the high spirits of your son with a letter more conciliatory than that former one, that the church of God may rejoice in tranquil devotion and that the empire may glory in its sublimity, with the mediation and help of Him who is the 'mediator between God and man, the man Christ Jesus'.*[21]

Adrian understood the awkward position that the bishops were in and their need for diplomatic niceties and, though disappointed, he was not surprised that they positioned themselves closer to the emperor than to him.

Frederick too was willing to lower the temperature now that he had the German bishops on his side. He wrote to them again crediting to Adrian 'our father the reverence that is his due' but emphasising that it was the college of the seven prince-electors of the Holy Roman Empire to whom he owed his crown, not the pope, who only provided his final anointing as a formality.

Frederick continued his letter to the bishops by justifying his search of the cardinals' luggage, insisting that it was not done 'to show disrespect for our

---

*   1 Timothy 2:5.

most beloved and reverend father' but to prevent the emissaries using blank letters 'to the disgrace and shame of our empire'. Frederick denied that he had closed access to Rome:

> We have not closed the way in and out of Italy by edict, nor do we wish in any way to close it to those going to the Roman see as pilgrims or on their own necessary business, in reasonable fashion, with testimonials from their bishops and prelates.

Frederick had still not forgotten the Lateran Palace portrait of Pope Innocent and Emperor Lothair, adding, 'we shall not endure it'. In particular, he regarded the inscription below as degrading the imperial crown:

> Let the pictures be destroyed, let the inscription be withdrawn, that they may not remain as eternal memorials of enmity between the royal and papal office.[22]

The offending picture remained in the Lateran until at least the sixteenth century, albeit with the inscription removed.[23]

✠ ✠ ✠

Frederick had been planning his second expedition to Italy since early 1157 in order to quell the rising challenges to his authority in Lombardy, and after these latest exchanges he was intent on confronting the pope too. There was nothing Adrian could have done to stop him. At the beginning of 1158 Frederick dispatched his chancellor, Rainald, and Otto of Wittelsbach, the headstrong man who had nearly spilt blood at the Diet of Besançon, to plan for his arrival in north Italy. These two hardliners had a small force with them and they accepted the capitulation of the fortress at Rivoli, which protected the pass of Verona, along which Frederick's army would soon follow. They also won the loyalty and sworn support of German-favouring towns in northern Italy including Mantua, Cremona and Pavia.

Having been disappointed by the lukewarm support of the German bishops, Adrian felt obliged to address the disputed word in his original letter. With Otto and Rainald already in Italy and winning support in north Italy for Frederick, he wanted to draw a line under the Besançon exchange and prepare to deal with whatever Frederick had in mind. He chose two new ambassadors, Cardinal Henry of SS Nereus and Achilles, and Cardinal Hyacinth of St Mary, whom he deemed to be of calmer temperament and better suited to meet with Frederick's envoys, Otto and Rainald. The two cardinals reached Ferrara but by then Frederick's envoys had returned to Modena, 50 miles to the southwest. Rather than wait for the emperor's ambassadors to come to them, they 'made show of humility, hitherto rare, and went directly to them'.[24]

At Modena goodwill broke out. Rainald and Otto were satisfied by the cardinals' humbler approach and thought that Adrian's latest message would find favour with Frederick. They allowed the cardinals to continue their way and meet Frederick at Augsburg in Bavaria, albeit the boastful Rainald and Otto did this disparagingly by telling Frederick that 'God had so improved the state of his affairs that if he chose he could both destroy Rome and work his will with regard to the pope and the cardinals'.[25]

They also slighted the cardinals by declining to provide them with any armed escort. The cardinals had to rely on Albert, Archbishop of Trent, to help safeguard them through the dangerous Alpine passes. Their northward route from Verona took them through the valley of Trent and the unprotected cardinals fell into the hands of the robber-barons Frederick and Henry of Tyrol. The barons knew of the troubles between pope and emperor and thought they could seize the cardinals with impunity. They were wrong. Cardinal Hyacinth's brother, a member of a powerful Roman family, first offered himself to the barons as a hostage in return for the release of the cardinals. Then, hearing of the outrage, Henry the Lion, the same Henry who had saved Frederick's life during the fighting in Rome at the time of Frederick's coronation, intervened, forcing the two barons to release their hostage and return to them their stolen goods.

Free of their captors, the cardinals pressed on to Augsburg, where Frederick was gathering his main army and which they reached in June 1158. Frederick had already been briefed by Otto and Rainald and the cardinals, adopting a reverential tone, were received kindly. Calm prevailed, perhaps because each side was missing its strongman, Chancellor Rainald for Frederick and Cardinal Roland for Adrian. The cardinals gave Otto of Freising Adrian's latest letter to read out. Adrian first made the point that his emissaries at Besançon, Cardinal Roland and Cardinal Bernard, were 'two of our best and most distinguished brothers' and his letter continued with a measured complaint about the treatment of the two cardinals, 'Not without great surprise did we learn that they were treated otherwise than became the imperial dignity.'[26]

For the first time Adrian went on to give his direct explanation of the offending word:

For your heart was stirred to anger, it is said, by the use of a certain word, namely 'beneficium', which should not have vexed the heart of even one in lowly station, to say nothing of a great man. For although this word 'beneficium' is by some interpreted in a different significance than it has by derivation, it should nevertheless have been understood in the meaning which we ourselves put upon it, and which it is known to have possessed from the beginning. For this word is formed of 'bonus' (good) and 'factum' (deed), and among us 'beneficium' means not a fief but a good deed.

He then explained that the imperial crown was 'conferred' on Frederick in the sense that it was 'placed' on his head:

And indeed your magnificence clearly recognises that we placed the emblem of imperial dignity upon your head in so good and honourable a fashion that merits recognition by all as a good deed. Hence when certain people have tried to twist that word and the phrase 'we have conferred upon you the emblem of the imperial crown' from its own proper meaning to another, they have done this not on the merits of the case, but of their own desire and at the instigation of those who by no means love the concord between the realm and the Church.

Adrian was eager to end the dispute but nonetheless complained about Frederick's ban on German clerics visiting Rome:

As for the report that you afterwards ordered the turning back of ecclesiastical persons from due visitation to the Holy Roman Church, if it be so, we believe that your discretion, very dear son in Christ, must realise how unseemly an act that was. For if you harboured any bitterness toward us, it should have been intimated to us by your envoys and letters, and we would have taken care to safeguard your honour, as that of our very dear son.

He closed with a sincere plea for a fresh start between Church and empire:

Now therefore, as we have, at the advice of our beloved son Henry, Duke of Bavaria and Saxony, sent into your presence two of our brothers, Henry, cardinal priest of the title of Sts Nero and Aquilleo, and Hyacinth, cardinal deacon of St Maria in Cosmedin, truly wise and estimable men, we urge and exhort your highness in the Lord to receive them with honour and kindness; and your excellency should also know that what is imparted to your magnificence by them on our behalf has proceeded from the sincerity of our heart; and therefore may your highness so strive to reach an agreement with these our sons, through the mediation of our aforesaid son, the duke, that there may remain no seed of discord between you and your mother, the Holy Roman Church.[27]

Adrian's letter was carefully nuanced. There was no admission of guilt on his part, nor apology, but it did the trick. We can never know if he had used the offending word deliberately or whether it was no more than a faux pas. Adrian knew that Frederick was planning a campaign against Milan and would hardly have wanted to provoke him into going further and attacking the Patrimony.

The incident at Besançon has been used by many writers to show Adrian in a poor light, but it is more likely that the German reaction to his letter was deliberately engineered and Frederick's anger had always been calculated to make his point. Anne Duggan's paraphrasing of the sense of Adrian's letter to Frederick is quite plausible:

I've done all I can for you, but your failure to act against the brigands who have seized and maltreated an eminent prelate travelling back from the Apostolic See looks like deliberate contempt in response to our rapprochement with the Sicilian King. We hope this isn't true, since we gladly conferred on you the crown, and would willingly have done more, to cement the goodwill between the empire and the Church.[28]

At least Adrian had been smart enough, having dug a hole, to extricate himself and some sort of honour was maintained on both sides. The new legates had cleared up the mess left by the previous cardinals and they returned to Adrian with gifts.

Whether engineered or not, Frederick would have been pleased that the quarrel was publicly seen to have been settled before he reached Italy. Open hostility to the pope would have proved an unnecessary impediment for him in winning renewed loyalty from the Italian cities. However, Besançon marked the point when Frederick, egged on by Rainald, adopted a harder line in his dealings with Adrian. The relationship between pope and emperor was always fragile and it would have been better for Adrian if the Besançon dispute had never happened. To that extent, Adrian came out of the incident as the loser.

A clear casualty of Besançon was Cardinal Roland, the first papal envoy, who might have drafted the offending letter himself. Frederick would take much longer to forgive him. On Adrian's death, Roland became Pope Alexander III and Frederick carried the grudge against him for eighteen years by refusing to accept him as pope.

The battle over vocabulary had ended, but the underlying cause, the incompatible views of the relative positions of papacy and empire, remained. Adrian and Frederick both knew that a break between them had not been avoided, only postponed.

LOMBARDY

Milan Surrenders to the Emperor

His courage was truly English; it lay not so much in the fury of attack as in the obstinacy of defence.

J.D. Mackie
The Lothian Essay, 1907[1]

Adrian's hard-won accommodation with Frederick was both shallow and short-lived. The next dispute that he had to contend with concerned the property of Countess Matilda of Tuscany. This impressive lady had been a powerful ruler in northern Italy in the latter part of the eleventh century and was a significant supporter of Pope Gregory VII during his fierce Investiture Controversy with Emperor Henry IV. In 1076 she had inherited substantial territories that included Lombardy, Emilia, the Romagna and Tuscany from her mother, who was a first cousin of Emperor Henry III.

In 1089 Matilda, then in her early forties, married Welf V, who was not then 20 years old. This brought together two rich territories. Welf was heir to the Duchy of Bavaria and a member of the Welf dynasty, also spelt Guelph. This marriage annoyed Emperor Henry IV, who was a member of the rival Ghibelline dynasty, and it sparked a fresh outbreak of war between the Guelphs and the Ghibellines.

The Guelphs and the Ghibellines were rival German parties. Broadly speaking, Guelphs were drawn from the wealthy mercantile families and Ghibellines were those whose wealth came from ownership of land. They were loosely the twelfth-century equivalents of England's eighteenth-century Whigs and Tories. The Guelphs and the Ghibellines took sides in Adrian and Frederick's struggle to control the city-states of central and northern Italy. When Frederick sought to expand imperial power in Italy, the Ghibellines readily supported him; the Guelphs thus endorsed the pope. The Guelphs continued their endorsement of popes well into the fifteenth century.

Henry IV invaded Italy in 1090, intent on defeating the reformist papacy of Urban II. He needed to pass through Matilda's lands to reach Rome, and the two armies met in battle outside Mantua, in northern Lombardy. Initially, the Mantuan citizens stood by Matilda but were then seduced by additional concessions from Henry in their so-called Holy Thursday betrayal. Matilda escaped to her stronghold at Canossa, a castle in the mountains about 60 miles west of Bologna.

At Canossa, the tables were turned. This time Matilda's men, much more familiar with the high mountains, defeated the larger imperial army. Emboldened by this victory, several cities, including Milan, Cremona, Lodi and Piacenza, sided with Matilda and Henry retreated to Germany.

In 1095 Matilda's short and childless marriage to Welf ended but she remained a force to be reckoned with, dominating the territories in the north of the Patrimony. In that same year, Henry returned to Italy and attempted to seize Matilda's castle of Nogara, 60 miles south-west of Venice, but Matilda again forced him to retreat. In 1097, a chastened Henry withdrew from Italy altogether and Matilda then reigned virtually unchallenged.

Henry died in 1106 and Matilda came to terms with his successor, Henry V, who married one of the many other twelfth-century Matildas, this one being the daughter of Henry I of England. In 1111 Countess Matilda of Tuscany had been crowned Imperial Vicar and Vice-Queen of Italy by Henry V. Matilda did not hold this grand title long and died of gout in 1115. In 1645 her remains were reinterred in St Peter's, making her one of only six women buried in the basilica. Her monument by Bernini displays a sarcophagus carved with an image of the 'Submission of the Emperor Henry IV to Pope Gregory VII' at her castle in Canossa in 1077.

The Church was adamant that Matilda had bequeathed her extensive freehold lands to the pope, but no record of her will remains. In the vacuum following her death, the citizens in some of her cities took control, beginning the era of the city-states in northern Italy. In 1125, after Henry V's death, his successors continued to acknowledge the papal title to these lands and held them as fief, but Frederick was not so amenable. On succeeding to the throne in 1154, he claimed the Matildine lands back for the empire and immediately bestowed them on his uncle, Welf VIII, as part of the steps he took to win support for his own kingship in Germany.

Adrian and Frederick would now compete for control and ownership of the Matildine lands in Lombardy, and in particular their principal cities of Milan and Pavia. Together with Lodi, Cremona, Verona and Genoa, these walled cities had become comfortable with their effective independence and were not about to submit willingly to imperial rule. They did not help themselves by constantly fighting with each other, which over the years had allowed invading emperors to pick them off one by one. They had made their resistance to the empire clear enough during Frederick's first Italian campaign in 1155, and the whole of Lombardy had been restless ever since. It was the struggle for control of these wealthy city-states that led to Frederick's second foray into Italy.

Frederick had forced the cities of Lombardy to submit during that first Italian campaign, but they had never been cowed, and as soon as he was out of sight he was ignored. Adrian was adamant about the papacy's superior claim to these Matildine cities and it suited him to lend them tacit support as a bulwark against further German incursions. Frederick knew the Lombards to be hardy fighters and well remembered that in 1155 the men of tiny Tortona had resisted his imperial army for two months. Tortona's spirit of resistance was typical of other cities. The Lombards had good control of the road from the north to Rome, which gave Adrian some comfort and protection as he waited in the Lateran Palace to see what Frederick's army would do.

Ever since his accord with the pope at Benevento, William of Sicily's forces had been helping to guard Rome. Adrian was safe for the moment but concerned that when he needed Sicilian help, William might have had to draw his forces back to deal with any new Byzantine threats to Brindisi. If that happened, Rome would be defenceless and open to the Germans, so Adrian needed additional support from somewhere; even more reason for him to do what he could to help the threatened people of Lombardy. An anti-Frederick alliance was coming together.

✠ ✠ ✠

Milan took the lead in the defence of Lombardy. Its hardy men had never lost their fighting spirit, and in Frederick's absence since 1155, Milan had been rebuilding its alliances, by force when necessary. Brescia, Crema, Parma, Piacenza and Modena had already signed up for Milan. Lodi proved more difficult. Milan insisted that all the citizens of Lodi over the age of 15 swear an oath of loyalty to Milan. The men of Lodi were uncomfortable about this since only two years earlier they had pledged their allegiance to Frederick. They faced equally hard alternatives.

Adrian, worried by this in-fighting between his potential allies, sent two cardinals, Orditio of Rivoltella and Otto of Brescia, to Lodi to reconcile the two cities. The cardinals' sympathies lay with the men of Lodi and they managed to broker a compromise whereby the men of Lodi took the oath in favour of Milan, but included a clause whereby they swore obedience to Frederick. That this entreaty to the awkward citizens of Milan succeeded when others had failed showed the influence Adrian carried in Milan.

It had been three years since Frederick had last been in Italy and he was not happy with the news that reached him from his advance party. His prime target was Milan, as he had never forgotten that in 1155 he had not been strong enough to subdue the Milanese and he was still livid that they had insolently trampled on his seal. It did not help that in continuous inter-city wars Milan's ally Brescia had also overcome the emperor's ally Bergamo in 1156. Frederick had been further incensed when Milan ravaged Lodi first, in 1157 and again in 1158, and then subdued both Pavia and Como by force. Now that Frederick had more troops, and the benefit of the experience that he had gained on his first Italian campaign, he was keener than ever to defeat what he regarded to be rebellious cities. In anticipation of Frederick's wrath, Milan had spent more than 500,000 marks in preparing for his return, rebuilding its fortifications and bridges.[2] A day of reckoning could not be far off.

Chancellor Rainald and Otto of Wittelsbach, the envoys sent ahead of Frederick to Italy, had quickly forced Rivoli's surrender; on seeing this, the citizens of Verona, Mantua, Cremona and Pavia all timidly swore an oath of fealty to Frederick rather than fight. Northern cities were taking sides and Adrian watched with dismay, impotent to offer them any material help. Next, the envoys moved to Ravenna on the Adriatic coast, where they were not unwelcome. They discovered that agents of the Byzantine Emperor were again at Ancona, 90 miles further down the coast. Perhaps they had never left: Emperor Manuel still nursed his aspiration to regain a foothold on the Italian mainland. They were once more stirring up support for Byzantine control of the eastern coastal cities, notwithstanding their overwhelming defeat by William at Brindisi in April 1156.

Summoning the Byzantine agents to their presence, Rainald and Otto, backed up by a local military force, demanded that they explain themselves. The agents knew that Frederick was not far behind his envoys and that they needed to tread carefully. In fear for their lives, they denied any treachery and, after handing over gifts for Frederick, they were fortunate to be allowed to go free. Adrian had been loath to ally with the Greeks in 1156 but, aware of their continuing presence in Italy, he might now have had in mind the possibility of some deal that would reduce the threat posed by Frederick's imminent arrival.

Adrian needed to keep all his options open. Frederick's envoys succeeded in turning Milan's ally Piacenza and other cities to the emperor's cause, all of which agreed to provide troops to assist the siege of Milan and make provisions available for Frederick's approaching army. Both sides, Milan and Frederick, had done what they could in preparation for the forthcoming battles.

Frederick now took centre stage. He crossed into Italy in June 1158 with much more strength than before. He had drawn troops from throughout central Europe, fielding fighting Franks, Saxons, Rhinelanders, Burgundians, Swabians, Bavarians, Lorrainers, Bohemians, Hungarians and Carinthians, all 'valiant men, warriors in untold numbers, with varied equipment of arms, young men strong and unafraid of war'.[3]

Due to the sheer numbers moving through narrow passes, Frederick's army had divided into four distinct forces, which also made good strategic sense. Frederick, with his brother Conrad, Count Palatine of the Rhine, and Ladislaus, King of Bohemia, marched over the Brenner Pass, heading due south towards Verona. Duke Henry of Carinthia, Duke Henry of Austria and the Hungarians entered Italy further to the east, through the Val Canale heading south-west for Verona. Frederick IV, Duke of Swabia, Frederick's cousin, supported by men from Franconia and the Rhineland, crossed the River Splugen and entered Italy at Chiavenna, then headed due south direct for Milan. Finally, Berthold IV, Duke of Zähringhen, and the men of Lorraine followed the route Julius Caesar had taken, over the Great St Bernard Pass to Aosta and approached Milan from the west. For now Adrian himself was safe, ensconced at Sutri, but was alarmed by regular reports of the swarming invaders.

At first Frederick met no resistance, receiving support from those cities of Lombardy that had felt threatened by Milan's aggression. He reached Verona at the same time as the Hungarian forces; its citizens wisely persuaded Frederick to leave them in peace and instead attack Brescia, an ally of Milan. The men of Bergamo, sandwiched between Milan and Brescia, were also happy to join in the rout of Brescia, their traditional enemy. Cities began falling to Frederick like ninepins and Adrian could only watch in horror. Too weak to do anything other than surrender, the Brescians switched their allegiance to Frederick and agreed to commit what troops they had to join the coming assault of Milan. In the face of the host that Frederick had assembled it was impossible for the smaller cities to do anything other than submit.

Frederick was always a strict disciplinarian, and he had issued tough orders to his troops to protect Italian non-combatants. Keeping the peace was not just about winning over hearts and minds. He did not want to destroy the very wealth he was intent on controlling, but this afforded an anxious Adrian no comfort at all.

Adrian had always been aware of Frederick's strength, but only as the imperial forces gathered did the Milanese realise the magnitude of the threat and begin to have second thoughts. They sent envoys to Frederick in an eleventh-hour attempt to buy peace, but by now Frederick's army of 15,000 knights and even more foot soldiers had too much momentum. The Milanese entreaties were dismissed out of hand and Frederick ordered his men to encircle Milan.

His first check came on 23 July 1158 when he faced the Milanese army across the River Adda at Cassano, some 20 miles east of the city. Milanese knights held the west bank and Frederick's army the east. Torrents fed by melting snow had destroyed the three bridges over the swollen river and it seemed as though this natural barrier would let Milan carry the day.

It was not to be. King Ladislaus and Count Conrad found a place to the south of the fallen bridges where they thought the river was shallow enough to swim across. They succeeded in doing so, even though some sixty men drowned in the process. Those who had crossed triumphantly attacked the flank of the Milanese army, who fled for their lives back to safety behind Milan's walls.[4] Frederick gave chase, supported by the homeless men of Como and Lodi, who delighted at the prospect of taking their revenge against Milan.

At the beginning of August Frederick tightened the noose, moving his main force towards Milan. He again refused peace entreaties from the Milanese citizens. Just as had happened in 1155, some of his own princes were in favour of brokering a deal as they were once again exhausted by the heat of Italy and already wanting to return to Germany, but Frederick was not about to quit. Encouraged by the hardline Archbishop Anselm of Havelberg, and holding all the cards, he rallied his troops with the cry that Milan's rebellion against the empire was a just cause for war, and on 6 August the full siege of Milan began. Anselm died suddenly six days later and some Germans saw this as a bad omen.

Siege was the textbook approach to overcoming a walled city. Altogether the best part of 100,000 men surrounded Milan's walls, yet there were still not quite enough to completely cover the full circumference. The walls were old, dating back to the fourth century, and not particularly high, although the Milanese had recently added a moat, which helped to protect them further.[5] The defending knights, mostly Milanese, were far fewer in number, perhaps 3,000 with about 9,000 supporting foot soldiers. Normally, the defenders would have the advantage in a siege, and indeed the Milanese held firm and successfully mounted several sallies against the besiegers. Neither side showed compassion and captives taken by each side were executed mercilessly.

Frederick's own troops were stationed in front of Milan's main city gate, the Porta Romana, and they managed to capture the fourth-century Roman triumphal arch that stood just outside the gate. The room on top of the arch was big enough to house about forty men, giving whoever occupied it good sight either into the city or over the besiegers. The arch was too strong to be shattered by stones, but Frederick's accurate archers succeeded in picking off many of the defenders and the remaining few surrendered. Having then occupied it themselves, the Germans were able to hurl stones at the Porta Romana, but the defenders built their own wooden siege tower and responded in kind.

Despite holding their own, the capture of the arch marked a turning point for the defenders. The Milanese had seen the besieging army devastating the surrounding countryside and morale in the city was draining away. Some citizens, in particular Count Guido of Biandrate, who had welcomed Frederick to nearby Novara in 1154 during Frederick's first Italian campaign, could only see one outcome and argued eloquently for surrender and terms to be agreed:

> There is great hope for us in the mercy of an emperor who will not be angry
> with us to the end, unless we ourselves have defied him to the very end.

Count Guido argued that although the city's walls could not be breached quickly, famine and pestilence would make Milan's ultimate defeat inevitable. He pleaded on behalf of the children, wives and parents who all stood to lose their lives. Guido was no coward himself, making it clear that if necessary he was 'prepared to die for my people, for my city, and I shall gladly pay my blood as the price of your safety'.[6]

Guido was the ideal candidate to intercede for the city, as he had long been a supporter of Frederick and had been a member of his team at the negotiations which had led to the Treaty of Constance in 1153. His presence showed that there was a pro-imperial faction in Milan.[7] An anonymous poet describes in epic style this pressure for surrender:

> Now there is hardly room for graves, and dread
> And sorrow fill the city. God himself,
> Who used to favour us before, seems angry,
> And choirs of saints have left us and our temples.
> So listen to the way we should be thinking.

Since we could not retain the ancient honour,
And God himself opposes us, submit.
Let not our shame inhibit us from seeking
To make a peace and keep what we possess.
The Roman leader has the legal right,
If we but speak the truth, to govern us.[8]

With hardman Anselm now dead, the Germans too wanted to bring the fighting to an end. Adrian was desolate about Milan's predicament but he was at Narni, about 65 miles north of Rome, too far away from the action, and in no position to help either with the fighting or with any negotiations.

Guido's counsel to sue for peace won the day. Supported by a majority in the city who had no appetite for the hardships of a long siege whose outcome was inevitable, Milan capitulated on 1 September after a siege of twenty-five days.

Their surrender did not get them off lightly: Frederick, in no mood to be generous, exacted a heavy price. First, Como and Lodi were granted liberty from Milanese control, and Milan was forced to agree to rebuild both towns which they had destroyed. Next, he imposed a ransom of 9,000 marks and took 300 Milanese hostages, half of them nobles and half commoners, against the city's observance of his conditions, and whom he promised to release no later than Christmas 1159. Finally, every Milanese man between the ages of 14 and 70 had to swear fealty to the emperor. All Milan's market and transit taxes now fell to Frederick and the Milanese agreed to build a palace in the city for his use.

This was not enough for Frederick, who also wanted to make a show of the defeated Milanese. He was travelling with an elaborate tent, which had been a gift from King Henry II of England:

King Henry of England who bestowed … a pavilion, very large in extent and of the finest quality. If you ask its size it could not be raised except by machinery, and a special sort of instrument and props; if you ask its quality, I should imagine that neither in material nor in workmanship will it ever be surpassed by any equipment of this kind.[9]

There is a story behind Henry's gift. His mother Matilda was first married to Emperor Henry V of Germany. When she left Germany to marry Geoffrey of Anjou, Henry's father, she brought with her a holy relic, the hand of St James. Henry set great store by his mother's relic, and invariably carried it as a safeguard whenever he crossed the Channel which, given that it split his kingdom, he did frequently. In 1157 Frederick asked for the hand back but Henry was not prepared to let it go. Instead, and to maintain the emperor's goodwill, he gave Frederick the elaborate tent.[10]

Frederick had the tent erected close to the city walls and flew his imperial banner from Milan's tower of St Ambrose, which at the time was the highest tower in Italy. On 8 September, the feast of the nativity of the Virgin, and in front of his assembled soldiers, Frederick forced twelve of the Milanese consuls to make a humiliating public obeisance to him, barefoot and bareheaded, approaching him at his tent two by two. Drawn swords were held at their necks to demonstrate that they merited execution.

Adrian was aghast when he received the news. The fall of Milan, the largest city in the disputed Matildine lands, did not augur well for the papal claims to that territory. On the other hand, his nemesis Frederick was well pleased. He had won the victory he had sought, and Milan could consider itself lucky to be permitted to keep its army and its alliances with other cities. Its city walls and churches remained intact and Milan could continue to appoint its own consuls. In that sense, it was not a total defeat for Milan and Frederick would live to rue not destroying its defences. Having helped to persuade the Milanese to concede, Count Guido's optimism proved correct and he retained Frederick's favour.

In late September Frederick moved to Monza, only 15 miles north of Milan and the traditional capital of Lombard kings, and ordered its cathedral, almost destroyed by the Pavians, to be rebuilt at his own expense; Adrian could not have cavilled at that. The Milanese had destroyed Old Lodi completely in April that year and Frederick granted them land and funds to build New Lodi by the River Adda, which would enjoy the protection of the empire. Adrian did see this as threatening but took some comfort from the fact that Frederick was reducing his forces. The emperor was now confident enough to allow a large part of his army, including King Ladislaus and Duke Berthold IV of Burgundy, who had been restless to leave before the siege of Milan, to travel home.

✠   ✠   ✠

Frederick was not yet done. Open rebellion might be over, but resentment of the empire was only just below the surface. He moved south and crossed the Po. Adrian's hope that the fall of Milan would mark the end of Frederick's campaign was dashed. The pope was now in Albano and was fearful when he heard that Frederick moved deeper still into the disputed Matildine territory.

Frederick was intent on another showcase. He set up camp at the traditional rendezvous for imperial armies in north Italy at the Plain of Roncaglia, half-way between Milan and Bologna, where he had mustered his troops back in December 1154. Frederick and his Germans were camped on the south side of the Po, with his Italian supporters on the north side, and a bridge was built to connect the two sides. Such was the logistical support within Frederick's army that this substantial wooden bridge was completed in only two days.

On the feast of Martinmas, 11 November 1158, Frederick summoned all the bishops and local leaders to a diet at Roncaglia. Over the years, imperial rights had fallen into neglect and Frederick needed to deprive the various cities of their individual laws if he was to establish his own authority throughout northern Italy. His new universal laws had been endorsed by sympathetic and learned lawyers from Bologna, the leading centre of legal studies in Europe.

Frederick had first met the 'four doctors of law', Bulgar, Martin, James and Hugh, at Bologna in 1155 when he placed Bologna's law students under his protection. Cleverly, and with the help of these Bologna lawyers, Frederick repurposed previous Roman laws to replace the hotch-potch administrations that had evolved in the various cities.

Only a brave man disregarded an imperial summons. There was no way that Adrian was going to participate but he did send a legate instead, who, much to Adrian's annoyance, was received rudely. Bishops were there in abundance, including those from Frederick's entourage, the German bishops of Cologne, Bamberg, Eichstadt, Prague, Würzburg, Verden and Augsburg. Since most Italian cities were bishoprics, the Germans were outnumbered by the bishops of Crema, Aquileia, Milan, Turin, Alba, Ivrea, Asti, Novara, Vercelli, Tortona, Pavia, Como, Lodi, Cremona, Piacenza, Reggio, Modena, Bologna, Mantua, Verona, Brescia, Bergamo and Concordia. For three days Frederick shared with all these prelates and his senior German princes the details of his new regime by which 'the royal power and glory of the empire might be advanced with due honour'.[11]

On the fourth day he widened the diet to include all the assembled city leaders and formally introduced the new laws. Frederick loved playing the grand theatre and in a dramatic climax, on that evening, he presented himself as the true Emperor of Rome, here to reclaim all the imperial rights. This was a direct challenge to Adrian's authority but it was time, Frederick said, for peace. Rahewin assures us that all the assembled great and good were favour-ably impressed, but he was writing as Frederick's man. He tells us that the bishops and nobles queued up to give speeches of support which lasted until nightfall and that the Archbishop of newly defeated Milan magnanimously summed up a glorious day with a quotation from the psalms: 'This is the day that the Lord hath made; we will rejoice and be glad in it.'*

It was now that Frederick named his empire as *sacrum* for the first time, the Holy Roman Empire. In November 1158, Caesar was reborn at Roncaglia. Adrian could only shudder.

Frederick and the lawyers spent the following days ruling on those cases brought to them and dispensing justice. The new laws were comprehensive and focused not only on good order but of course on producing income for the empire. Frederick was hardly going to return home without a prize. His laws confirmed imperial rights to all public roads, rivers and harbours. All fisheries, salt works and mines became imperial monopolies with all taxes on them due to the emperor. Homage was to be paid to the emperor by bishops and nobles. Imperial troops were to be supplied with free forage and the emperor claimed the right to levy special taxes to fund imperial expeditions. In every city the emperor would appoint the supreme magistrate, called the *podesta*, with the consent of its citizens. One half of any treasure found on imperial or Church land would belong to the emperor. Finally, and ominously for Adrian, the Roncaglian Diet established that all lordships in Italy were held by royal grant from the empire and so held in fief, in total disregard of both the papacy and the position that his three preceding German kings had taken. This total package gave Frederick much more than a fair share of Italy's wealth.

Adrian was in no position to challenge militarily but he picked up his pen and took Frederick to task for the lack of respect shown to his legate at Roncaglia and complained of the pillage of some papal *castra* by imperial troops, a breach of his coronation oath to protect the Holy Roman Church and contrary to the instructions that Frederick had given to his own men. Adrian also warned Frederick not to interfere in a local dispute that had arisen between the churches of Brescia and Bergamo.[12]

Frederick was not going to take a lecture from the pope and regarded Adrian's letter as an unwarranted interference. He accused Adrian of entrusting his letter to an 'unworthy messenger – a low fellow'.[13] Adrian had sent an emissary of lower rank to save his cardinals from the insults and mistreatment they had previously suffered at the German court. Rahewin, ever loyal to the emperor, is likely to have exaggerated this story, as was his wont. Despite his anger, Frederick's reply was even tempered except for an opening allocution deliberately calculated to offend. Formal letters to the pope would invariably address him in the polite form, but Frederick now adopted the over-familiar

---

* Psalms 118:24.

singular. This hardly seems significant now but, as at Besançon, niceties of vocabulary mattered enormously.

Winter was setting in and, after the Diet of Roncaglia had closed, Frederick lingered in Bologna. From there he dispatched envoys throughout the cities to collect the *fodrum* and install his new magistrates, the *podestas*. Frederick had decreed the new laws and now he had to set about enforcing them. As bearers of unwelcome news, his envoys realised that they would be unpopular, especially in proud Milan, which had not been intimidated despite its recent surrender. The new regime appalled not just Milan but all the northern cities, which immediately appealed for help from Adrian. Frederick's new laws trampled all over papal rights but Adrian still could not do anything to help directly at this stage. However, he was using this time while in Rome to strengthen the relationship with his ally, King William. He hoped that somehow William might be able to help his friends in Lombardy in a way that he, on his own, could not.

Frederick spent Christmas at Alba in Piedmont, midway between Genoa and Turin and close to what is now the French border. The Archbishop of Ravenna had died during the siege of Milan and in early 1159 Frederick unilaterally appointed Guido, a local noble, to be Ravenna's new archbishop. Guido was the son of Count Guido of Biandrate, who had helped arrange the surrender of Milan to the emperor, and doubtless this appointment was a reward to his family for his loyalty. Frederick dispatched the Bishop of Vercelli to Rome to insist that Adrian ratify Guido as Ravenna's archbishop.

Guido was already a sub-deacon in the Church in Rome, and he could not accept an appointment in another diocese without the pope's express permission. That was not going to happen. Adrian could hardly agree to a senior Church appointment being made by the emperor, and especially of someone so close to the emperor. Rather than giving an outright refusal, Adrian tactfully sent a measured reply to Frederick explaining that he was intending Guido for higher things in Rome and could not part with such a valued colleague. Angrily, Frederick sent a second envoy to Adrian in the form of Herman, the Bishop of Verdun, to try again to persuade Adrian to agree to the appointment, but Adrian still did not budge. Frederick had wanted a staunch imperialist in the Archdiocese of Ravenna, second in importance in Italy only to Rome, to strengthen his support in the north. Unfortunately for Frederick, his scheme was thwarted.

Frederick was not chastened. Soon afterwards, in February 1159, he promoted his hardline chancellor, Rainald, to the vacant Archbishopric of Cologne, again without prior reference to the pope. This royal appointment of a senior churchman was a direct breach of the Diet of Worms, which Frederick had vowed to respect. In the poor post-Besançon atmosphere, Frederick seemed to be deliberately challenging the pope at every opportunity. All pretence of respect had evaporated.

Frederick was not getting everything his own way, and his new order for the post-Roncaglia peace was proving not to be so peaceful. The years of imperial neglect in Italy had worn away its feudal control there. Those Italian cities that had supported him so far had done so only to avenge themselves against their neighbouring enemy cities. As they realised that Frederick's new controlling laws would constrain them too, restlessness grew throughout Lombardy. Its countryside was already desolate after the recent fighting, and the people were starving to death. Adrian, all too aware of the sufferings of the Milanese in particular, continued to provide them with his moral support as he pondered how best to challenge Frederick. He had not hesitated to use the powerful weapon of excommunication against both the city of Rome and King William, and he was prepared to use it again – but not just yet. He did not want excommunication to trigger all-out war between Church and empire.

✠   ✠   ✠

Nonetheless, a wider war was looking inevitable. Milan had been overcome by Frederick in the siege, but almost as soon as Frederick's army was out of sight it had resumed its challenge to the empire. The citizens had noticed that Frederick's supporting troops had reduced in number and they felt emboldened enough to recapture the *castrum* of Frezzo on the River Adda.

Milan also led the opposition to Frederick's new laws of Roncaglia. His two trusted envoys, Otto and Rainald, reached Milan in January 1159, charged with appointing two *podestas* for Milan. Otto and Rainald were accompanied by Count Guido, who had led Milan's peace negotiations in August the previous year, in the hope that he would smooth their reception. Guido could not, and Otto and Rainald stepped into a hornets' nest. The imperial appointment of a *podesta* in Milan was a blatant breach of the recent September treaty. If that were not bad enough, Frederick's ban on associations between cities decreed at Roncaglia was also counter to the agreement that Milan could keep its alliances.

The envoys evaded an angry mob, but only as far as their lodgings, which were then surrounded and stoned. Guido was powerless to restrain the rabble. Otto and Rainald, having no armed support, and their horses having been stolen, sought sanctuary in St Mary's Church. The Consuls of Milan knew full well that this attack on the envoys could only end badly and rushed to the scene, trying to quieten the mob. Assisted by Count Guido, they pleaded with Otto and Rainald not to inform the emperor of the riot but, indignant at their rough treatment, the envoys could not be appeased. They escaped the city unharmed and immediately reported back to Frederick.

On 2 February 1159, Adrian was celebrating the feast of Candlemas at the Lateran Basilica, at the same time as Frederick received Otto and Rainald at his camp, now at Vercelli, 50 miles west of Milan. Frederick regarded the treatment of his ambassadors as outrageous treachery and it was certainly a gross violation of diplomatic custom. Milan, still regretting its impetuousness, sent their own envoys to Frederick offering financial compensation for their breach of hospitality, while complaining that the emperor had broken the September peace treaty. Frederick answered firmly that the new laws 'agreed' at Roncaglia superseded the September agreement. On being asked why they had broken their oaths to the empire, Rahewin reports that the envoys replied with amazing cheek, 'We did, indeed, swear but we did not promise to keep our oaths'.[14] These fateful words triggered a new war between Milan and the empire that would last for three years.

Frederick had realised that an all-out war was coming and during Lent in 1159 he had been busy strengthening his bases around Milan including New Lodi, which was only 20 miles away from Milan. He had an enormous defensive moat dug around the town and installed strong gates. Frederick spent Easter at Modena, then moved south-east to Bologna and summoned the Milanese leaders to appear there before him. They ignored this order and Frederick continued preparations for the coming conflict, securing what troops he had in strongholds at Verruca, Serralonga and New Lodi. He also ensured that Milan's former ally, Piacenza, would remain loyal to the empire.

On hearing of the incident in Milan, the King of Hungary offered to send Frederick more supporting troops. Frederick declined that offer but he did send a summons to Henry the Lion, Duke of Saxony and Bavaria, for more armed support. Critically, it would be spring in the following year before these extra forces could be gathered and reach Italy.

Frederick had scrambled around for additional militia, but he still did not have sufficient troops to mount another complete siege of Milan. Instead, he planned to starve the city of food; once again, he laid waste the surrounding lands and blocked shipments of grain into Milan. Vineyards were destroyed and fruit trees stripped of their bark. In plain sight of the defenders of Milan, Frederick executed some of the 300 hostages taken after his previous defeat of the city. He had captured some *castra* surrounding Milan but was caught unaware by a Milanese attack on the still only half-rebuilt New Lodi on Whit Sunday, 31 May 1159. The attackers drove off cattle as booty before a force of Germans, led by the Bishop of Mantua, put them to flight. Several of the attackers were killed and sixteen prominent Milanese knights were taken captive.[15] Frederick was incensed that the Milanese had made an attack on one of the holiest days of the year, a breach of twelfth-century etiquette.

Frederick was right to be concerned that cities that had supported him would break ranks. In June, fickle Brescia reneged on its July 1158 oath of imperial loyalty and renewed its alliance with Milan. The men of Brescia felt strong enough to mount an attack on still loyal Cremona, but they lost the element of surprise, having been spotted by scouts, and they were repulsed. By now the positions of the various adversaries in Lombardy were almost back to square one.

Frederick knew that Adrian was supportive of the northern cities and that the prospect of direct armed conflict between him and the pope was now palpable – but, like Adrian, he did not want to take the first step. For now, the weapons were yet more letters. First, Cardinal Henry of Nereus and Achilles, doubtless writing with Adrian's blessing, wrote to Bishop Eberhard of Bamberg in northern Bavaria, who was with Frederick in his camp. Henry asked Eberhard to guide the emperor along a course of peace and honour, imploring the bishop to work to prevent the quarrel and to stand fast for the honour of God and the freedom of the Church. Eberhard was no more willing to take sides than had been the German bishops after Besançon but he replied in a way that showed that his sympathies lay with Frederick. He claimed ignorance of Frederick's slight in addressing Adrian in the informal and countered that Adrian's letter on the Church dispute between Brescia and Bergamo was unnecessarily harsh. Eberhard begged the cardinal to mediate not with bitterness but with love.

There was no comfort here for cardinal or pope. Eberhard also wrote to Adrian directly and more forthrightly, warning that the slightest spark would ignite a conflict but:

> Putting aside such matters as may be interpreted in different ways by different persons, may you, as a father, deign to write again, gently and kindly, to your son, our lord emperor, and with paternal affection recall him to himself, for he is ready to show you all reverence. Let Samuel embrace his David.[16]

This brewing war in Lombardy put Adrian and Frederick in full public gaze. The watchers included Louis VII of France and Henry II of England. The relationship between these two kings had been tense ever since Eleanor of Aquitaine's divorce from Louis in 1152 and her immediate remarriage to Henry. However, this spat had not prevented the two kings from conceiving a joint plan in early 1159 to invade Castile and drive out the remaining Saracens. Louis had taken part in the disastrous Second Crusade and wanted to redeem his reputation as a zealous campaigner for the Church. The proposed invasion had been triggered by the death of King Sancho III of Castile, who had bequeathed the throne to his 2-year-old son Alfonso VIII, leaving Castile in chaos. This vacuum was seen by Louis and Henry as a chance to make a mark by intervening to drive the Saracens out of Spain.

The kings sought Adrian's blessing for such a campaign and were surprised to find the pope circumspect. Adrian was pleased to see a new friendship between Louis and Henry, but told them firmly that it would not be prudent or safe to invade a foreign country without the consent of its lords and people. The kings should first seek out what support there was in Spain before embarking on an adventure. Adrian wrote to both Henry and Louis with his decision but only his letter to Louis survives:

> Your Highness should recall how the Crusade to Palestine miscarried through neglect of ordinary precautions, and how its disastrous end involved the Roman Church herself, which was charged with having counselled the enterprise, and assisted in its execution, and everywhere accusations have been levied at her with much bitterness for having caused so great a misfortune. These considerations oblige us to postpone giving that consent which the Bishop of Evreux has asked of us, until such time as the prayers of the Spaniards themselves shall justify it.[17]

Henry and Louis had expected more support from Adrian, but they had misjudged the pope. During his time in Catalonia in 1148 he had developed a soft spot for Spain and was determined to protect it from invasion. Furthermore, the pope already had too much on his plate. They could not have picked a worse time to seek his approval. He was in the middle of preparations for war against the imperial forces and the last thing Adrian needed was another conflict. His wise decision arguably saved Spain from chaos.

With Spain saved, Adrian could turn his attention back to the battle for control of the Matildine lands in Lombardy.

ANAGNI
Thwarted by Death

He picked up the burden of St Peter; exhausted himself in the unremitting toil of that the office imposed; and maintained and defended the claims of Peter's see at a moment of great crisis.

Anne Duggan
'*Servus Servorum Dei*'[1]

Adrian spent the final ten weeks of his life at the hill retreat of Anagni. He had wisely moved to the cooler hills outside Rome to escape the summer heat, as popes still do today. He arrived there on 15 June 1159, just as events in Lombardy were coming to a climax, but already he was not a well man. Adrian had brought with him the 'Sicilian' cardinals, a move which Frederick saw as provocative, and further evidence of his plotting against him with William. In fact, the switch from imperial protection to Sicilian support had already happened at Benevento and the benefits to Adrian of that treaty in 1156 were now obvious.

Adrian was expecting William's help, and he had every reason to do so. The papacy could not afford to let Frederick run amok in Lombardy or its fate could then be Rome's fate. It has been suggested that Adrian had deliberately left the 'German' cardinals behind so that he could more easily foment trouble for Frederick in Milan but Adrian cannot be held responsible for the dissent raging in Lombardy. Frederick had brought this on himself by his introduction of the unpopular laws of Roncaglia. The imposition of two *podestas* in Milan by Frederick's envoys had been the final straw.

For safety Adrian had moved further away, but, ill as he was, he was by no means backing off. He wrote again, this time bluntly. Frederick received this letter at Bologna on 24 June 1159. Adrian cut to the quick, using strong words to condemn Frederick's insolence to the representative of Christ:

> My son in the Lord. The law of God promises long life to those who honour: threatens death to those who speak evil of their father and mother.[2]

Adrian reminded Frederick of the oath he had sworn at his coronation in St Peter's, to be the defender of the Holy Roman Church. Having presented Frederick with his crown, he now threatened to take it away from him. Adrian's tone was courageous. He was facing a much more powerful adversary yet he could not have been more direct, hurling at Frederick the same quotation from St Luke that Boso had used about him when he turned down William's peace offerings at Benevento in February 1156:

> Everyone that exalteth himself shall be humbled, and he that humbleth him-self shall be exalted.*

Frederick gave as good as he got. Relations had become so bitter that in public he called for Adrian's deposition because he was an 'uncanonical pope', being the son of a priest.[3] If Frederick really thought that was the case, then his own imperial coronation would have been a fraud. In no uncertain terms, Frederick ordered the pope to confine himself to the humble doctrines of Christ, and adamantly insisted that he was entitled to feudal oaths from all the bishops. He asked rhetorically whether Pope Sylvester had any power to govern in Constantine's time, pointedly claiming that subsequent popes owed whatever temporal powers they had to the generosity of Constantine and successive emperors, of which he was the latest. Yet again, any relationship between the two was made impossible by the circular argument that had been running ever since Sutri: as a Christian, Frederick was subject to the pope, but as a subject of the empire, Adrian owed political allegiance to the emperor, yet it was the pope who had conferred the crown on the emperor.

There was no chance of peace and neither Adrian nor Frederick could have expected it. Adrian was never going to back down but was too careful a man not to exhaust all opportunities for a reconciliation. Fighting had to be the last resort and in his certain mind it would represent failure, whatever the outcome.

---

*   Luke 18:14.

The rebels in Rome were also watching. Just as they had done in 1155, and knowing of the tension between pope and emperor, they took their chance to seek favours from the emperor. During June, the Commune dispatched a new embassy to Frederick's court. The Romans were concerned that the pope's ally, William, was a threat to them in Rome and believed that it was in Frederick's best interest to help them to remove that danger. This time their embassy was better chosen and included Peter, the Prefect of Rome, who was a nephew of Frederick's supporter, Cardinal Octavian.[4] For the first time Frederick received them with sympathy, seeing that the Romans could indeed be useful allies in the expected battle against the pope.

The embassy returned to Rome with Frederick's encouragement and gifts, and accompanied by three of Frederick's senior advisers, Otto of Wittelsbach, Aribert of Aqua and Guido of Biandrate. The cunning Frederick was keeping all his options open, thinking that there was still an outside chance that Adrian would capitulate. He told his envoys to drop their contacts with the Roman Commune if he reached a settlement with Adrian. His sceptical envoys thought that any such deal was most unlikely, and once they were in Rome they did what they could to undermine the pope's authority. Their mischief included briefing the 'German' cardinals, who would lead the schism on Adrian's death, setting them against their own pope. In another sign that he was buying influence in anticipation of a possible papal election, Frederick granted the resident canons of St Peter's Basilica his imperial protection.

Adrian was close to all-out hostilities with the empire but, in a last throw of the dice and prompted by Bishop Eberhard, in June or July he selected four senior cardinals for a final embassy to negotiate for peace with Frederick, who was now back at Bologna. These four were Octavian of St Cecilia; Henry of St Nereus; William, Archdeacon of Pavia; and Guido of Crema. Adrian's search for an eleventh-hour peace was genuine: he deliberately included two cardinals, Octavian and Guido, who had always supported closer links between the papacy and the empire.

The cardinals offered only harsh terms to Frederick. First, the papacy's absolute dominion over Rome must be acknowledged. This meant that the emperor must send no officers into Rome without papal permission and all Roman monopolies and royalties must be recognised as belonging to the papacy alone. Secondly, the emperor must cease making levies or taxes on any papal domains other than on the coronation of a new emperor. Thirdly, bishops might swear allegiance to the emperor but were not to do homage to him. Fourthly, imperial envoys must cease taking lodgings in bishops' palaces.

Finally, the title to all the Matildine lands as well as the Duchy of Spoleto and both Corsica and Sardinia were to be handed over to the papacy.

These were surprising demands from the English pope with limited resources to the mightiest armed monarch in Europe. Mackie considered the ultimatum to be no less than a declaration of war.[5] Amazingly, Frederick did not dismiss the demands out of hand, although he answered them with scarcely hidden mockery. In a contemptuous reply, he agreed that his officers would not lodge in episcopal palaces unless those palaces were built on imperial land. He would also waive the homage of bishops provided they restored to him the fiefs they held from the emperor in Italy. The bishops must also agree not to obey the pope as regards any disobedience to the emperor. Frederick refused point blank to concede any temporal power for the papacy in Rome itself, even though in 1155 he had explicitly recognised the pope's possession of Rome and his men had even spilt blood to help Adrian regain it. Frederick's position now was that, as he was the Roman Emperor, authority over Rome was unshakably his, and if he did not hold Rome, his imperial title would be a hollow one.[6] He also complained that papal legates had entered his empire without permission.

Negotiations were not quite at an end. In a reversal of roles, Frederick suggested a compromise to the four cardinals. He proposed that a conference of twelve – six bishops chosen by him and six cardinals chosen by the pope – should meet to decide on the remaining points. Adrian dug his heels in and stood by his demands. He refused to accept a compromise, particularly about the pope's temporal authority over Rome. Instead, he insisted that Frederick comply with the Treaty of Constance that he had made with Pope Eugenius, which explicitly recognised the pope's lordship of Rome. Frederick's angry counter was that the treaty had died when Adrian made his own pact with William in 1156.

This was the final impasse. Opinions have always differed as to whether it was Adrian or Frederick who forced this final confrontation, and from this distance it is difficult to discern. Adrian could never have been expected to agree to Frederick's proposed conference. Had a meeting of twelve arbiters gone ahead, they might well have concluded the authority over Rome in Adrian's favour, but it was a risk he could not afford to take. Submitting the papacy to close control of the German Empire and the loss of its authority over Rome could not be contemplated for one minute. For his part, Frederick must have known that he had imposed an impossible request, and that by insisting on his own absolute authority in Rome he was in blatant breach, not just of the Treaty of Constance, but of his coronation oath.

Furthermore, it was Frederick, not Adrian, who had triggered the current unrest in Lombardy. Both leaders were stubborn men, but Frederick must take the blame for the consequences.

Adrian turned his attention elsewhere, having no confidence that any more exchanges with Frederick would serve any purpose. It is possible that, during these final days in Anagni, Adrian had invited William to take over as ruler of all Italy, as a fief of the pope, seeing this as the only way to protect the Church. Adrian sent his chancellor, Cardinal Roland, to William with the blessed banner of St Peter, a strong sign that William and the Church could work yet more closely together. In this, Adrian had the support of most, but not all, of his cardinals.

Imarus of Tusculum, Octavian of St Cecilia, Guido of Crema and John of St Martin all vehemently opposed these latest overtures to William. Having succumbed to the blandishments of Frederick's three envoys in Rome, Otto, Aribert and Guido, they remained convinced that only the emperor could safeguard the Church. This split among the cardinals, first seen at Benevento in 1156 and again after the furore at Besançon in 1157, was now an open breach. To Adrian's dismay, these diametrically opposed views were undoing all his attempts to keep his cardinals united. His waning health perhaps contributed to his failure to hold them together. Adrian had forced through a major change in papal policy by favouring Sicily, and some opposition was an inevitable consequence. Adrian's poor health would have been known to the cardinals and they were taking positions for the growing possibility of an election for a new pope.

Frederick also looked elsewhere. Ever since that incident over 'papal benefits' at Besançon, Frederick had been scheming to replace the pope but now he realised that he might not need to. Adrian had probably been unwell since about March and Frederick too may already have known this and started manoeuvring to influence the succession. It was obvious who Frederick had in mind. Throughout Adrian's papacy, Cardinal Octavian had been at the forefront of those cardinals wanting to maintain close ties to the empire, and Frederick would benefit if Octavian became pope. Frederick granted Octavian and his three brothers the Umbrian city of Terni as an imperial fief, an estate which controlled access from the north to the roads to Rome, a useful power base for a future pope.[7]

On 2 July, Frederick launched a siege of Crema, Milan's secret ally, in retaliation for its attempted attack on New Lodi on the preceding Whit Sunday. Other towns, encouraged by Milan, had also declared themselves to be republics, free of the empire, and Adrian stood by them. Frederick became aware of letters from Adrian to Milan and other cities encouraging revolt against the empire. Without Frederick's knowledge, Adrian had indeed endorsed a secret pact between Milan, Brescia, Piacenza and Crema whereby all four cities agreed not to make any peace with Frederick without the permission of the pope. Adrian wanted to help them further and he started gathering what troops he could.

This marks the point when pope, Sicilian king and those northern cities, acting in concert, took the fight to the empire. Adrian openly hosted meetings between representatives of the Lombards and the Sicilians, telling them that he was about to wield his big stick. Adrian took his cue from his role model, Pope Gregory VII, who had strongly held the view that an emperor only held his power so that he could work for the good of the Church, and if he acted against the interest of the Church the emperor could be rebuked, excommunicated or even deposed.[8] Gregory had attempted to do just that against Emperor Henry IV in 1076 and Adrian was now ready to treat Henry's successor in the same way. He told his allies that he planned to excommunicate Frederick in forty days' time. He was even willing to seek support for Lombardy from the Byzantine Emperor, and because Frederick was making only slow progress in the north, he had time to do so.

Adrian's direct intervention in the war between Frederick and the cities in Lombardy was explosive. For the second time in less than 100 years the papacy was pitted directly against the empire, and just as Frederick's army was being reinforced. In late July additional troops, led by Henry the Lion, arrived from Germany and strengthened the besieging force at Crema. Nonetheless, Crema was able to hold out until January 1160.

Adrian wrote no more letters to Frederick, but he did go over his head in a fiery letter to the German archbishops of Treves, Mentz and Cologne which he used as a proxy attack on Frederick. In it, he blamed Frederick for the breakdown, calling him a 'fox who thinks to lay waste the Lord's vineyard'. Adrian returned to the nub of the Besançon furore, writing that 'before his consecration he is but king'. The pope reminded the archbishops of the founding of the Holy Roman Empire by a pope, and ended with a repeated threat to uncrown him:

> From whence then the Emperor but from us? Remember what these German kings were, drawn about in wagons by oxen like any poor philosopher, before Pope Zacharius I exalted Charles [Charlemagne] to the Empire and gave him a name great above all names. That which we bestowed on the faithful German we may take away from the disloyal German.[9]

Adrian pointedly told the archbishops that they 'also will be involved in ruin' if there was a permanent split between Church and empire. Adrian never did excommunicate Frederick. His sudden death at Anagni intervened.

✠ ✠ ✠

Stricken by quinsy, and perhaps suffering from angina, Adrian died on 1 September 1159. The full circumstances of his death are not known. There have been accounts of poisoning but no evidence for this has ever been found. Frederick's supporters claimed that he choked on a fly as he drank at a fountain, but this is no more than a whimsical explanation of the likeliest cause, quinsy. Now called peri-tonsillitis, quinsy is an abscess behind the tonsil and in the absence of antibiotics can cause a blockage of the airway. It suited Frederick's supporters to explain Adrian's death as divine retribution for preparing his excommunication. Not so, of course, but his enemies would have taken some comfort from believing this.

The cardinals' first thought was to bury Adrian in Anagni and hold the papal election there. Frederick's envoys were still in Rome, and the cardinals were wary of the Roman senators, who were more supportive of the German-favouring cardinals than the majority of the cardinals who had approved of the reconciliation with William of Sicily. They also knew that Frederick had been buying influence in Rome. However, when news of Adrian's death reached Rome the senators rushed to Anagni and somehow persuaded the cardinals to hold the election in Rome.[10]

Adrian's body was carried to Rome for his funeral on 4 September, held in the presence of the three imperial envoys, Otto, Aribert and Guido. Whatever their disagreements, Frederick respected his brave adversary after death. Adrian was entombed in a third-century red marble sarcophagus in the nave of St Peter's Basilica and alongside his predecessor and mentor, Pope Eugenius. In 1607, when the old St Peter's was demolished and the current basilica built, Adrian's tomb was removed to the crypt of St Peter's. His coffin was opened at the time and Adrian's body was found to be well preserved and dressed in a dark silk chasuble. He was described as 'an undersized man, wearing Turkish slippers on his feet and, on his hand, a ring, with a large emerald'.[11]

His sarcophagus remains in the crypt, marked by the classical designs of an ox skull and two flowers. One writer claimed the ox was a deer and a sign of his roots in St Albans, with the flowers being roses, representing Adrian's native England. The simple inscription is 'Adrianus Papa IIII'. On the side of the niche is an inscription placed by the Royal Norwegian Society of Science and Letters on the 900th anniversary of Adrian's mission to Norway in 1152.

John of Salisbury, forlorn at Adrian's early and unexpected death, spoke touchingly of his beloved friend. His grief was genuine and clear, shining through his own somewhat immodest words:

> The death, too, of our lord, Pope Adrian, which disturbed all nations and peoples, has moved with yet more violent a grief the England whence he took his origin. All, indeed, wept, and none more than I, for when he had a mother and brother of his own, yet he loved me with a nearer affection than all.[12]

John seems to have had a premonition of Adrian's early death. In a letter to Pope Adrian two years earlier, he signed off with:

> May you fare well forever father – and bear in mind what all know, but very few declare in your hearing, that a Roman pontiff cannot long be Pope.[13]

Not long enough. John had a strong personal reason to rue the early death of his mentor. It is quite likely that Adrian had intended to raise John to the College of Cardinals, and John would have known this. Adrian may have given John this impression during the time that they spent together at Benevento, but after John unwittingly upset King Henry over the Irish question, Adrian was probably loath to upset Henry further by rewarding John too quickly. Regretfully for John, he never got his red hat.

✠   ✠   ✠

Adrian's long journey and short life were over. If he had been given more time, much more might have been possible. We can never know. The archives of his pontificate are not extensive, but by following this journey through his life it is possible to take a good measure of the man.

From an early age Adrian had been a self-starter. He knew as a boy that he needed education to improve himself and he knew that finding a school would not be easy, but patience and determination were his bywords. Matthew Paris and William of Newburgh told us that in his youth Adrian was a handsome man with courteous manners, which would have helped him to get on in life. Nevertheless, it still took courage to leave not just the familiarity of St Albans but England too. He was clearly intelligent, and he was determined to make something of himself. Whether or not he succeeded in the schools of Paris or only later at Arles, he proved a diligent student. It was his education that opened the door to his future positions of authority, but it was by his own efforts that he achieved that education. He could never have bought his way into office and, unlike most churchmen of the era, he had no helpful family connections.

At all the stages in his journeys he made an instant good impression. He was not a large man, but he had presence. His character and skills were honed through a succession of promotions, all of which were achieved entirely on his own merits. The monks at St Ruf, the small but prestigious abbey, had quickly elected him to office. They may have regretted their decision, but they would not have elected a nonentity. Monks in a community get to know each other very well and they must have seen leadership qualities and a personable manner.

It took Pope Eugenius no time to spot the same qualities in the 40-something-year-old, taking him into his own service in short order. That Adrian's path crossed with Eugenius was fortuitous and not the consequence of ruthless ambition. Eugenius had head-hunted the English abbot with care, seeing a young man of firm resolution. Adrian never let Eugenius down and performed his duties in Catalonia well and his talents then attracted wider attention.

Eugenius, taking the advice of the other cardinals, promoted him to the College of Cardinals, and straight in at the top rank, as a cardinal bishop no less. There would have been no shortage of talent and experience among Eugenius's cardinals, but he had no hesitation in entrusting his new cardinal with the major diplomatic role in Scandinavia. The pope may have lighted on Adrian because he was a northerner, but he would not have sent him on such an important mission had he not thought he was up to it.

Adrian's greatest achievement before becoming pope was in Scandinavia, not simply by his reorganisation of its dioceses but also by bringing the Church in Scandinavia out of its isolation and into line with western Christian culture. His work benefitted both the Church that had sent him there and Scandinavia itself. He was always even-handed in his judgements, as when balancing the loss to Lund of its supremacy over the Church in Norway against its continuing authority over the Swedish Church. He is now better remembered in Scandinavia than he is in England, regarded fondly there as the founder of the still-flourishing cathedral schools in Bergen, Hamar and Trondheim. Every year, Trondheim Cathedral School hosts a Breakspear lecture organised by Norway's oldest learned society, the Royal Norwegian Society of Science and

Letters. You can still order an '*entrecote* Breakspear' in Trondheim restaurants. His success in Scandinavia was rewarded by his fellow cardinals when they unanimously elected him pope.

Adrian can never have anticipated becoming pope. For him to have done so would have been ridiculous. He was just an Englishman abroad who had always done his best in whatever task was given to him, and with determination even if not always with relish. The papacy was never his dream, but his progress proved unstoppable. Less than ten years since becoming an abbot in Provence, he sat on St Peter's throne in Rome. This was spectacular progress, and all the more so for his being a foreigner who had not served office in the Curia. His work in St Ruf, Catalonia and Scandinavia all demonstrated nothing less than purposeful leadership. At no stage did he settle for an easy option. He was never intimidated by those stronger and more experienced than he was. No scandal about his personal integrity was ever suggested, then or since. His self-confidence was impressive, and it took him all the way to the throne of thorns.

Some commentaries have characterised Adrian as weak and pliable, but such a man could not have made such meteoric progress. The cardinals who voted unanimously for him knew what difficulties faced the next pope and knew for whom they were voting. Once elected, Adrian proved to be the strong leader that they expected.

From the very start in 1155 he dealt firmly with the rebels of Rome, a nettle his predecessor had not grasped. The Romans had thought that the new young foreign pope would be a pushover, but they could not have been more wrong. His spontaneous use of an interdict against Rome soon had them caving in. Adrian's strong faith in the eternal redemption offered by the Church defeated the rebels and led to Arnold's fall. His courage in facing up to difficult meetings with Frederick, a mighty emperor, at Sutri and later with King William at Benevento, are not in any doubt.

But was Adrian a proud man? He had flashes of pride, a necessary adjunct of leadership, but any sin of pride was tempered by his humility and restraint which were never more visible than in his dealings with Frederick.

Adrian's judgements were not always perfect. Perhaps he had been too stubborn when he first met Frederick at Sutri; had he not made an issue of the stirrup, he might have developed a good working relationship with the emperor. On the other hand, a pliable pope could too easily have become a mere German puppet. The events that unfolded proved that Frederick was always going to put his own imperial ambitions ahead of his care for the Church and that Adrian had been right to be wary. Adrian had to concede defeat to William at Benevento after rejecting the king's earlier and better terms, but this decision had been a collective decision of the cardinals. The fiasco of the letters at Besançon was at worst careless. At all times there is a powerful sense that he stood up for the dignity of the Church and his office, rather than for himself.

Behind his strong leadership there was an equally formidable team. Adrian was a good judge of others and a particularly good team player. He needed to be. His rapid promotion meant that when he became pope he had had little experience of the Curia and its workings. His confidence in cardinals Roland and Boso, the key members of his team in the Curia, was well placed. Adrian managed people well and his instinct was collegiate, rather than autocratic, as his role model Pope Gregory VII had been. He worked hard to bring his cardinals with him on the big decisions and only towards the end of his papacy, and strained by war, the split between the 'Sicilian' and 'German' cardinals became unmanageable and erupted on his death. It is hard to see, even with hindsight, how he could have satisfied the 'German' cardinals without submitting the papacy to the direct control of the Holy Roman Empire.

It is not difficult to form a view on Adrian's lasting achievements as pope. Bartolomeo Platini, a fifteenth-century humanist employed in the Curia, could not have been more direct:

He died in the fourth year and tenth month of his pontificate, leaving the Roman Church greatly enriched.[14]

Adrian was a man of action living in an age of change, a loyal supporter of the traditions of the Church in all that he did but he was not an innovator. Aided by his well-chosen team of close advisers, he much improved the fabric of the Patrimony. He was not on the papal throne long enough ever to have called a council, and so left few reforming legacies for the Church itself. We have no records of his sermons, which would have opened a window on his Christian thinking. Nor has Adrian left us any significant theological teachings, but he did leave his mark on the Church. He was diligent, as shown by his large output of letters and judgements. Adrian had an excellent sense of right and wrong, and was compassionate. He left wise rulings on the marriage of serfs and removing tax advantages on new lands acquired by wealthy monasteries. These judgements stood the test of time, finding their way into canon law.

Adrian was kept busy on English matters, but they were only a small proportion of the disputes that he was called on to judge. The Curia received constant demands for papal permissions and Adrian played his part to the full. He issued his first privilege only eight days after his election, and throughout his pontificate of four years and eight months he issued 653 formal letters and decretals, which works out at an average of 140 a year.[15] Together with a further 200 less formal documents, this was a heavy load for a pope and showed Adrian to be conscientious. By this measure, Adrian was busier than his predecessor Pope Eugenius had been, although later popes did more. His constant travelling around Italy never disrupted the work of the Curia. Furthermore, and despite his continuing arguments with Emperor Frederick, about a quarter of Adrian's rulings concerned imperial lands.

Adrian was pleased to have Frederick's help in removing Arnold in 1155. We now see Arnold as a political agitator, but Adrian's treatment of him appears ruthless only to the modern eye, and we do not know if the execution was carried out with his knowledge. Adrian could be ruthless, and any twelfth-century leader had to be. This was not a gentle age and he had the necessary courage to face up to external military threats and by so doing left an improved situation for the popes who followed him.

Adrian would not be seen as a man of peace today, but for him war was always a last resort. As pope he was not shy in leading armies into battle and encouraging others to fight to defend the papacy's interests, but Adrian never wanted a drama to grow into a crisis. Throughout his papacy he was restrained, resorting to extreme measures only after all other means had failed. This was never clearer than in his final struggle in Lombardy. At least three times after the Besançon incident he sought to negotiate with Frederick rather than confront him.

His aversion to fighting had been clear ever since his time in Scandinavia, when he advised King Sweyne in Denmark to avoid the futility of war. If not lasting peace, Adrian brought calm to Norway. He had supported the fighting against the Moors in Spain during the Second Crusade, and played his part, but his Church necessarily saw that as a just war. However, he would not support the kings of France and England in their later wish to invade Castile, instead insisting that intervention could only happen if there was support within the country. It is likely that he took a similar view of Henry's ambitions in Ireland but that is less clear. Some will always insist that Adrian shares the blame for the later English domination of Ireland.

More than anything else, Adrian's reign was dominated by his relationship with Frederick. The sixteenth-century Protestant *Foxe's Book of Martyrs* put it well: 'Much trouble had good Fridericus with the Pope.'[16] It was Adrian's bad luck that he had to spend most of his papacy facing up to the ambitious and

energetic German Emperor. Like the rebels of Rome, Frederick had expected
the new foreign, low-born pope to be a soft touch but instead he had found
out the hard way of Adrian's inner steel and his physical and moral courage.
When they met for the first time at Sutri, Frederick had been stunned to find
Adrian pushing back against his lack of diplomatic protocol. It was Frederick
who had given way in that first tussle, and from then on Frederick knew that
he could take nothing for granted with this man.

Adrian has been blamed for the split between the papacy and the empire.
Writers of the eighteenth and nineteenth centuries mostly took Frederick's
side, seeing Adrian's objectives as anti-imperialist by design rather than of
necessity. Most of the contemporary accounts of Adrian's time were written
by Frederick's supporters and their criticisms about his break with Frederick
stuck. Throughout their struggles, each claimed the moral high ground of the
Treaty of Constance of 1153, both saying that it was the other who broke it
first. The modern consensus is that this was Frederick. Once Frederick had
got his hands on the imperial crown he no longer needed anything from
Adrian and regarded his obligations to the papacy as having been completed.
Although he had his reasons for leaving Adrian in the lurch at Tivoli, his troops
being exhausted, the fact remains that Frederick left Adrian to face the threat
of William's advances on his own. Had he fulfilled the obligations he had
signed up to and faced up to William's threat to papal lands in 1155, the story,
and the relationship, could have been different.

Instead, Frederick went on to stir up the barons in Apulia and did nothing
to dissuade the Greeks from their joint venture. Denied Frederick's active
support, the defeats at Brindisi and Bari left Adrian no choice but to accept
William's terms at Benevento. Whatever Frederick claimed, Adrian had not
made an accommodation with William of his own volition. As it happened,
this alliance with the Normans proved a more natural alliance than one with
Frederick, lasting forty years. Events at Benevento in 1156 marked the decisive
break between papacy and empire. The Besançon episode in 1157 was a clash
of egos between two stubborn men. By then, both had accepted that the Treaty
of Constance was dead, but each was still trying to pin the blame on the other.

Adrian was not chastened, never settling for a quiet life, and he tackled
Frederick over the kidnap of Archbishop Eskil. He refused to be bullied by
Frederick's attempts to impose his own man as Archbishop of Ravenna. Adrian
never defeated Frederick, but he contained the emperor's grab for control of
the papacy.

Nor can Adrian be blamed for the final break with empire in 1159 when
he gave his support to Milan and the other northern cities. Frederick was

the architect of the post–Roncaglia uprisings in Lombardy. His imposition of *podestas* on the northern cities was part of the imperial plan to usurp not just Adrian's authority but that of succeeding popes too. Adrian did not shape events but rather was forced to react to them, always doing what he could to protect the Curia from the threats that surrounded it. The allegiances Adrian forged shifted in response to events and were never made by design.

In relying on the fake 'Donation of Constantine' in the Investiture Controversy, Adrian did no more than popes had done before him and would do after him. It was the essential role of the pope to protect the interests of the Church and Adrian cannot be faulted for striving his utmost to do so. Had he given way to Frederick, especially his demands for authority over Rome itself, any pretence of partnership between empire and papacy would have disappeared, not just in Rome but throughout Italy. The popes in Rome would have been no more than puppets, 'glorified German chaplains', a term coined by Thomas Noble when writing of eighth-century popes.[17]

Adrian had become pope at a challenging time. In his mere four years and eight months, he achieved much to protect the independence of the Church. The papacy as an institution in the late Middle Ages was more important than whoever was the pope in person. Adrian served his Church well and it was only the brevity of his reign that prevented him from being seen as a great pope. Adrian's chosen motto, 'My eyes are always upon the Lord',[18] demonstrated that for Adrian, the Church and the Lord were one, and his eyes never wavered. The only English pope could not have done more to protect the throne of St Peter.

Not only those who share Adrian's faith pay tribute to him. Even those who now disapprove of the institution of the papacy can still recognise his selfless service, his throne full of thorns. England can be proud of its illustrious but neglected son.

EPILOGUE
Succession and Schism

The Englishman initiated the age of the great mediaeval popes. Adrian, the pope of action, ranks in importance in no wise below the popes of theory. He is, as it were, theory made eminently practical. His pontificate begins the steep ascent of the papacy to the dizzy heights of the Innocentian era.

Walter Ullmann
'The Pontificate of Adrian IV'[1]

It was not unusual for a pope to have expressed a preference for his successor before his own death, and it was sometimes helpful that he do so. One witness reported that Adrian had nominated Cardinal Bernard of Porto.* Bernard and Roland were the two cardinals who had represented Adrian at the fateful Diet of Besançon in 1157. Adrian had high regard for Bernard and had promoted him to cardinal bishop in 1159. Even if he had been Adrian's preferred successor, Bernard did not get the job, but there is no clue as to why he did not. Unlike Roland, Bernard always maintained good relations with the emperor. Frederick likely would have found Bernard an acceptable successor to Adrian and, if he had been elected, the schism on Adrian's death might never have happened.

At the time of his death, Adrian had just about completed the coalition of the papacy with the Lombards and the Sicilians which would in time wreck

---

* Cardinal Priest Bernard of St Clemente had been promoted to Cardinal Bishop of Porto in 1159.

Frederick's Italian ambitions, but this anti-imperial alliance contributed to the schism over Adrian's successor. Both sets of cardinals wanted the new pope in their camp. The first, the 'Sicilian' group, approved of the new relationship with William and the Lombards, and felt threatened by Frederick's ambitions for Italy. The second, the smaller 'German' group, sympathised with Frederick and wanted to restore the imperial alliance as it had been up to 1156. It was not a sharp distinction, and some cardinals would not have seen themselves in either group.

The cardinals would have wanted to reach a consensus. Rahewin, no friend to the 'Sicilian' cardinals, writes of their initial good intentions:

> The cardinals had agreed to return to Rome and to elect in harmony some one of themselves. If they could not do so, they would seek some outside person. If, however, they could not agree on one, they would postpone the election until they could find a suitable person whom they could elect harmoniously. And this was unanimously ratified.[2]

The power struggle emerged quickly. A dispute was inevitable whenever a pope and emperor had fallen out. Rahewin tells us that, while Cardinal Octavian went to pay his respects over Adrian's body, other cardinals 'sent Boso, that author of evil, that first born of Satan, on ahead to occupy the castle of St Peter [Castel Sant'Angelo], whose garrison had sworn fidelity to him while Pope Adrian was still alive'.[3]

With Boso occupying the Castel Sant'Angelo, the 'German' cardinals were wary of accepting a summons there for the election, for fear of being taken prisoner. After a stand-off lasting two days, the election was held, not in the castle, but behind the altar in St Peter's itself. It descended into chaos. Each group of cardinals elected its own pope, and an undignified fight broke out over the robe of office, as each party in turn snatched it from the other. Both groups complained of the other's election procedures and it is not possible so long after the event to see who was in the right. The 'Sicilian' group had the strength of numbers, making up about two-thirds of the complement of thirty-one cardinals. A simple majority of cardinals was all that was required; it was only after the Third Lateran Council in 1179 that the required majority was increased to two-thirds.

The 'Sicilian' group elected Cardinal Roland, Adrian's faithful chancellor and perhaps the architect of Adrian's accommodation with William, who took the title of Pope Alexander III. The 'German' group, encouraged by Frederick, elected Cardinal Octavian, who chose the name Victor IV. Octavian was the cardinal who had always had strong German leanings and whom Boso had accused of plotting a schism as far back as Sutri in 1155. Antipope Victor's cardinal supporters soon fell to as few as five, and included only one of the cardinal bishops, Imarus of Tusculum. These five continued to accuse the 'Sicilian' cardinals of plotting to persuade Adrian to excommunicate Frederick, refusing to accept defeat.

It has been suggested that Adrian had stacked the college with 'Sicilian' sympathisers, but if that were true then he would not have appointed Guido of Crema cardinal little more than a year earlier. Adrian knew that Guido's sympathies lay with Octavian, to whom he was related. It had been events, not plots, that had driven Adrian's recognition of William's kingship at Benevento in 1156. Had there been a plot running, Adrian would not have let the cardinals persuade him to reject William's offer in August 1155.

Roland hailed from Sienna and had been a teacher of law at Bologna before entering papal service for Pope Eugenius in 1148. His work as Adrian's chancellor had been impressive and he would have been an obvious candidate. His adversary, Antipope Victor was no straw man, though; he too had had a distinguished career in the Church and was a member of one of Rome's aristocratic families. Neither Roland nor Octavian was willing to step down, and not for the first time the Church ended up with two popes. This schism ran longer than the previous two, lasting twenty-one years from 1159 to 1180. Victor had fewer supporters but a powerful one in Frederick and he enjoyed the possession of the Leonine City, the papal stronghold across the Tiber from Rome.

Frederick at first gained the upper hand in the fighting with Lombardy, which broke out as Adrian died. He defeated Milan in 1162 and this time razed it to the ground. After its surrender Frederick boldly summoned a council in Pavia to decide who was the authentic pope. The council, which was attended by over fifty bishops, found in favour of Victor. Pope Alexander had no doubt that he was the rightful heir to St Peter and that Frederick had no right to summon a Church council. He responded by excommunicating Frederick, just as Adrian had intended to do in 1159. Alexander had the support of the Lombards and Sicily from the start and, despite Frederick's best efforts to prevent it, he had also won the powerful support of Emperor Manuel, as well as both France and England in 1160. The Norwegian clergy, remembering their good supporter Nicholas Breakspear, also supported Alexander, but their Danish counterparts took the German side and supported Victor.

Victor was always on the back foot and his death in 1164 was a blow to Frederick's ambitions. Victor's successor was his relation, Guido of Crema, who became Antipope Paschal III, but already support for the schism was ebbing away, even within Germany. Alexander felt secure enough to return to Rome in 1165 but Frederick was not yet done. He mounted yet another expedition to Rome in 1167, successfully occupying the Leonine City and installing Paschal there.

Fate now played a hand as the curse of Italy's climate struck again. A mysterious infection, probably malaria, decimated Frederick's army and killed several of his leaders, including his aggressive chancellor, Rainald. This encouraged the Lombards to re-form their alliance, marked by the founding of a new town called Alessandria in honour of the pope, a blatant challenge to Frederick's authority.[4]

Paschal died in 1168 and Antipope Callixtus III replaced him. Still Frederick persisted with his ambition to control Italy and returned with his army yet again in 1174, but he was defeated by the Lombards at the decisive Battle of Legnano in 1176. After this defeat Frederick had no choice but to agree to the resignation of Callixtus and accept Alexander as the true pope.

The approach Adrian had adopted to stand firm against Frederick was finally vindicated. Adrian did not live to see the consequences of his policy, but it proved successful and Frederick never again threatened the Church. Since Adrian's death, much of the Patrimony had been seized by Frederick and it was not until 1198 that the papacy regained control of Adrian's *castra*.

Adrian's loyal lieutenant and successor died in 1181 after a successful reign of twenty-two years. Roland proved an excellent choice for the Church. He had always been a loyal supporter of Adrian and he continued the struggle against empire. As Alexander, he lived to see Frederick's recognition of both himself as the legitimate pope and the papacy's temporal rights over Rome. Thanks to Adrian's forcefulness in Sutri in 1151, Frederick had not hesitated to hold the stirrup for Alexander when they sealed their reconciliation at the basilica of St Mark the Evangelist in Venice in 1177.[5]

Some laid the blame for this twenty-one-year schism on Adrian. Godfrey of Viterbo had no doubt that he was responsible, saying 'he himself was the grizzly head of schism',[6] but he was a close supporter of Frederick and so would naturally favour him. That Adrian had to stand up to Frederick does not make him responsible for the schism that followed his death. Frederick must take the blame for that too. He could have accepted the clear wish of the majority of cardinals in 1159 and made a fresh start with Roland as pope, but he chose not to do so. He wanted his puppet pope and backed the less well-supported 'German' candidate. It was Frederick, not Adrian, who was the 'grizzly head of schism', using his weight for twenty-one years in a doomed attempt to back a minority candidate with little international support.

✠ ✠ ✠

In 1189, Frederick accepted leadership of the Third Crusade. The following March, his army of over 12,000 crusaders, including at least 3,000 knights, pushed through Anatolia reaching Celician Armenia. Frederick accepted the local Armenians' advice to follow a shortcut along the Saleph River while his army took the mountain path. On 10 June 1190, he decided to bathe in the river and drowned. The icy mountain water was a fatal shock to the 68-year-old emperor. His unexpected death left the Third Crusade under the uneasy command of the rivals King Philip II of France and King Richard of England.

King William of Sicily lived until 1166, enduring constant internal power struggles. He was succeeded by his son William II, known now as 'William the Good', who enjoyed the internal peace denied to his father. He remained a staunch supporter of the papacy and continued the opposition to Frederick. He died one year before Frederick, in 1189, and without issue. His aunt Constance was the sole heir to the throne but had been confined to a monastery until 1184, when she was betrothed to Henry, Frederick's eldest son, the future Emperor Henry VI.

William had named Constance and Henry his heirs, but the Sicilian noblemen had no wish to be ruled by a German. Tancred, the illegitimate grandson of Roger II, was crowned King of Sicily. In 1191 Tancred had formed a brief friendship with King Richard the Lionheart, who was on his way to the Third Crusade. Richard gave Tancred an impressive gift, a sword that he claimed was King Arthur's Excalibur which had recently been found at Glastonbury.[7]

In 1192, Pope Celestine III agreed to invest Tancred's kingship but in return forced Tancred to concede the rights over Church appointments in Sicily that Adrian had had to surrender in Benevento in 1156. Excalibur failed to save Tancred's throne. Beset by internal and external threats, the Norman kingdom declined and Constance and Henry prevailed. In 1194 the kingdom fell to Henry. The lands lost by Adrian at Benevento in 1156 were eventually regained by Pope Innocent III early in the thirteenth century.

Henry II of England also died in 1189, at the age of 56, having spent thirty-five years on the throne. Henry gained an unexpected benefit from the papal schism that started on Adrian's death. In 1160 Henry was keen for his son, Young Henry, to be married to Margaret, daughter of King Louis VII of France, even though he was only 5 years old and she just 2. Henry's chancellor, Thomas Becket, had arranged the betrothal of the two infants in 1158. A speedy marriage would allow King Henry to win control of the Vexin, an area in north-west France and close to Paris, which Louis had offered as Margaret's dowry. Marriage at such a young age was a breach of Church law and Louis had thought the dowry was safe in his hands until Young Henry was at least 15. However, a wily Henry II took advantage of the legates who asked him in 1160 to support Pope Alexander III in the schism; in return for Henry's support the legates agreed to allow the marriage of the 5-year-old prince.[8]

Henry had proved a good king and arguably strengthened the English monarchy internally. He also planted the roots of English Common Law and the national exchequer. His quarrel with Becket blemished his reign, and the Irish will never forgive him for his invasion of Ireland in 1171. His reign ended sadly, Henry having difficult relationships with his surviving sons, Richard and John, and the French King Philip II. It was after Henry's death that the new King Richard left on the Third Crusade where he covered himself in glory. However, on his return from the Holy Land, Henry II's son was held hostage by Frederick Barbarossa's son, Emperor Henry VI of Germany, and freed only after an enormous ransom was raised and paid. Henry VI used that ransom money to pay for his defeat of Sicily.[9]

The Byzantine emperor Manuel Comnenus never did re-establish significant authority in Italy. His amicable relationship with Frederick had died in 1159 along with Manuel's German wife, Bertha of Sulzbach. In 1171 he even fell out badly with his close ally Venice, although Frederick's defeat at Legnano in 1176 did help restore his relationship with Venice. Manuel paid for the restoration of the walls of Milan after they had been demolished by the Germans in 1162 and the Byzantines had good relations with several cities including Genoa, Pisa, Cremona and Pavia. Ancona even accepted Manuel as sovereign, and the Byzantines maintained a presence there. Manuel had spent enormous quantities of gold on his Italian adventures yet had little to show for it. When Manuel died in 1180 he left the Byzantine Empire as a great power, secure within its frontiers. However, his son Alexios was a minor and his unpopular regency was soon overthrown.

✠   ✠   ✠

It was Adrian's work in Norway that had taken him to the papacy. Pope Alexander III corresponded regularly with kings and bishops in the north, and in 1163 or 1164 he sent Stephen of Orvieto to Norway as his legate to ensure that the Norwegian Church would support him in the papal schism that followed Adrian's death in 1159, which it did. Adrian's work in that country had not been forgotten.

Adrian had backed a winner in supporting Inge, who emerged as the sole King of Norway after his half-brothers Sigurd and Eystein died in 1155 and 1157 respectively. Inge himself died in 1161. The calm that Adrian had brought to Norway did not last long, but blame cannot be laid at his door.

Peace is incremental and absolute peace was unattainable in the twelfth century. Thirty years after Adrian's mission, Norway descended into chaos. Pope Clement III demanded that the Norwegian clergy respect Adrian's order to refrain from the use of arms but the Norwegian kings continued to fight for their thrones. King Sverre of Norway (1184–1202) had been ordained a priest but lost his calling and overthrew King Magnus in 1184. Archbishop Eystein, who had been installed in Nidaros in 1161, fled to exile in England but returned to Norway in 1183 and reached an accommodation with Sverre. On his deathbed in 1202, Sverre quoted Adrian in encouraging his heir Haakon to make peace with the Church:

> Make peace with the Church – as was appointed by Cardinal Breakspear …
> as was sworn by the three brothers Sigurd, Eystein and Inge.[10]

Fifty years after Adrian's visit, a repentant king remembered his achievements. Haakon heeded his father's advice and was reconciled to the Church. Adrian's peace returned at last to Norway.

Adrian was a successful non-Italian pope. Bernard of Clairvaux had advised Pope Eugenius to appoint non-Italian cardinals, and following Adrian there were eighteen non-Italian popes until 1503, when an unbroken run of forty-five Italian popes started, ended by Polish Pope John Paul II in 1978. Since then, there have been no Italian popes. There has not been another Englishman after Adrian, although there have been two near misses. Thomas Wolsey had papal ambitions but only obtained seven votes in the election of 1522. Reginald Pole, the last Catholic Archbishop of Canterbury during Mary I's reign, was made a cardinal in 1536 and did rather better. In 1549 he nearly secured the two-thirds majority needed to become pope. Pole declined to vote for himself; had he done so he would have been elected.

A third possibility could have been the longest-ever serving cardinal. Henry Stuart, the younger brother of the Young Pretender, who might himself have become King Henry IX of England and Henry I of Scotland, served as a cardinal for sixty years, during which time he took part in four papal elections. It is believed that the late Basil Hume, Archbishop of Westminster, was a credible candidate for the papacy in 1978 even though he had only been a cardinal for two years.

Adrian remains England's only pope. Some 860 years after his death, St Albans remains proud of its son. The stone screen above the altar in its cathedral was built by William Wallingford in 1484 and the Victorian patron of the abbey, Lord Aldenham, restored it to its present glorious state. Pope Adrian's statue is included in this screen, where he stands second from the right in the upper tier. Nicholas Breakspear is back home.

ACKNOWLEDGEMENTS

I knew nothing of Nicholas Breakspear before embarking on this book, other than his being the answer to the Trivial Pursuit question 'Who was the only English pope?' I suspect my Catholic Lancashire parents named me Adrian for the English pope. I thank them for sowing that seed which germinated soon after I retired when I stumbled across the plaque to Breakspear and Becket on the ruins of Merton Priory in Morden Park, which proclaimed they both attended its school. I asked Google if this was so (it proved unlikely) and in the process discovered that, while Becket's life is well documented, much less is known about Breakspear. I wanted to right that national omission.

The writers who have gone before me provided details that I would not have found otherwise. All have been helpful, and they are acknowledged in the bibliography. The most helpful modern source on Adrian has been the scholarly tome *Adrian IV: The English Pope (1154–1159)*, a series of essays edited by Brenda Bolton and Anne Duggan and published twenty years ago. My book would have been much thinner had it not been able to draw on their collective knowledge and that of the authors whom they commissioned.

My working life as an actuary depended on the use of figures, and turning to letters has been a learning experience. I reached the end of this journey only due to the skill and patience of my first editor, Anne-Marie Walker (herself married to an actuary and so knowing well just how much help I would need). My re-education was completed by Professor Pamela Pilbeam at Birkbeck University. Once I had a draft that I dared let others see, people who might not otherwise have had the biography of a pope on their reading list helped to improve the text and provided encouragement. My grateful thanks for this to my children, Robert, Ella and Edward, my brother Bernard Waddingham, sister-in-law Philippa Anderson, and supportive friends Beth Gillam, Nick Lee, Peter Rice, Peter Tompkins,

Andrew Vaughan, David Wilkie, Sir Thomas Woodcock, Paul Worsley QC and Jonathan Phillips, Professor of Crusading History at Royal Holloway College. My agent, Robert Gwyn Palmer, introduced me to the terrific team at The History Press who provided the final polish: Simon Wright, Jezz Palmer and Cynthia Hamilton, as well as freelance editor Catherine Hanley, who made several important corrections. Any remaining solecisms are entirely my responsibility.

It has been a delight to discover the many public institutions with generous staff ever-willing to assist an author, including Lambeth Palace Library, the British Library, the Hudson Library at St Albans Cathedral, Merton Historical Society, Abbots Langley Local History Society, the Municipal Archives and Bibliothèque Ceccano in Avignon, the Municipal Archives in Arles, Øystein Ekroll, the Trondheim Cathedral archaeologist, and Maurizio Bianchi at the Cathedral Museum in Benevento. They could not have been more helpful.

My final thanks are to my wife Angela, who never withheld her encouragement.

Adrian Waddingham
Silverdale, Lancashire

CHRONOLOGY

22 June 305	St Alban martyred
793	St Alban's Abbey founded by King Offa of Mercia
25 December 800	Charlemagne crowned Roman Emperor
1039	Monastery of St Ruf founded at Avignon
1054	The Great Schism between the Roman and Orthodox Churches
1059	Abbey of St Ruf in Avignon re-formed
1060	The Normans invade Sicily
1076	The Investiture Controversy between Gregory VII and Henry IV starts
1086	Domesday Book produced in England
1090	St Bernard of Clairvaux born
1096–1099	First Crusade
c. 1100	Nicholas Breakspear's birth
2 August 1100	Death of King William Rufus
5 August 1100	Coronation of King Henry I
28 September 1106	King Henry defeats his brother, Duke Robert of Normandy, at Tinchebrai
28 December 1115	Dedication of the abbey church at St Albans
1117	Merton Abbey founded in Surrey

25 November 1120	Prince William Adelin drowns when the *Blanche Nef* sinks
1122	Concordat at Worms
25 December 1130	Roger II crowned King of Sicily
1 December 1135	King Henry dies and is succeeded by King Stephen
1137	Breakspear elected prior at St Ruf
1139	Breakspear accompanies Archbishop William of Arles to Barcelona
8 April 1143	Manuel Comnenus crowned Byzantine Emperor
1143	The Roman Commune establishes a senate
1144	Robert Pullen becomes the first English cardinal
15 February 1145	Pope Eugenius III elected
c. 1145	Breakspear elected Abbot of St Ruf sometime between 1143 and 1147
1146	Pope Eugenius dismisses the complaints of the monks of St Ruf
1146	Breakspear becomes a papal aide
1147	Arnold of Brescia becomes leader of the Republicans in Rome
1147	Council of Reims, at which Breakspear is asked to go to Catalonia
1147	The start of the Second Crusade
30 December 1148	Fall of Tortosa in the Iberian Crusade
17 December 1149	Breakspear installed as Cardinal Bishop of Albano

1150	Eugenius appoints a legation to Ireland to draw the Irish Church closer to Rome
March 1152	Breakspear asked to go as papal legate to Scandinavia
4 March 1152	Frederick Barbarossa crowned King of Germany
18 July 1152	Breakspear lands in Norway
January 1153	Treaty of Constance between Frederick Barbarossa and Pope Eugenius
8 July 1153	Pope Eugenius dies
12 July 1153	Pope Anastasius elected
20 August 1153	Death of St Bernard of Clairvaux
1153	Cardinal Breakspear calls the Council of Nidaros, Norway
26 February 1154	King William I of Sicily crowned
Summer 1154	Cardinal Breakspear calls the assembly at Lynkoping, Sweden
October 1154	Frederick Barbarossa enters Italy on his first Italian campaign
November 1154	Breakspear returns to Rome from Scandinavia
3 December 1154	Death of Pope Anastasius IV
4 December 1154	Breakspear elected Pope Adrian IV
19 December 1154	King Henry II crowned in England
20 March 1155	Pope Adrian places Rome under interdict
18 April 1155	Frederick Barbarossa captures Tortona after a long siege
8 June 1155	Pope Adrian and Frederick Barbarossa quarrel at Sutri
18 June 1155	Frederick Barbarossa crowned Roman Emperor by Pope Adrian

29 September 1155	Adrian sets out for Benevento to wage war on William I of Sicily
30 April 1156	Brindisi recaptured from the Greek army by King William I
June 1156	King William I forces the Treaty of Benevento on Pope Adrian
July–October 1156	Adrian travels from Benevento to Monte Cassino, to Ferentino, on to Narni, Orvieto and Viterbo before returning to Rome
12 November 1156	Adrian re-establishes the Curia in the Lateran Palace
October 1157	Frederick Barbarossa summons the Diet of Besançon
June 1158	Frederick Barbarossa's second Italian campaign starts
1 September 1158	Milan falls to Frederick Barbarossa
11 November 1158	Frederick Barbarossa summons the Diet of Roncaglia where he declares himself Holy Roman Emperor for the first time
15 June 1159	Adrian arrives at the summer retreat of Anagni
1 September 1159	Pope Adrian dies at Anagni
4 September 1159	Cardinal Roland elected Pope Alexander III
7 May 1166	Death of King William I of Sicily
29 December 1170	Murder of Thomas Becket
1171	King Henry II subdues Ireland
29 May 1176	The Lombard League defeats Frederick Barbarossa at Legnano
24 September 1180	Death of Emperor Manuel Comnenus
10 June 1190	Death of Frederick Barbarossa

NOTES

Preface

1   Edward Gibbon, *The Decline and Fall of the Roman Empire*, Everyman (Dent), 1910, Vol. 6, p. 534.
2   Simon Webb, *Nicholas Breakspear: The Pope from England*, Langley Press, 2016; Brenda Bolton and Anne Duggan, *Adrian IV: The English Pope (1154–1159)*, Ashgate, 2003; Edith M. Almedingen, *The English Pope (Adrian IV)*, Heath Cranton, 1925.
3   L.C. Casartelli, *Sketches in History*, St Pius Press, 1905, p. 53.
4   *Manchester Guardian*, December 1896.
5   William of Newburgh, *Historia rerum Anglicarum*, Appendix 3 in Bolton and Duggan (eds), *Adrian IV*, p. 273.
6   Matthew Paris, '*Gesta abbatum S. Albani*', Appendix 6b in Bolton and Duggan (eds), *Adrian IV*, p. 290.
7   Horace K. Mann, *Nicholas Breakspear: Hadrian IV*, Keegan Paul, 1914; A.H. Tarleton, *Nicholas Breakspear (Adrian IV)*, Chiswick Press, 1896; Almedingen, *The English*; Richard Raby, *Pope Adrian IV*, Amazon reprint, 2010; Louis Casartelli, *Sketches in History*, St Pius Press, 1906.
8   John Freed, *Frederick Barbarossa: The Prince and the Myth*, Yale University Press, 2016.

Chapter 1: St Albans

1   Thomas Fuller, *The History of the Worthies of England*, Tegg, London, 1842, Vol. 2, p. 42.
2   Robert Bartlett, *The Hanged Man*, Princeton University Press, 2004, p. 63.
3   J.A. Froude, *History of England*, ed. E.H. Blakeney, Macmillan, 1972, Ch. 1, p. 53.
4   Paris, '*Gesta abbatum S. Albani*', p. 291.
5   C.N.L. Brooke, 'Adrian IV and John of Salisbury', in Bolton and Duggan (eds), *Adrian IV*, p. 5; M.A. Mayer, *The Culture of Christendom: Essays in Medieval History*, London, 1993, p. 133.

6   Alfred Henry Tarleton, *Nicholas Breakspear: Englishman and Pope*, Hanse Reprints, 1896, p. 15.
7   F.A. Gasquet, *English Monastic Life*, Methuen, 1904, p. 101.
8   William of Newburgh, *Historia rerum Anglicarum*, p. 273.
9   Horace Mann, *The Lives of the Popes in the Early Middle Ages*, Kegan Paul, 1914, Vol. 9, p. 237.
10   John of Salisbury, *Metalogicon*, Book IV, p. 274.
11   Jane E. Sayers, *Oxford Dictionary of National Biography*, 23 September 2004.
12   Boso, '*Vita Adriani IV*', in Bolton and Duggan (eds), *Adrian IV*, Appendix 1, p. 214.
13   H.E.J. Cowdrey, *Pope Gregory VII*, Oxford, 1998, p. 28.
14   Paris, '*Gesta abbatum S. Albani*', p. 291; Thomas Fuller, *The History of the Worthies of England*, Tegg, London, 1842, Vol. 2, p. 42.
15   Domesday Book, Hertfordshire, folio 8.
16   William of Newburgh, *Historia rerum Anglicarum*, p. 273.
17   Bede, *The Ecclesiastical History of the English People*, ed. Colgrave and Mynors, Oxford Medieval Texts, 1972, p. 35.
18   Leopold Ranke, *The Popes of Rome*, John Murray, 1841, p. 15.
19   Roger of Wendover, *Flowers of History*, tr. J.A. Giles, Henry G. Bohn, 1849, p. 467.
20   Brenda Bolton, 'St Albans' Loyal Son', in Bolton and Duggan (eds), *Adrian IV*, p. 76.
21   Richard North, *Fools for God*, Collins, 1987, p. 300.
22   Seb Falk, *The Light Ages*, Allen Lane, 2020, p. 22.
23   MS Arundel 249 in *A Fifteenth Century Schoolbook*, ed. William Nelson, Clarendon Press, 1956, pp. viii–ix.
24   Paris, '*Gesta abbatum S. Albani*', p. 291.
25   E. Trollope, 'Memoir of the Life of Adrian the Fourth', *Archaelogica*, 1857, Vol. 37, p. 40; John Bale, Illust. Brit. Centur. II, N.90, p. 197.
26   William of Newburgh, *Historia rerum Anglicarum*, p. 273.
27   Ibid.

Chapter 2: Paris

1   Matthew Paris, '*Gesta abbatum S. Albani*', p. 291.
2   R.L. Poole, *Studies in Chronology and History*, Clarendon Press, 1934, p. 295.
3   Peter Newcombe, *The History of the Ancient and Royal Foundation, called the Abbey of St Albans*, London, 1793, p. 64.
4   Alfred Heales, *The Records of Merton Priory*, Oxford University Press, 1898, p. 1.
5   Lionel Butler and Chris Given-Wilson, *Medieval Monasteries of Great Britain*, Michael Joseph, 1979, p. 76.
6   Poole, *Studies in Chronology and History*, p. 293.
7   *The Letters of John of Salisbury*, ed. and tr. Millor and Butler, Thomas Nelson and Sons, 1955, Vol. 1, Letter 50, p. 87.
8   Richard Chellow, *The Influence of Merton Priory*, Merton Historical Society, 2014, p. 6.

9   Lionel Green, *Daughter Houses of Merton Priory*, Merton Historical Society, 2002, p. 22.
10   Orderic Vitalis, *The Ecclesiastical History VI*, ed. M. Chibnall, Clarendon Press, 1975, Book XI.
11   John of Salisbury, *Policraticus*, Bk VIII, Ch. 23, p. 224.

Chapter 3: Provence

1   Boso, '*Vita Adriani IV*', p. 215.
2   Almedingen, *The English Pope*, p. 8.
3   Casartelli, *Sketches in History*, p. 57.
4   William of Newburgh, *Historia rerum Anglicarum*, p. 273 .
5   Paris, '*Gesta abbatum S. Albani*', p. 291.
6   Boso, '*Vita Adriani IV*', p. 215.
7   Casartelli, *Sketches in History*, p. 57.
8   Christoph Egger, 'The Canon Regular', in Bolton and Duggan (eds), *Adrian IV*, p. 24.
9   Boso, '*Vita Adriani IV*', p. 215.
10   David Knowles and Dimitri Obolensky, *The Christian Centuries*, Dartman, Longman & Todd, 1972, Vol. 2, p. 191.
11   Robert Bailly, *Avignon hors les Murs*, Imp Horta Avignon, 1967, p. 66.
12   William of Newburgh, *Historia rerum Anglicarum*, p. 273.
13   Boso, '*Vita Adriani IV*', p. 215.
14   Poole, *Studies in Chronology and History*, p. 294.
15   William of Newburgh, *Historia rerum Anglicarum*, p. 275.
16   Ibid.
17   Egger, 'The Canon Regular', p. 26.
18   William of Newburgh, *Historia rerum Anglicarum*, p. 275.
19   Boso, '*Vita Adriani IV*', p. 215.

Chapter 4: Catalonia

1   Jonathan Phillips, *The Second Crusade*, Yale University Press, 2007, Appendix 1, p. 281.
2   John Julius Norwich, *The Popes*, Vintage, 2012, p. 132.
3   Otto of Freising, *The Deeds of Frederick Barbarossa*, tr. Mierow, Columbia University Press, 1953, p. 71.
4   Phillips, *The Second Crusade*, Appendix 1, p. 281.
5   Tarleton, *Nicholas Breakspear*, p. 46.
6   Phillips, *The Second Crusade*, p. 136.
7   Ibid., p. 165.
8   I.S. Robinson, *The Papacy 1073–1198*, Cambridge University Press, 1990, p. 136.
9   John of Salisbury, *Historia Pontificalis*, ed. and tr. Marjorie Chibnall, Nelson's Medieval Texts, 1956, p. 5.
10   Ibid. p. 7.
11   *Anglo-Saxon Chronicle*, tr. G.N. Garmonsway, Everyman's Library, Dent, 1953, E1137, p. 265.

12 Damian J. Smith, 'The Abbot-Crusader', in Bolton and Duggan (eds), *Adrian IV*, p. 33.
13 Egger, 'The Canon Regular', p. 24.
14 Smith, 'The Abbot-Crusader', p. 33.
15 Phillips, *The Second Crusade*, p. 263.
16 Dan Jones, *In the Reign of King John*, Head of Zeus, 2015, p. 245.
17 Phillips, *The Second Crusade*, p. 255.
18 Smith, 'The Abbot-Crusader', p. 35.
19 Richard Raby, *Pope Adrian IV*, Chapter 7.
20 Poole, *Studies in Chronology and History*, p. 295.
21 Wikipedia.org, 'Robert Pullen'.
22 Knowles and Obolensky, *The Christian Centuries*, p. 231.
23 Egger, 'The Canon Regular', p. 26.
24 Poole, *Studies in Chronology and History*, p. 295.
25 Egger, 'The Canon Regular', p. 26.
26 Ibid., 27.
27 C.N.L. Brooke, 'Adrian IV and John of Salisbury', p. 7.
28 Phillips, *The Second Crusade*, p. 271.
29 Knowles and Obolensky, *The Christian Centuries*, p. 230.
30 Boso, '*Vita Adriani IV*', p. 217.
31 John of Salisbury, *Policraticus*, vi 19, p. 122.
32 M. Foster Farley, 'Adrian IV: England's Only Pope', *History Today*, 1978, Vol. 28, p. 530.
33 John Gran, 'English Influence on Norwegian Monasticism', *The Month*, 1959, Vol. 22.
34 William of Newburgh, *Historia rerum Anglicarum*, p. 275.

Chapter 5: Norway

1 Boso, '*Vita Adriani IV*', p. 215.
2 Saxo Grammaticus, *The History of the Danes*, tr. Peter Fisher, Clarendon, 2015, Book xiv, 11.1, p. 1041.
3 Henry of Huntingdon, *Acts of King Stephen Book II*, tr. Forrester, Henry G. Bohn, London, 1853, p. 418.
4 Snorri Sturlason, *Heimskringla*, Book 13, Chapter 24, Amazon, p. 341.
5 Anders Winroth, *The Conversion of Scandinavia*, Yale University Press, 2012, p. 2.
6 Hallfreor Ottarson, *Sagas of Warrior-Poets*, tr. Whaley, Penguin Classics, 2002, p. 85.
7 Adam of Bremen, *Gesta*, ed. Schmeidler, tr. Tschan, Columbia Press, New York, 1959, Ch. 2.26.
8 Sturlason, *Heimskringla*, Book 12, Ch. 7, p. 331.
9 Ibid., Book 13, Ch. 12, p. 337.
10 Ibid., Ch. 22, p. 341.
11 Ibid.
12 A. Bergquist, 'The Papal Legate', in Bolton and Duggan (eds), *Adrian IV*, p. 44.

13 Sturlason, *Heimskringla*, Book 13, Ch. 24, p. 341.
14 J.D. Mackie, *Pope Adrian IV: The Lothian Essay*, Blackwell, 1907, p. 23.
15 Almedingen, *The English Pope*, p. 122.
16 Sverre Bagge, *Cross and Sceptre*, Princeton University Press, 2014, p. 80.
17 Almedingen, *The English Pope*, p. 183.
18 Mackie, *Pope Adrian IV*, p. 21.
19 Almedingen, *The English Pope*, p. 122.
20 Sturlason, *Heimskringla*, Book 13, Ch. 23, p. 341
21 Isaksen, *Hellig Krig Om Norges Krone*, p. 127.
22 Almedingen, *The English Pope*, p. 179.
23 Sturlason, *Heimskringla*, Book 13, Ch. 23, p. 341.
24 Almedingen, *The English Pope*, p. 193.

Chapter 6: Sweden

1 Grammaticus, *History of the Danes*, Vol. 2, Book xiv, 11.1, p. 1043.
2 Ibid.
3 Sverre Bagge, *Cross & Sceptre*, Princeton University Press, 2014, p. 81.

Chapter 7: Denmark

1 Grammaticus, *History of the Danes*, Vol. 2, Book xiv, 11.1, p. 1043.
2 Ibid.
3 Ibid.
4 Bergquist, 'The Papal Legate', p. 46.
5 Grammaticus, *History of the Danes*, Vol. 2, Book xiv, 11.2, p. 1045.
6 Ibid., 12.2, p. 1047.
7 Sturlason, *Heimskringla*, Book 13, Ch. 23, p. 341.

Chapter 8: Rome

1 Sturlason, *Heimskringla*, Book 13, Ch. 23, p. 341.
2 Almedingen, *The English Pope*, p. 141.
3 Robinson, *The Papacy*, p. 78.
4 Boso, '*Vita Adriani IV*', p. 215.
5 John of Salisbury, *Policraticus*, Bk VIII, Ch. 23, p. 224.
6 Boso, '*Vita Adriani IV*', p. 217.
7 Tarleton, *Nicholas Breakspear*, p. 65.
8 Fuller, *The History of the Worthies of England*, p. 42.
9 Poole, *Studies in Chronology and History*, p. 161.
10 Kenneth Clark, *Civilisation: A Personal View*, BBC documentary, 1969.
11 Colin Morris, *The Papal Monarchy: The Western Church from 1050 to 1250*, Oxford University Press, 1989, p. 431.
12 John of Salisbury, *Policraticus*, Book VIII, Ch. 23, p. 224.
13 Tarleton, *Nicholas Breakspear*, p. 83.

14   John of Salisbury, *Historia Pontificalis*, p. 60.
15   Bernard of Clairvaux, *De Consideratione*, lib iv, cap 2.
16   John of Salisbury, *Historia Pontificalis*, p. 65.
17   Raby, *Pope Adrian IV*, Chapter III.
18   Boso, '*Vita Adriani IV*', p. 217.
19   Ibid.
20   Susan E. Twyman, '*Summus Pontifex*', in Bolton and Duggan (eds), *Adrian IV*, p. 51.
21   Webb, *Nicholas Breakspear*, p. 10.
22   Robinson, *The Papacy*, p. 4.
23   Twyman, '*Summus Pontifex*', p. 71.
24   Robinson, *The Papacy*, p. 24.

Chapter 9: Beyond Rome

1   Mackie, *Pope Adrian IV*, p. 23.
2   Freed, *Frederick Barbarossa*, p. xxiii.
3   Ibid., p. xix.
4   Otto of Freising, *The Deeds of Frederick Barbarossa*, Book 2, xiii, p. 127.
5   Ibid., p. 128.
6   Claudia Gold, *The King of the North Wind*, William Collins, 2018, p. 62.
7   Otto of Freising, *The Deeds of Frederick Barbarossa*, p. 120.
8   Dante Aligheri, *Inferno*, canto 19, lines 115–17.
9   Hugh Falcandus, *History of the Tyrants of Sicily 1154–69*, tr. Loud & Wiedermann, Manchester University Press, 1998, p. 1.
10   John Julius Norwich, *The Kingdom in the Sun*, Faber and Faber, 2018, p. 169.
11   Paul Magdalino, *The Empire of Manuel Komnenos 1143–1180*, Cambridge University Press, 1993, p. 56.
12   Maria Patrizia Carrieri, 'Longevity of Popes and Artists Between the 13th and the 19th Century', *International Journal of Epidemiology*, 2005, Vol. 34, pp. 1435–6.
13   Norwich, *The Kingdom in the Sun*, p. 173.
14   Freed, *Frederick Barbarossa*, p. 123.
15   Mackie, *Pope Adrian IV*, p. 38.

Chapter 10: Sutri

1   *Barbarossa in Italy*, ed. Bergamo Master, tr. Thomas Carson, Italica Press, 1994, lines 67–72, p. 3.
2   Walter Ullmann, *A Short History of the Papacy in the Middle Ages*, Routledge, 1972, p. 191.
3   Otto of Freising, *The Deeds of Frederick Barbarossa*, p. 130.
4   *Barbarossa in Italy*, lines 366–72, p. 13.
5   Anne Duggan, 'The Pope and the Princes', in Bolton and Duggan (eds), *Adrian IV*, p. 114.
6   Boso, '*Vita Adriani IV*', p. 217.

7   Mackie, *Pope Adrian IV*, p. 41.
8   Boso, '*Vita Adriani IV*', p. 219.
9   Robinson, *The Papacy*, p. 12.
10 Boso, '*Vita Adriani IV*', p. 219.
11 Norwich, *The Popes*, p. 143.
12 Gibbon, *Decline and Fall*, p. 484. Gibbon's translation of Otto of Freising's *Gesta Frederici Imperatoris* is abridged with 'freedom yet fidelity'.
13 Boso, '*Vita Adriani IV*', p. 221.
14 John of Salisbury, *Historia Pontificalis*, p. 75.
15 Boso, '*Vita Adriani IV*', p. 223.
16 Ibid.

Chapter 11: The Leonine City

1   Boso, '*Vita Adriani IV*', p. 223.
2   Otto of Freising, *The Deeds of Frederick Barbarossa*, Book 2, xxviii, p. 144.
3   Ibid., xxxi, p. 149.
4   Ibid., xxxii, p. 150.
5   *Barbarossa in Italy*, lines 657–61, p. 23.
6   Boso, '*Vita Adriani IV*', p. 223.
7   Mann, *The Lives of the Popes in the Early Middle Ages*, Vol. 9, p. 264.
8   Ibid., p. 265.
9   Ibid.
10 Freed, *Frederick Barbarossa*, p. 58.
11 Ullmann, *A Short History of the Papacy*, p. 185.
12 Walter Ullmann, 'The Pontificate of Adrian IV', *The Cambridge Historical Journal*, 1955, Vol. XI, No. 3.
13 Freed, *Frederick Barbarossa*, p. 148.
14 Otto of Freising, *The Deeds of Frederick Barbarossa*, Book 2, xxxiii, p. 151.
15 Boso, '*Vita Adriani IV*', p. 225.
16 Otto of Freising, *The Deeds of Frederick Barbarossa*, Book 2, xxxiv, p. 152.
17 Boso, '*Vita Adriani IV*', p. 225.
18 Freed, *Frederick Barbarossa*, p. 157.

Chapter 12: Benevento

1   Norwich, *The Kingdom in the Sun*, p. 188.
2   Dan Jones, *The Templars*, Head of Zeus, 2017, p. 34.
3   Morris, *The Papal Monarchy*, p. 214.
4   Duggan, 'The Pope and the Princes', p. 116.
5   Boso, '*Vita Adriani IV*', p. 215.
6   Robinson, *The Papacy*, p. 116.
7   Norwich, *The Kingdom in the Sun*, p. 196.
8   Ibid., p. 200.
9   Ibid., p. 199.
10 Peter Partner, *The Lands of St Peter*, University of California Press, 1972, p. 199.

11 Paris, 'Gesta Abbatum', p. 293.
12 Ibid.
13 William of Newburgh, *Historia rerum Anglicarum*, Book II, Ch. 7.
14 Oliver J. Thatcher, *Studies Concerning Adrian IV*, Forgotten Books, 2018, p. 31.
15 Paris, 'Gesta Abbatum', p. 295.
16 Ibid.
17 Ibid.
18 Newcombe, *History of the Ancient and Royal Foundation*, p. 65.
19 Matthew Paris, *Liber Additamentorum*, Cotton MS Nero D1, British Library.
20 John of Salisbury, *Policraticus*, Book VI, Ch. 24, p. 132.
21 Ibid., p. 133.
22 Ibid., p. 134.
23 William Shakespeare, *Coriolanus*, Act I, Scene i.
24 John of Salisbury, *Policraticus*, Book VIII, Ch. 23, p. 224.
25 Ibid., Ch. 24, p. 225.
26 Poole, *Studies in Chronology and History*, p. 249.
27 Anne Duggan, 'Servus servorum Dei', in Bolton and Duggan (eds), *Adrian IV*, p. 192.

Chapter 13: Ireland

1 John of Salisbury, *Metalogicon*, p. 274.
2 Paris, 'Gesta Abbatum', p. 293.
3 Duggan, 'The Pope and the Princes', p. 144.
4 John of Salisbury, *Metalogicon*, p. 274.
5 Gerald of Wales, 'Expugnatio Hibernica', in Bolton and Duggan (eds), *Adrian IV*, p. 287.
6 Thatcher, *Studies Concerning Adrian IV*, p. 26.
7 Ibid., p. 17.
8 *The Letters of John of Salisbury*, ed. Millor and Butler, Nelson's Mediaeval Texts, 1955, Vol. 1, Letter 30, p. 48.
9 Anne Duggan, 'Henry II, the English Church and the Papacy', in Harper-Bill et al., *Henry II: New Interpretations*, Boydell Press, 2007, p. 159.
10 Gerald of Wales, 'Expugnatio Hibernica', p. 285.
11 Duggan, 'The Pope and the Princes', p. 138.
12 Tarleton, *Nicholas Breakspear*, p. 178.
13 Gerald of Wales, 'Expugnatio Hibernica', p. 287.
14 Ibid.
15 Thatcher, *Studies Concerning Adrian IV*, p. 3.

Chapter 14: Ferentino

1 Mann, *The Lives of the Popes in the Early Middle Ages*, p. 274.
2 William of Tyre, *A History of Deeds Done Beyond the Sea*, tr. E.A. Babcock, Columbia University Press, Vol. 2, Book 18, Ch. 6, p. 246.

3   Ibid., Ch. 3, p. 239.
4   Ibid., p. 240.
5   Ibid.
6   Ibid., Ch. 7, p. 248.
7   *The Letters of John of Salisbury*, Letter 91, p. 140.
8   Mann, *The Lives of the Popes in the Early Middle Ages*, p. 338.
9   Duggan, '*Servus servorum Dei*', p. 195.
10 Ibid., p. 196.
11 Mann, *The Lives of the Popes in the Early Middle Ages*, p. 274.
12 Thomas F. Madden, *Venice: A New History*, Penguin, 2012, p. 80.
13 Brenda Bolton, 'Adrian IV and the Patrimony', in Bolton and Duggan (eds), *Adrian IV*, p. 168.
14 Boso, '*Vita Adriani IV*', p. 231.

Chapter 15: England

1   Adrian's letter to Abbot Robert, '*Incomprehensibilis*', in Bolton and Duggan (eds), *Adrian IV*, pp. 313–15.
2   Duggan, '*Servus servorum Dei*', p. 193.
3   *The Letters of John of Salisbury*, Letter 11, p. 18.
4   Matthew Strickland, *Henry the Young King*, Yale University Press, 2016, p. 35.
5   *The Letters of John of Salisbury*, Letter 87, p. 135.
6   G.G. Coulton, *The Medieval Village*, Cambridge University Press, 1926, p. 469.
7   Duggan, '*Servus servorum Dei*', p. 189.
8   Ibid., p. 187.
9   John of Salisbuy, *Policraticus*, Book VII, p. 173.
10 David Knowles, *The Monastic Order in England*, Cambridge University Press, 1950, p. 589.
11 Adrian, '*Incomprehensibilis*', p. 313.
12 Bolton, 'St Albans' Loyal Son', p. 87.
13 Ibid., p. 96.
14 Paris, '*Gesta Abbatum*', p. 301.
15 Bolton, 'St Albans' Loyal Son', p. 96.
16 Gerald of Wales, '*Speculum ecclesiae*', in Bolton and Duggan (eds), *Adrian IV*, p. 281.
17 '*Religiosam uitam*', Adrian IV to Abbot Robert of St Albans, Lateran, 14 May 1157, in Bolton and Duggan (eds), *Adrian IV*, p. 323.
18 F. Rushbrooke Williams, *The History of the Abbey of St Albans*, Longmans, 1917, p. 72.
19 Gerald of Wales, '*Speculum ecclesiae*', p. 281.
20 *The Letters of John of Salisbury*, Letter 50, p. 87.
21 Mann, *The Lives of the Popes in the Early Middle Ages*, p. 320.
22 *The Letters of John of Salisbury*, Letter 15, p. 25.
23 Poole, *Studies in Chronology and History*, p. 272.
24 *The Letters of John of Salisbury*, Letters 40 and 41, pp. 74–6; Poole, *Studies in Chronology and History*, p. 273.

25 *The Letters of John of Salisbury*, Letter 16, p. 26.
26 *The Letters of John of Salisbury*, Letters 9 and 26, pp. 15 and 43; Poole, *Studies in Chronology and History*, p. 277.
27 *The Letters of John of Salisbury*, Letter 67, p. 26.
28 Ibid., Letter 57, p. 98.
29 Tarleton, *Nicholas Breakspear*, p. 254.

Chapter 16: The Patrimony

1   Partner, *The Lands of St Peter*, p. 135.
2   Norwich, *The Popes*, p. 110.
3   Ullmann, *A Short History of the Papacy*, p. 181.
4   Partner, *The Lands of St Peter*, p. 442.
5   Robinson, *The Papacy*, p. 31.
6   Bolton, 'Adrian IV and the Patrimony', p. 162.
7   Ibid., p. 177.
8   *The Letters of John of Salisbury*, Letter 49, p. 86.
9   Duggan, '*Servus servorum Dei*', p. 183.
10 Tarleton, *Nicholas Breakspear*, p. 270.
11 Morris, *The Papal Monarchy*, p. 111.
12 Norwich, *The Popes*, p. 105.
13 William of Malmesbury, *Gesta regum Angolorum*, G. Bell and Sons, Book IV, Ch. 2, p. 371.
14 Chris Wickham, *Medieval Rome: Stability and Crisis of a City*, Oxford University Press, 2015, p. 228.
15 Knowles and Obolensky, *The Christian Centuries*, Vol. 2, p. 386.
16 Mann, *The Lives of the Popes in the Early Middle Ages*, p. 282.
17 Boso, '*Vita Adriani IV*', p. 231.
18 Ibid.
19 Bolton, 'Adrian IV and the Patrimony', p. 176.
20 Ibid.
21 Boso, '*Vita Adriani IV*', p. 233.

Chapter 17: Besançon

1   Otto of Freising, *The Deeds of Frederick Barbarossa*, Book 3, viii, p. 180.
2   Freed, *Frederick Barbarossa*, p. 199.
3   Robinson, *The Papacy*, p. 465.
4   Freed, *Frederick Barbarossa*, p. 45.
5   Ibid., p. 50.
6   Otto of Freising, *The Deeds of Frederick Barbarossa*, Book 3, viii, p. 181.
7   Ibid., Book 3, ix, p. 182.
8   Freed, *Frederick Barbarossa*, p. 33.
9   Otto of Freising, *The Deeds of Frederick Barbarossa*, Book 3, x, p. 183.
10 Ibid., p. 184.
11 Ibid.
12 Mackie, *Pope Adrian IV*, p. 79.

13   Ullmann, *The Pontificate of Adrian IV*, p. 245.
14   Otto of Freising, *The Deeds of Frederick Barbarossa*, Book 3, xi, p. 186.
15   Ullmann, *The Pontificate of Adrian IV*, p. 244.
16   Freed, *Frederick Barbarossa*, p. 54.
17   Otto of Freising, *The Deeds of Frederick Barbarossa*, Book 3, xi, p. 185.
18   Boso, '*Vita Adriani IV*', p. 221.
19   Otto of Freising, *The Deeds of Frederick Barbarossa*, Book 3, xvi, p. 191.
20   Ibid., xvii, p. 192.
21   Ibid., p. 194.
22   Ibid., p. 193.
23   J.L. Jong, *The Power and the Glorification: Papal Pretensions and the Art of Propaganda*, Penn State Press, 2013, p. 163.
24   Otto of Freising, *The Deeds of Frederick Barbarossa*, Book 3, xxi, p. 198.
25   Mann, *The Lives of the Popes in the Early Middle Ages*, p. 292.
26   Otto of Freising, *The Deeds of Frederick Barbarossa*, Book 3, xxiii, p. 199.
27   Ibid., p. 200.
28   Duggan, 'The Pope and the Princes', p. 130.

Chapter 18: Lombardy

1   Mackie, *Pope Adrian IV*, p. 120.
2   Freed, *Frederick Barbarossa*, p. 217.
3   Otto of Freising, *The Deeds of Frederick Barbarossa*, Book 3, xxvi, p. 201.
4   Ibid., p. 208.
5   Freed, *Frederick Barbarossa*, p. 224.
6   Otto of Freising, *The Deeds of Frederick Barbarossa*, Book 3, xlvi, p. 220.
7   Freed, *Frederick Barbarossa*, p. 227.
8   *Barbarossa in Italy*, lines 2500–10, p. 88.
9   Otto of Freising, *The Deeds of Frederick Barbarossa*, Book 3, vii, p. 178.
10   Gold, *The King of the North Wind*, p. 102.
11   Otto of Freising, *The Deeds of Frederick Barbarossa*, Book 4, iii, p. 234.
12   Ibid., xviii, p. 252. Rahewin's chronology may be mistaken and it is more likely that the Brescia/Bergamo quarrel took place in the summer of 1158. See Mackie, *Pope Adrian IV*, p. 98.
13   Ibid., xviii, p. 252.
14   Ibid., p. 265.
15   Ibid., xl, p. 275.
16   Ibid., xxii, p. 260.
17   F.M. Steele, *The Story of the English Pope*, London, 1908, p. 169.

Chapter 19: Anagni

1   Duggan, '*Servus servorum Dei*', p. 202.
2   Tarleton, *Nicholas Breakspear*, p. 238.
3   Ullmann, *The Pontificate of Adrian IV*, p. 245.
4   Freed, *Frederick Barbarossa*, p. 256.

5   Mackie, *Pope Adrian IV*, p. 101.
6   Otto of Freising, *The Deeds of Frederick Barbarossa*, Book 4, xxxv, p. 271.
7   Duggan, 'The Pope and the Princes', p. 138.
8   Knowles and Obolensky, *The Christian Centuries*, p. 331.
9   Tarleton, *Nicholas Breakspear*, p. 244.
10   Mann, *The Lives of the Popes in the Early Middle Ages*, p. 311.
11   Norwich, *The Kingdom in the Sun*, p. 208.
12   John of Salisbury, *Metalogicon*, Book IV, p. 274.
13   *The Letters of John of Salisbury*, Letter 41, p. 76.
14   Bartolomeo Platina, 'Adrian IIII', Appendix 8 in Bolton and Duggan
     (eds), *Adrian IV*, p. 309.
15   Duggan, '*Servus servorum Dei*', p. 184.
16   John Foxe, *Book of Martyrs*, John Day, 1563.
17   Thomas Noble, *The Republic of St Peter: The Birth of the Papal State
     680–825*, Philadelphia, 1984, p. 335.
18   Ciaconius, *Vitae et gesta romanorum pontificum et cardinalium*, 1599.

Epilogue

1   Ullmann, *The Pontificate of Adrian IV*, p. 233.
2   Otto of Freising, *The Deeds of Frederick Barbarossa*, Book 4, lxxvi, p. 310.
3   Ibid.
4   Morris, *The Papal Monarchy*, p. 195.
5   Norwich, *The Popes*, p. 157.
6   Godfrey of Viterbo, '*Gesta Friderici I*', Appendix 4 in Bolton and Duggan
     (eds), *Adrian IV*, p. 279.
7   Norwich, *The Kingdom in the Sun*, p. 372.
8   Strickland, *Henry the Young King*, p. 29.
9   Jones, *The Templars*, p. 259.
10   Almedingen, *The English Pope*, p. 182.

BIBLIOGRAPHY

Published Primary Sources

Adam of Bremen, *Gesta*, ed. Schmeidler, tr. Tschan, Columbia Press, New York, 1959.

Anglo-Saxon Chronicle, tr. G.N. Garmonsway, Everyman's Library, Dent, 1953.

Barbarossa in Italy, ed. Bergamo Master, tr. Thomas Carson, Italica Press, 1994.

Bede, *The Ecclesiastical History of the English People*, ed. Colgrave and Mynors, Oxford Medieval Texts, 1972.

Bernard of Clairvaux, *De Consideratione*, Lib iv.

Boso, Cardinal, '*Vita Adriani IV*', Appendix 1 in *Adrian IV: The English Pope (1154–1159): Studies and Texts*, ed. Brenda Bolton and Anne Duggan, Ashgate, 2003, pp. 215–33.

Falcandus, Hugh, *History of the Tyrants of Sicily 1154–69*, tr. Loud & Wiedermann, Manchester University Press, 1998.

Gerald of Wales, '*Expugnatio Hibernica*', Appendix 5b in *Adrian IV: The English Pope (1154–1159): Studies and Texts*, ed. Brenda Bolton and Anne Duggan, Ashgate, 2003, pp. 285–7.

——, '*Speculum Ecclesiae*', Appendix 5a in *Adrian IV: The English Pope (1154–1159): Studies and Texts*, ed. Brenda Bolton and Anne Duggan, Ashgate, 2003, pp. 281–3.

Godfrey of Viterbo, 'Deeds of the Emperor Frederick I', Appendix 4 in *Adrian IV: The English Pope (1154–1159): Studies and Texts*, ed. Brenda Bolton and Anne Duggan, Ashgate, 2003, pp. 277–9.

Henry of Huntingdon, *Acts of King Stephen Book II*, tr. Forrester, Henry G. Bohn, London, 1853.

——, *The History of the English People 1000–1154*, tr. Diana Greenway, Oxford University Press, 1996.

John of Salisbury, *Historia Pontificalis*, ed. and tr. Marjorie Chibnall, Nelson's Medieval Texts, 1956.

——, *The Letters of John of Salisbury*, ed. W.J. Millor and H.E. Butler, Nelson, 1955, Vol. 1.

——, *Metalogicon*, tr. Daniel McGarry, University of California Press, 1955.

——, *Policraticus*, ed. and tr. Cary J. Nederman, Cambridge University Press, 1990.

Ottarson, Hallfreor, *Sagas of Warrior Poets*, tr. Whalley, Penguin Classics, 2002.

Otto of Freising, *The Deeds of Frederick Barbarossa*, ed. C.C. Mierow, Columbia University Press, 1953.

Paris, Matthew, '*Gesta Abbatum*', Appendix 6b in *Adrian IV: The English Pope (1154–1159): Studies and Texts*, ed. Brenda Bolton and Anne Duggan, Ashgate, 2003, pp. 291–303.

——, '*Historia Anglorum*', Appendix 6a in *Adrian IV: The English Pope (1154–1159): Studies and Texts*, ed. Brenda Bolton and Anne Duggan, Ashgate, 2003, p. 289.

Plattina, Bartolomeo, 'Adrian IIII', Appendix 6a in *Adrian IV: The English Pope (1154–1159): Studies and Texts*, ed. Brenda Bolton and Anne Duggan, Ashgate, 2003.

Roger of Wendover, *Flowers of History*, tr. J.A. Giles, Henry G. Bohn, 1849.

Saxo Grammaticus, *The History of the Danes, Book XI*, tr. Peter Fisher, Clarendon, 2015.

Sturlason, Snorri, *Heimskringala*, Amazon, 2014.

Vitalis, Orderic, *The Ecclesiastical History*, ed. and tr. Marjorie Chibnall, Oxford Clarendon Press, 1975, Vol. VI, Book XI.

William of Malmesbury, *Gesta regum Angolorum*, G. Bell and Sons, 1883.

William of Newburgh, '*Historia rerum Anglicarum*', Appendix 3 in *Adrian IV: The English Pope (1154–1159): Studies and Texts*, ed. Brenda Bolton and Anne Duggan, Ashgate, 2003, pp. 273–5.

William of Tyre, *A History of Deeds Done Beyond the Sea*, tr. Babcock, Columbia University Press, 1943, Vol. 2.

Published Secondary Sources

Almedingen, Edith M., *The English Pope (Adrian IV)*, Heath Cranton, 1925.

Bagge, Sverre, *Cross and Scepter*, Princeton University Press, 2014.

Bailly, Robert, *Avignon hors les Murs*, Imp Horta Avignon, 1967.

Barber, Malcolm, *The Two Cities*, Routledge, 1992.

Barber, Richard, *Henry II: A Prince Among Princes*, Allen Lane, 2015.

Barlow, Frank, *The Feudal Kingdom of England 1042–1216*, Longman, 1988.

Bartlett, Robert, *The Hanged Man*, Princeton University Press, 2004.

Bellenger, Dominic, and Stella Fletcher, *Princes of the Church: A History of the English Cardinals*, Sutton, 2001.

Bergquist, Anders, 'The Papal Legate: Nicholas Breakspear's Scandinavian Mission', in Bolton and Duggan (eds), *Adrian IV: the English Pope (1154–1159)*.

Birt, Henry Norbert, 'Boso Breakspear', *The Catholic Encyclopedia*, Robert Appleton Company, 1907, Vol. 12.

Bolton, Brenda, 'Adrian IV and the Patrimony', in Bolton and Duggan (eds), *Adrian IV: The English Pope (1154–1159)*.

——, 'St Alban's Loyal Son', in Bolton and Duggan (eds), *Adrian IV: The English Pope (1154–1159)*.

Bolton, Brenda, and Anne Duggan (eds), *Adrian IV: The English Pope (1154–1159): Studies and Texts*, Ashgate, 2003.

Brooke, C.N.L., *The Saxon and Norman Kings*, B.T. Batsford, 1963.

——, 'Adrian IV and John of Salisbury', in Bolton and Duggan (eds), *Adrian IV: The English Pope (1154–1159)*.

Bury, J.B., *The Cambridge Medieval History, Volume 5: The Contest of Empire and Papacy*, Cambridge University Press, 1948.

Butler, Lionel, and Chris Given-Wilson, *Medieval Monasteries of Great Britain*, Michael Joseph, 1979.

Carpenter, David, *The Struggle for Mastery*, Penguin, 2003.

Carrieri, Maria Patrizia, *International Journal of Epidemiology*, 2005, Vol. 34.

Casartelli, Louis *Sketches in History*, St Pius X Press, 1905.

Chellow, Richard, *The Influence of Merton Priory*, Merton Historical Society, 2014.

Constable, Giles, *Crusaders and Crusading in the Twelfth Century*, Routledge, 2016.

Coulton, G.G., *The Medieval Village*, Cambridge University Press, 1926.

Cowdrey, H.E.J., *Pope Gregory VII*, Oxford, 1998.

Dickinson, John Compton, *The Origins of the Austin Canons*, Hassell Street Press, 2021.

Duggan, Anne, 'The Pope and the Princes', in Bolton and Duggan (eds), *Adrian IV: The English Pope (1154–1159)*.

——, 'Servus Servorum Dei', in Bolton and Duggan (eds), *Adrian IV: The English Pope (1154–1159)*.

Egger, Christoph, 'The Cannon Regular', in Bolton and Duggan (eds), *Adrian IV: The English Pope (1154–1159)*.

Falk, Seb, *The Light Ages*, Allen Lane, 2020.

Farley, M. Foster, 'Adrian IV: England's Only Pope', *History Today*, 1978, Vol. 28, pp. 530–6.

Foxe, John, *Foxe's Book of Martyrs*, London.

Freed, John B., *Frederick Barbarossa: The Prince and the Myth*, Yale University Press, 2016.

Froude, J.A., *History of England*, ed. E.H. Blakeney, Macmillan, 1972.

Fuller, Thomas, *The History of the Worthies of England*, Tegg, 1840.

Gasquet, Cardinal, *English Monastic Life*, Methuen, 1924.

Gibbon, Edward, *The Decline and Fall of the Roman Empire*, 1910, Everyman, Dent, Vol. 6.

Ginnell, Laurence, *The Doubtful Grant of Ireland*, Fallon & Co., 1899.

Glasby, Michael, and Gail Thomas, *Matthew Paris: Monk and Chronicler of St Albans Abbey*, The Fraternity & Friends of St Albans Abbey, 2018.

Gold, Claudia, *King of the North Wind*, William Collins, 2018.

Gran, John, 'English Influence on Norwegian Monasticism', *The Month*, 1959, Vol. 22, pp. 121–8.

Green, Lionel, *Daughter Houses of Merton Priory*, Merton Historical Society, 2002.

——, *A Priory Revealed: Merton Priory*, Merton Historical Society, 2005.

Haren, Michael, *Laudabiliter: Text and Context*, Palgrave Macmillan, 2005.

Harper-Bill, Christopher, and Nicholas Vincent, *Henry II: New Interpretations*, Boydell Press, 2007.

Heales, Alfred, *Records of Merton Priory*, Oxford University Press, 1898.

Herbert, Ailsa, Pam Martin, and Gail Thomas, *St Albans Cathedral and Abbey*, Scala Arts and Heritage Publishers, 2015.

Isaksen, Trond Noren, *Hellig Krig om Norges Krone*, Historie & Kultur, Oslo, 2017.

Jones, Dan, *In the Reign of King John*, Head of Zeus, 2015.

——, *The Templars*, Head of Zeus, 2017.

Jong, J.L., *The Power and the Glorification: Papal Pretensions and the Art of Propaganda*, Penn State Press, 2013.

Kedar, Benjamin, Johnathan Phillips, and Jonathan Riley-Smith, *Crusades*, 2009, Routledge, Vol. 8.

Kelsall, Jane, *Christina of Markyate*, Friends of St Albans Abbey, 2013.

Kippis, Andrew, *Biographia Britannica*, 1778.

Knowles, David, *The Monastic Order in England*, Cambridge University Press, 1950.

——, 'Nicholas Breakspeare in Norway', *The Month*, 1959, Vol. 21, pp 88–94.

Knowles, David, and Dimitri Obolensky, *The Christian Centuries, Volume 2: The Middle Ages*, Darton, Longman & Todd, 1972.

Mackie, J.D., *Pope Adrian IV: The Lothian Essay*, Blackwell, 1907.

McKitterick, W., *Lasting Letters*, Cambridge Cardozo Kinderley Editions, 1992.

Madden, Thomas, *Venice: A New History*, Penguin, 2012.

Magdalino, Paul, *The Empire of Manuel Komnenos 1143–1180*, Cambridge University Press, 1993.

Mann, Horace K., *The Lives of the Popes in the Early Middle Ages*, Keegan Paul, 1914.

Mayer, *The Culture of Christendom: Essays in Medieval History*, London, 1993.

Milman, H.H., *History of Latin Christianity*, Widdleton, 1870.

Morris, Colin, *The Papal Monarchy: The Western Church from 1050 to 1250*, Oxford University Press, 1989.

Newcombe, Reverend Peter, *The History of the Ancient & Royal Foundation called the Abbey of St Albans*, J. Nichols, 1795.

Noble, Thomas, *The Republic of St Peter: The Birth of the Papal State 680–825*, Philadelphia, 1984.

Noonan, J.C., *The Church Visible*, Viking, 1966.

Norgate, Kate, 'The Bull Laudabiliter', *English Historical Review*, 1893, Vol. 8, No. 29, pp. 18–52.

North, Richard, *Fools for God*, Collins, 1987.

Norwich, John Julius, *The Kingdom in the Sun*, Faber and Faber, 2018.

——, *The Popes*, Vintage, 2012.

Partner, Peter, *The Lands of Saint Peter*, University of California Press, 1972.

Phillips, Jonathan, *The Second Crusade*, Yale University Press, 2007.

Polack, Gillian, and Katrin Kania, *The Middle Ages Unlocked*, Amberley, 2015.

Poole, A.L., *From Domesday Book to Magna Carta*, Clarendon Press, 1954.

Poole, R.L., *Studies in Chronology and History*, Oxford University Press, 1934.

Raby, Richard, *Pope Adrian IV: An Historical Sketch*, Amazon reprint, 2015.

Ranke, Leopold, *The Popes of Rome*, John Murray, 1841.

Richards, Jeffrey, *The Popes and the Papacy in the Early Middle Ages*, Routledge and Kegan Paul, 1979.

Robinson, I.S., *The Papacy 1073–1198*, Cambridge University Press, 1990.

Rose, E.M., *The Murder of William of Norwich*, Oxford University Press, 2015.

Royidis, Emmanuel, *Pope Joan*, tr. Lawrence Durrell, Peter Owen Publishers, 1999.

Scharma, Simon, *A History of Britain: At the Edge of the World?*, Bodley Head, 2009.

Sheehy, M.P., 'The Bull Laudabiliter: A Problem in Medieval Diplomatique and History', *Journal of the Galway Archaeological and Historical Society*, 1961, Vol. 29, Nos 3–4, pp. 45–70.

Smith, Damian, 'The Abbot-Crusader', in Bolton and Duggan (eds), *Adrian IV: The English Pope (1154–1159)*.

Spencer, Charles, *The White Ship*, William Collins, 2020.

Steele, F.M., *The Story of the English Pope*, London, 1908.

Strickland, Matthew, *Henry the Young King*, Yale University Press, 2016.

Tarleton, Alfred Henry, *Nicholas Breakspear (Adrian IV)*, Chiswick Press, 1896.

Thatcher, Oliver J., *Studies Concerning Adrian IV*, Forgotten Books, 1903.

Tout, Thomas, *Essays in Medieval History*, Essay 5, Manchester, 1925.

Trollope, E., 'Memoir of the Life of Adrian the Fourth', *Archaeologica*, 1857, Vol. 37.

Twyman, Susan, '*Summus Pontifex*', in Bolton and Duggan (eds), *Adrian IV: The English Pope (1154–1159)*.

Ullmann, Walter, 'The Pontificate of Adrian IV', *The Cambridge Historical Journal*, 1955, Vol. 11, No. 3.

——, *A Short History of the Papacy in the Middle Ages*, Routledge, 1972.

Vaughan, Richard, *Matthew Paris*, Cambridge University Press, 1958.

Walsh, Michael, *The Popes*, Marshall Cavendish, 1980.

Watkins, Carl, *Stephen: The Reign of Anarchy*, Allen Lane, 2015.

Watt, J.A., 'Laudabiliter in Mediaeval Diplomacy and Propaganda', *Irish Ecclesiastical Record*, 1957, Ser. 5, Vol. LXXXVII, pp. 420–32.

Webb, Simon, *Nicholas Breakspear: The Pope from England*, Langley Press, 2016.

Wickham, C., *Medieval Rome: Stability and Crisis of a City*, Oxford University Press, 2015.

Williams, F. Rushbrook, *The History of the Abbey of St Alban*, Longmans, 1917.

Winroth, Anders, *The Conversion of Scandinavia*, Yale University Press, 2012.

INDEX

Note: the suffix 'n' indicates a note.

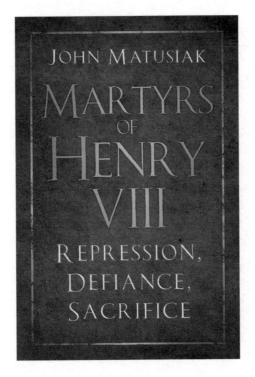

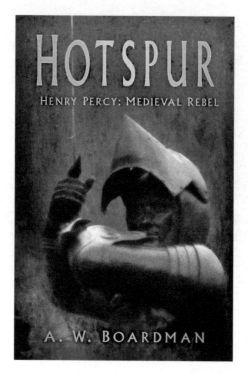